The Red Smith Reader

Also by Red Smith

Out of the Red
Views of Sport
Red Smith on Fishing
Red Smith's 1961 Sports Annual
The Best of Red Smith
Strawberries in the Wintertime

The
RED
SMITH
Reader

edited by Dave Anderson

with a foreword by Terence Smith

Random House New York

Library of Congress Cataloging in Publication Data

Smith, Red, 1905–1982.
    The Red Smith reader.

    A collection of the author's newspaper columns
which appeared between 1934 and 1982.
    1. Sports—Addresses, essays, lectures. I. An-
derson, Dave. II. Title.
GV707.S63 1982   796   82–40124
ISBN 0–394–52811–5   AACR2

Manufactured in the United States of America
4689753

Foreword by
Terence Smith

When I was growing up, it seemed to me that my father was always writing a column. I can remember him working in every imaginable setting: football press boxes, at the track, in hotel rooms, at fight camps in the Catskills, in summer cottages in Wisconsin, on airplanes and on the road. Very often when the family was driving somewhere, someone else would be at the wheel and Pop would be in the passenger seat with a light portable cradled on his knees, tapping the keys with two fingers.

Everything we did together or as a family became grist for a column. In the years when Pop was writing seven a week, it had to be. Our summer vacations in Door County, Wisconsin; fishing in the stream near our house in Connecticut; the time we tried to enter our overindulged dachshund in a local dog show (a haughty judge took one look at the plump pooch and told my mother: "This is a show for dogs, madam, not pigs")—all these became columns over the years. The actual writing of a column might take only a few hours, but it was a twenty-four-hour-a-day occupation. Pop would no sooner finish one than he would begin to wonder aloud what he would write the next day. He and his great friend and colleague Joe H. Palmer, the racing columnist for the *New York Herald Tribune*, even rewrote the Lord's Prayer to read: "Give us this day our daily plinth . . ." a play on the Greek word for the base of a classical column.

One lazy summer afternoon in 1977 Pop took my son, Chris, who was then five, fishing on a pond near his summer house in Martha's Vineyard. The conversation between them produced a lovely column that opened with Chris, watching his silver-haired grandfather climb through a barbed-wire fence, asking: "Grandpa, did you *grow* old, or were you *made* old?" Thirty years earlier, another column had been built around a similar fishing expedition, this time with father and son in fruitless pursuit of smallmouth bass on a Wisconsin lake. In that piece, the boy is quoted as saying: "Gee, Dad, this is the life, isn't it? Fishing and eating in saloons."

It follows, then, that in later years, when I was abroad as a foreign correspondent for *The New York Times,* that Pop's columns continued to serve as a kind of family chronicle and newsletter. (We both wrote for a living, but not for leisure; we were lousy correspondents.) His column, appearing in the *International Herald Tribune,* was a way for me to follow his movements and what he was up to. Similarly, he would track my bylines and datelines and would call or write to see what was wrong if they disappeared for too long.

Pop was able to find column material in the least likely places. Once, when he came to Jerusalem, where I was the *Times'* bureau chief, we drove down to Jericho and came across an abandoned racetrack where the princes and playboys of the Hashemite court had raced camels and gambled at a casino on the shore of the Dead Sea prior to the 1967 Arab-Israel war. The place was a shambles by then, but some local Bedouin told us stories about what it had been like and, naturally, their tales produced a column entitled "Life and Times at Dead Sea Downs."

Writing the column was my father's life, his livelihood and his therapy. In 1966, when we got word that my mother had contracted incurable cancer, I drove out to Connecticut to share the news with Pop. When he heard it, he broke down crying. Then he wrote a column. It was a good column—good for him to write, and good to read.

In the last years of my father's life, when his health and strength were fading, sustaining the column required a tremendous act of will. Yet he wanted nothing more than to keep at it. Pop regarded retirement as a kind of social disease. The column was his contract with life.

Out of concern for his health, I tried repeatedly to get him to slow down, to write three columns a week instead of four. It was an unrewarding task. Fewer columns, he argued, gave him fewer chances to be good. He cared as intensely about that at the age of seventy-six as he ever had. He titled his last column, in which he reluctantly advised his readers that he would be cutting back to three times a week, "Writing Less—and Better?"

After getting him to agree to trim his output, I upped the ante in our negotiations. I urged him, on the advice of his doctor, not to go to the Super Bowl that was scheduled for Detroit about three weeks later. Stay home and watch it on television, I argued, like millions of other Americans. Then write your column based on what they saw on their sets.

Now I had gone too far. "Nothing doing," he said, his voice suddenly louder and stronger. "I'm going to the Super Bowl, then I'm going to Las Vegas for a fight, then I'm going to Florida for spring training. If I can't do that, I'd better pack it in." Only death interrupted that schedule, and his determination to meet it.

Pop resisted with equal force repeated invitations to write his memoirs or, worse yet from his point of view, weighty works on the role of sports in American society. He didn't have much use for books like that, and he used to argue that he never wanted to write a book that he wouldn't read himself. But there was more to it than that. After all those years of condensing his thoughts into column-length units, he was uncertain, even insecure, about attempting a book. "I'm good at writing the column," he said to me during one long, post-midnight conversation in Martha's Vineyard three years before he died. "I think I'll stick with what I know I can do well."

Lord knows he did that.

Contents

Foreword by Terence Smith   v

Introduction by Dave Anderson   xi

"I'd Like to Be Called a Good Reporter"   1

1   Olympics   17

2   Racing   55

3   Football   91

4   Baseball   113

5   Politics   167

6   Some Other Sports   183

7   Fishing   209

8   Offbeat   237

9   Boxing   263

10   Pals, Colleagues, and Himself   291

Introduction:
Collecting the Columns

by Dave Anderson

If you blindfolded yourself, reached into Red Smith's files, and yanked out 130 columns, *any* 130 columns, you would have a good collection. But in choosing these columns of America's best sportswriter, I preferred mostly those he wrote about big names, big events, big issues.

Clippings of the columns were stashed away in his little office in the gray barn that serves as a garage behind the white colonial home he shared with Phyllis on a quiet, leafy country road in New Canaan, Connecticut. Over his last decade, those columns he wrote at home were created in that little office on his Olympia typewriter or, in the last few months, on a video display terminal.

His columns from the last fifteen years had been slipped into clear plastic envelopes, month by month, and stacked in the lower left-hand drawer of his red tabletop desk. Those from previous years had been tucked into cardboard shoe boxes, year by year, inside a metal file cabinet. And those from early in his career had been pasted in a now tattered, yellowed scrapbook begun nearly half a century ago. In his devotion to accuracy, if a typographical or editing error had occurred, he had corrected it in the margin. But nowhere was a column framed or on display.

His gray wood-paneled office was as he left it before he died at age seventy-six on January 15, 1982.

Next to the window overlooking the grassy backyard and the gravel driveway, his typewriter was surrounded by a black telephone, a telephone-number card file and a mug of pens and pencils. Along the walls, shelves held perhaps 1,500 books, not all on sports. Not far from a Bobo Newsom bubble-gum card and a reddish trout fly under glass, complete sets of the *World Book* and the *Encyclopaedia Britannica* were within reach.

On the back of the office door, a *New Yorker* cartoon showed a husband and wife watching a TV quiz show. "If you know all the answers, Mr. Red Smith," the wife is saying, "why don't you try to get on?"

Photos, sketches and prints were everywhere—Joe Frazier flinging the left hook that crumpled Muhammad Ali in their first fight, a collage of boxing champions, Ted Williams leaning on a bat, Yogi Berra wearing most of his catcher's equipment as he sat on the steps of the Yankee dugout, Herman Hickman, Grantland Rice, Sunny Jim Fitzsimmons, his friend Jack Murphy on a fishing trip, old English racing scenes. And a plaque with a metallic photo of a horse named for him, W. W. Smith, high-stepping across the finish line at Saratoga Raceway. "World record 1:58.4," the plaque proclaims, "4-year-old pacing gelding ½-mile track 9/10/66." Near it was a Joe DiMaggio–model bat.

Near another window, sunlight shone across *Webster's New International Dictionary*, second edition, that was open to pages 1306 and 1307, from *liege* to *ligature.* The dominant word on those two pages, with all its derivatives, was "life."

"I'd Like to Be Called a Good Reporter"

This personal recollection by Red Smith appeared in No Cheering in the Press Box, *a collection of interviews with sportswriters recorded and edited by Jerome Holtzman.*

NEW CANAAN, CONNECTICUT, 1973

I never felt that I was a bug-eyed fan as such. I wasn't one of those who dreamed of being a sportswriter and going around the country traveling with ballplayers and getting into the games free and, oh, dear diary, what a break. I'm not pretending that I haven't enjoyed this hugely. I have. I've loved it. But I never had any soaring ambition to be a sportswriter, per se. I wanted to be a newspaperman, and came to realize I didn't really care which side of the paper I worked on.

I'm too lazy to change over now, to start something new at this stage. I just got so comfortable in so many years in sports. But otherwise I still feel that way. I never cared. When I went to Philadelphia I didn't know what side of the paper I'd be on. I had done three or four years of rewrite and general reporting in St. Louis when I accepted the offer in Philadelphia. I knew how many dollars a week I was going to get. That was the essential thing. I never asked what they wanted me to do.

The guy I admire most in the world is a good reporter. I respect a good reporter, and I'd like to be called that. I'd like to be considered good and honest and reasonably accurate. The reporter has one of the toughest jobs in the world—getting as near the truth as possible is a terribly tough job. I was a local side reporter in St. Louis and Milwaukee. I wasn't as good as some. I wasn't one of those who could go out and find the kidnapper and the child. But I got my facts straight and did a thorough job.

I like to report on the scene around me, on the little piece of the world as I see it, as it is in my time. And I like to do it in a way that gives the reader a little pleasure, a little entertainment. I've always had the notion that people go to spectator sports to have fun and then they grab the paper to read about it and have fun again.

I've always tried to remember—and this is an old line—that sports isn't Armageddon. These are just little games that little boys can play, and it really isn't important to the future of civilization whether the Athletics or the Browns win. If you can accept it as entertainment, and write it as entertainment, then I think that's what spectator sports are meant to be.

I've been having fun doing this seminar at Yale, once a week. They call it Sports in American Society. I don't know what that name means, but obviously it's a big, broad topic and I have got guys up to help me. It's a round-table discussion, eighteen students, but usually there are a couple missing so it's about fifteen. We bat around everything from the reserve system to amateurism and professionalism, and yesterday they wanted to talk about sports journalism, a subject I have been avoiding because I wanted them to do the talking. As a rule, I fire out a subject and say, "What do you think about this?" and they kick it around. I like that better. I knew that if I was alone I'd do all the talking, so I got Leonard Koppett of the *Times* up there to help. And Koppett said that generally speaking sportswriters aren't the most brilliant people in the world because really smart people do something else besides traveling with a ball club for twenty-five years. I don't know. Did you ever feel discontented, feel the need to do something that other people would say was more important?

During the war, World War II, I was of draft age. By that I mean I hadn't yet gotten to be thirty-eight. I was registered for the draft, but I had a family and didn't think I could afford to be a private in the army and I didn't want to go looking for one of those phony public relations commissions. So I just kept traveling with the last-place Philadelphia Athletics and, oh boy, more than once I thought, What the hell am I doing here? But that was during the war. Outside of that I never felt any prodding need to solve the problems of the world. You can help a little by writing about games, especially if you're writing a column.

Oh, I don't know if I've ever helped, but I have tried to stay aware of the world outside, beyond the fences, outside the playing field, and to let that awareness creep into the column sometimes. Occasionally, I've thrown a line about a Spiro Agnew or a Richard Nixon into a piece. I wouldn't imagine I had any effect, excepting to make an occasional reader write and say, "Stick to sports, you bum. What do you know about politics?"

Sure, I respect the Tom Wickers. He's certainly more effective. But somehow I have felt that my time wasn't altogether wasted. I haven't been ashamed of what I've done. I seem to be making apologies for it. I don't mean to, because I feel keeping the public informed in any area is a perfectly worthwhile way to spend your life. I think sports constitute a valid part of our culture, our civilization, and keeping the public informed and, if possible, a little entertained about sports is not an entirely useless thing.

I did get a kick out of covering an occasional political convention, but even then my approach to it was as a sportswriter viewing a very popular spectator sport, and I tried to have fun with it. I did the presidential conventions in '56 and again in '68. The 1956 Democratic convention in Chicago was a pretty good one. Happy Chandler was a candidate for the presidential nomination. They finally nominated Adlai Stevenson and almost nominated John Kennedy for Vice President. Kennedy was in the Stockyard Inn writing his acceptance speech when they decided to go for Coonskin Cap—Kefauver. Anyway, there was Happy Chandler. He was a good, soft touch for one column. There was Governor Clements of Tennessee. He made one of the great cornball keynote addresses of our time, and he was good for another column. Let me see, what else? Oh, yes, Truman came on. He looked like the old champ, trying to make a comeback, like Dempsey. Truman wasn't running for reelection, but he showed up at the convention and made for lively copy. On the whole I just felt loose and easy and free to write what I pleased, and it seemed to come off well.

Over the years people have said to me, "Isn't it dull covering baseball every day?" My answer used to be "It becomes dull only to dull minds." Today's game is always different from yesterday's game. If you have the perception and the interest to see it, and the wit to express it, your story is always different from yesterday's story. I thoroughly enjoyed covering baseball daily.

I still think every game is different, not that some of them aren't dull, but it's a rare person who lives his life without encountering dull spots. It's up to the writer to take a lively interest and see the difference. Of course most of my years I was with a club to which a pennant race was only a rumor—the Philadelphia Athletics. I did ten years with them. They were always last.

I don't agree with him, but yesterday, at Yale, Leonard Koppett said one of the great untrue clichés in sports is that the legs go first. He said that's not true. He insists that the enthusiasm, the desire go first. And he said this is generally true of the athlete and, of course, when the athlete gets above thirty-five or forty he just can't go on. He's physically unable to. The writer can go on, he is able to physically, but Leonard believes writers lose their enthusiasm, too. He thinks very few writers of forty-five have had the enthusiasm of their youth for the job. He said he didn't know how writers of sixty-five felt, and I said, "Neither do I, but I don't think I've lost my enthusiasm." If I did, I'd want to quit.

My enthusiasm is self-generating, self-renewing. My life, the way it's been going now, I see very few baseball games in the summer. I'll start with the opening of the season. I'll see the games then, but things like the Kentucky Derby and Preakness get in the way, and lately we've had a home up in Martha's Vineyard, where I like to spend as much of the summer as I can, working from there. By the time the World Series comes along I may feel that I've had very little baseball for the year. But I find that old enthusiasm renewing itself when I sit there at the playoffs.

I don't enjoy the actual labor of writing. I love my job, but I find one of the disadvantages is the several hours at the typewriter each day. That's how I pay for this nice job. And I pay pretty dearly. I sweat. I bleed. I'm a slow writer. Once, through necessity, I was a fast rewrite man, when I had to be. I had no choice.

But when I began doing a column, which is a much more personal thing, I found it wasn't something that I could rip off the top of my head. I had to do it painstakingly. I'm always unhappy, very unhappy, at anything that takes less than two hours. I can do it in two hours, if I must. But my usual answer to the question "How long does it take to write a column?" is "How much time do I have?" If I have six hours, I take it. I wish I could say that the ones that take six hours turn out better. Not necessarily. But I will say this: I do think that, over three hundred days, effort pays off. If you do the best you can every day, taking as much time as necessary, or as much time as you have, then it's going to be better than if you brushed it off.

It's not very often that I feel gratified with a piece I've just written. Very often I feel, "Well, this one is okay." Or "This one will get by." The next day when I read it in print, clean and in two-column measure, it often looks better. But sometimes I'm disappointed. If I think I've written a clinker, I'm terribly depressed for twenty-four hours. But when you write a good one, you feel set up, the adrenaline is flowing.

Arthur Daley once told me that Paul Gallico asked him, "How many good columns do you strive for?"

Arthur said, "One every day."

And Gallico said, "I'll settle for two a week."

In my later years I have sought to become simpler, straighter, and purer in my handling of the language. I've had many writing heroes, writers who have influenced me. Of the ones still alive, I can think of E. B. White. I certainly admire the pure, crystal stream of his prose. When I was very young as a sportswriter I knowingly and unashamedly imitated others. I had a series of heroes who would delight me for a while and I'd imitate them—Damon Runyon, Westbrook Pegler, Joe Williams. This may surprise you, but at the top of his game I thought Joe Williams was pretty good.

I think you pick up something from this guy and something from that. I know that I deliberately imitated those three guys, one by one, never together. I'd read one daily, faithfully, and be delighted by him and imitate him. Then someone else would catch my fancy. That's a shameful admission. But slowly, by what process I have no idea, your own writing tends to crystallize, to take shape. Yet you have learned some moves from all these guys and they are somehow incorporated into your own style. Pretty soon you're not imitating any longer.

I was a very shy, timid kid. Going to Notre Dame and living for four years with guys—no girls, of course, were around—was good for me. It gave me a feeling of comfort mixing with my peers, a sense of comfort I didn't have in grade school or in high school. But my defense mechanism has been at work so long I still find myself talking too much at parties, things like that. I know this is a defense to cover shyness. I often hear myself babbling on and wish I'd shut up. I know it's because I'm shy. It's a defensive mechanism that has developed and operated over the years.

I'm not a psychologist, but I do know, for example, that a fellow like Howard Cosell is the braggart that he is because of a massive insecurity. He has to be told every couple minutes how great he is because he's so insecure. And if you don't tell him, he tells you. He can't help this.

I was born in Green Bay, Wisconsin. My father, Walter P. Smith, was the third generation in a family business—wholesale produce and retail groceries. My mother was born and grew up in New York. Her name was Ida Richardson. On vacation one time, visiting a friend out in Green Bay, she met my father and they got married. She spent the rest of her life in Green Bay, virtually all of it. My great-grandfather had come out from New Jersey and cleared a cedar swamp and started truck gardens. They raised garden truck and bought from farmers around there and shipped to northern Wisconsin and the northern peninsula of Michigan. They supplied hotels, restaurants, and grocery stores and they ran a grocery store in Green Bay. They went broke during the Depression.

There were three kids. I was the second son. My brother, Art, is still alive. He lives in the Bronx, and I guess he is retired. My brother never went to college. He had fun in high school, dating the French teacher and that sort of thing, and didn't bother reading any books. So eventually, well, my father said, "Look, for gosh sakes, either you do something or you go to work." So Art went to work on the hometown newspaper. He was a newspaperman all of his life. He was essentially a rewrite man and worked all the papers—Chicago, Milwaukee, Detroit, St. Louis, and New York. In New York he did rod and gun for the *Daily News* and for the *Herald Tribune*. That was his last newspaper job. He is a bit more than a year older than I am. We had a little sister, Catherine. She died of tuberculosis at about nineteen, while I was in college.

My parents read all the time. They weren't scholars or anything, but they were literate and there were books in the house. I remember bookcases with the glass doors in front. I read everything in the house. Corny 1910 romances entitled *The Long Straight Road,* and *When Knighthood Was in Flower.* Everything that was there, I read.

I was a real dedicated small-boy baseball fan up to World War I. Let's see, I was nine when World War I started and the Wisconsin-Illinois League folded about that time. For years I tried never to miss a game when the Green Bay team played at home. Casey Stengel won the batting championship that year. He played for Aurora, Illinois. I don't remember Stengel, but I can still almost recite the lineup of the Green Bay team of 1912 or 1914, whatever year Casey won the championship. I remember George Mollwitz, the Green Bay first baseman. I met him many years later in Bradenton, Florida. Somehow, all old ball players go to Bradenton. Mollwitz had a cup of coffee with the Cincinnati Reds, so he'd be in the record books.

And, of course, I played all sports. Everybody did. We played football and baseball on our lawn and we tried to take a clothes pole and vault, the way all kids do. But I never had any proficiency in sports. I learned to swim and loved it. Pretty early in life I learned to enjoy fishing, which is still my dodge. If I'm a participant in any recreation, it's fishing.

I was always out in the woods, just a kid playing along the creek. I remember meeting a young man who was fly-casting. I had never seen a fly rod before, or anyone casting flies. He was about five years older and turned out to be a very amiable guy. He taught me how to cut a willow branch and make a very poor fly rod out of it and cast for chubs and minnows in the stream. He became a hero of mine. His name was Vince Engel. He was going to Notre Dame, studying journalism, and therefore I felt it was necessary for me to do the same. That was great. I'd be like him. And of course, later I realized that sitting on my duff pounding a typewriter was a pretty easy way to make a living. It seemed very attractive, a lot better than lifting things.

I remember one day in high school I had a Notre Dame catalogue which I was studying, and a senior who was going to go to Notre Dame borrowed it from me. This was Jimmy Crowley, the left halfback on the Four Horsemen. He was a year ahead of me and a big football star, and I remember him borrowing it. He didn't need a catalogue because some old Notre Damer was sending him to Rockne. But he was interested in looking at it.

I stayed out of school for one year—between high school and college—simply to get a few hundred bucks because we had no money. I was an order clerk, filled orders for the Morley-Murphy-Olfell Hardware Company in Green Bay, not a very responsible job. I scuffled my way through Notre Dame. I got a job waiting on tables in a restaurant in South Bend. I borrowed money from a cousin. I contrived this and that. I got involved in class politics and, by chance, belonged to the winning party which elected the class president, and so on. As a reward for my political activities I got elected editor of the *Dome* and that was worth five hundred bucks.

I took a general arts course with a major in journalism. The journalism school consisted of one man, a darling old guy, Dr. John Cooney. I hadn't written very much. I did write an essay in high school, when I was a senior, that was published in the annual, some silly little thing. If I remember correctly, and I do, it was about the debating team. It was supposed to be a humorous sketch. God, I'd hate to read that today. Then I worked a little bit on what they called the *Notre Dame Daily,* which came out two or three times a week. I probably did fragments of news. But I didn't work there very long, because it was a dull operation.

I knew Rockne, of course, but whether he knew me I don't know. I tried to run on his track team. He was the track coach as well as the football coach. He coached pretty near everything when I was at Notre Dame.

In order to graduate we were supposed to have one credit in physical education, which really meant that once or twice a week you went to gym class and took calisthenics unless you did something else. And that something else could be participation in any sport. You were excused from gym class for the season of your sport, if you participated.

I loathed this gym class and didn't like the instructor. He was a senior trackman who just said, "Up, down! Up, down! C'mon there, Smith, get the lead out!" and so I signed up for freshman track. I don't think I had any misconceptions about my speed. I tried to run the mile because I knew I couldn't run very fast. I thought maybe I could run long. But I was mistaken about that, too. For just a few weeks I trained with the track team. I remember the freshman-varsity handicap meet came along, starting the indoor season, and I finished last in the mile, that's last among many. Paul Kennedy, who was an upperclassman and the star miler, went in 4:21, which sounds slow, but this was a dirt track, twelve laps to the mile, and 4:21 was a fast mile in that day, on that track. I was many laps behind. I never did any sportswriting at Notre Dame, not even in the annual where you sum up the football season and so on.

When I finished at Notre Dame I wrote about—now I say a hundred—but maybe it was only fifty letters to newspapers I got out of the Ayers Directory. I got my first job on the *Milwaukee Sentinel.* That was in the summer of '27. I was a cub reporter, chasing fire engines. I didn't do much. I was mostly being used to cover conventions, speeches, luncheons, and dinners. Every once in a while I'd be the ninth guy covering a murder investigation and it was pretty exciting. It was a morning paper and I'd be up all night. I didn't get off until midnight. These were Prohibition times, and I'd go down into the Italian ward where they had speakeasies and nightclubs with three-piece combos and canaries. Those were the people I knew. And I thought it was the most exciting thing in the world.

I was being promised raises but still getting twenty-four dollars a week, and then I moved to St. Louis. A guy who had been on the *Sentinel* had gone to the *St. Louis Star,* and he wrote a letter back to the makeup editor at the *Sentinel* which said, "Come on down, they're looking for people." He was really looking for friends to join him. The makeup editor had a divorce case coming up and couldn't leave the state, so he showed me the letter. And I wired the *Star,* faking it, advertising myself as an all-around newspaperman with complete experience—and got an offer of forty dollars a week on the copy desk. I was terrified but I took it.

That fall the managing editor, a man named Frank Taylor, fired two guys in the sports department, and he came over to me on the copy desk and he said, "Did you ever work in sports?"

And I said, "No."

"Do you know anything about sports?"

And I said, "Just what the average fan knows."

"They tell me you're very good on football."

"Well, if you say so."

And he said, "Are you honest? If a fight promoter offered you ten dollars would you take it?"

I said, "Ten dollars is a lot of money."

And he said, "Report to the sports editor Monday."

I stayed in sports about four years. Then I moved back to the local side, doing rewrite and general reporting. This was an exciting time. A lot of things were happening in St. Louis. Roosevelt had been elected and in his first message to Congress he said, "Bring back beer" and they brought it back, in about June. For months I wrote nothing but beer. It was a running story.

Beer was one of the big industries in St. Louis. I was always interviewing Gus Busch and Alvin Griesedick. I lived in the breweries in those days, doing stories such as should the alcohol content of beer be 3.2 by volume or by weight? Anheuser-Busch is almost a city by itself down in South St. Louis. The night beer came back—you wouldn't believe it. Several hundred guests were invited to the bottling plant which had a big bar, a rathskeller sort of place. Thousands of St. Louisans jammed the streets, dancing and singing and celebrating the end of Prohibition. At 12:01 the first bottle came down the conveyor and everybody got Gussie Busch to autograph the label.

I had been Walter W. Smith in the sports department, but I was anonymous 99 percent of the time on the news side. Everybody was, except Harry T. Brundage, our star reporter. He was the crime chaser and glamour boy. If Frank Taylor, the managing editor, felt very indulgent he might give you an occasional byline. I remember seeing a note he wrote to the city desk, advising that I be sent to interview George M. Cohan, and it said, "If he writes a good story, give him a byline."

One time Taylor called me over and said, "I want you to go out in the sticks and get some old lady, some old doll who has never been to a city, who has never seen an electric light. Bring her to town as our guest. Get an old guy if you have to, but preferably get a woman."

I had just read a story about a strike of tiffminers in a place called Old Mines, Missouri, in the foothills of the Ozarks. This was an area settled by the French at about the same time the fur traders were coming up from New Orleans and settling St. Louis. These tiffminers were completely isolated—only I had read a travel piece about how the hard road had just come into Old Mines.

My wife and I drove to Old Mines. It wasn't more than seventy-five miles out of St. Louis. I went to strike headquarters there and told the guys what I wanted, and they said I should go see Old Lady Tygert, in Callico Creek Hollow. Susan Tygert. I found this old lady smoking a corncob pipe and wearing a black sunbonnet and living in a one-room shack with her husband, John. She was seventy-nine or eighty, at the least, and had never been out of Callico Creek Hollow. She had never ridden in an automobile, never turned on an electric light, had never used the telephone.

I had a hell of a time getting her to come to St. Louis. She liked my wife, and besides, I promised she could ride on a Mississippi riverboat. She wasn't in St. Louis more than four or five days, and every day I wrote a story about her. I took her to the zoo and to places like the Statler Roof, where there was dancing and a show. She was charming and colorful, smoking that corncob pipe and wearing that black sunbonnet. Everybody was daffy about her. The stories got a warm response.

But O. K. Bovard, who was the managing editor of the *St. Louis Post-Dispatch*—the rival paper—read them and said, "It's a movie scenario." Bovard simply decided I was a faker, had faked the whole thing.

A little while after that Ed Wray, the sports editor of the *Post-Dispatch,* made me an offer. But first I had to go see Bovard and he wouldn't see me. I could have gone to work there, anyway, but I decided even if I could beat down his resistance it would be unwise to be working for a managing editor who was convinced I was a faker.

I went to the *Philadelphia Record* instead and stayed there ten years, all in sports, covering the Phillies and Connie Mack's A's.

In those days New York dominated the newspaper business, far more than it does today. The big papers were all here, the headquarters of the syndicates, the magazines, the book publishers, everybody so far as paper and ink was concerned. I had to take my shot at it. It was the pure ham in me, I guess. It was like playing the Palace.

I got my shot on V-J Day. I had heard Stanley Woodward was after me—he was the sports editor of the *New York Herald Tribune*. Early in 1945, during the first few weeks of the baseball season, an old friend of mine, Garry Schumacher, a New York baseball writer, said to me, "Have you heard from Stanley Woodward?"

I said he had called the other day, but I was out and when I called back he was out. I thought he wanted to know how old Connie Mack was, or something, you know, for a story. And Garry said, "Well, get plenty. He's coming after you."

I waited all summer and I never heard a sound out of Stanley, and I was dying. Finally, the morning after V-J Day, he called. We dickered and then we made a deal. It wasn't to write a column. He just hired me to work in the sports department, to take assignments, but he told me later he hoped I would wind up doing a column. I came over on September 24, 1945, one day before my fortieth birthday. Stanley lied to the *Tribune* about my age. He told them I was in my early thirties.

When I first knew Stanley as a casual press box acquaintance, I guess I resented him a little bit. He was an iconoclast. He was never one to accept the handout. He wanted to know himself. Also, during the war he was dead against sports. He felt games were nonessential and that we all should be fighting the war, that there shouldn't be a sports page, no baseball or horse racing, not even football—and he loved football. Well, of course, there shouldn't be necktie salesmen or florists or any of the nonessential industries, if you're fighting an all-out, 100 percent war. I disagreed with him. I felt there was some morale value to games.

He was perhaps the most thoroughly competent, all-around newspaperman I've known, a fine reporter, a great editor, a man who could do anything on the paper. He would have been a great managing editor. But he was impolitic and absolutely refused to compromise. He got fired for telling Mrs. Reid that she didn't know anything about running a newspaper.

Soon after he hired me there was an economy wave on the paper and he was ordered to cut two people from his staff, two older men who were near retirement. He said, "Give me some time and I'll arrange their retirement and we won't fire anybody."

But they said, "No, you've got to do it right now."

He refused. He lost his temper and said, "All right then, fire Smith and Woodward."

In those days they had all sorts of forms for the personnel department—added to payroll, subtracted from payroll, and so on. He got one of these payroll forms, for dismissal, listing reasons from one to ten and he wrote "Incompetence" and sent it through and that night, down in the office saloon, he told me, with great glee, what he had done.

The last straw was the silliest thing in the world. *The New York Times,* which in those days had an awful lot of space, had a banner on one of the inside pages on a women's golf tournament in Westchester. It wasn't of interest to anybody but the players, but some of Mrs. Reid's Westchester friends were offended because the *Tribune* didn't carry anything about the tournament, and she raised cain.

So Stanley investigated, found it was a weekly tournament and would require so much space to publish the results. He wrote a very snotty memo to this effect to Mrs. Reid and said if she insisted on him wasting space and effort on this tripe he wanted two additional columns of space for the sports section. He also told her he wouldn't insult one of his staff members by sending him on such an assignment. He would send a copyboy. She lost her temper and had him fired.

Stanley was a great man, and a great newspaperman and was always trying to put out the best section possible. Once, after he had left the paper, I tried to explain this to Mrs. Reid. I told her, "Didn't you understand, he was fighting with you to help improve your paper?"

But she simply fluttered. She just said something fluttery. I didn't know what the hell she was talking about.

Unlike the normal pattern, I know I have grown more liberal as I've grown older. I have become more convinced that there is room for improvement in the world. I seem to be finding this a much less pretty world than it seemed when I was younger, and I feel things should be done about it and that sports are part of this world. Maybe I'm sounding too damn profound or maybe I'm taking bows when I shouldn't. I truly don't know. But I do know I am more liberal and probably one of the reasons is that I married not only Phyllis, who is younger and more of today than I was, but I married five stepchildren who are very much of the current generation. They are very good friends and very articulate, and I think that this association has helped me to have a younger and fresher view.

My sympathies almost always have been on the side of the underdog, or the guy I think is the underdog. There was a time when I was more inclined to go along with the establishment. It may be because I'm no longer traveling with a baseball club and no longer exposed to the establishment day in and day out. I supported the players this past season when they went on that historic thirteen-day strike. Now that I do a column, I can stand there, a little removed, and look at what the Charlie Finleys and Bowie Kuhns are doing.

When I first heard about Marvin Miller—the players' man—I didn't hear anything favorable. I heard complaints from owners and club executives about how these ballplayers were putting themselves into the hands of a bloody labor organizer, a steel mill guy. I remember hearing one player, Dick Groat, saying he was in Pittsburgh and how he saw some of the results of union operations and that he wasn't in favor of it. He voted against employing Miller, as some other ballplayers did.

Then I began to hear that Miller is a pretty smart guy, seems like a very nice guy. The owners and the hierarchy, like the league presidents and such, were beginning to be very discreet in their remarks about Marvin. I had never met him until the winter baseball meetings in Mexico City, in 1968. I introduced myself. Since then, when there has been a newsworthy dispute in baseball—and there have been a lot of them—I have found I get straighter answers from Marvin than from anyone else I know in baseball. I have yet to find any trace of evidence that he's ever told me an untruth.

There have been times when he has said, "I think I had better not talk about that now," which is understandable. I don't doubt for a moment that he knows he's talking for publication and he's going to tell me what he thinks will look good on his side of the argument. But as far as I know, it's the absolute truth. More honest than most. Sports promoters find lying to the press is part of their business. They have no hesitation at all about it.

This generally applies across the board. I was going to say it also includes league presidents, but I would hate to think of Chub Feeney lying. I think Joe Cronin would avoid a fact now and then, or evade one. As for the present commissioner, Bowie Kuhn, he doesn't tell you anything so I don't know whether he lies or not. But the sportswriter learns to adjust, to make allowances. When you're listening to these people, who are serving special interests, you simply adjust by taking a little off the top.

Over the years, of course, all sportswriters, especially those assigned to and traveling with ball clubs, have difficulties with a ballplayer, or ballplayers. I never had anything as crucial as an actual fist fight, but I did have some differences with Bill Werber. This was when I was in Philadelphia and when he was traded or sold. The A's sent him to the Cincinnati Reds, and when the deal was announced I think I probably wrote something to the general effect of "Good riddance." I'm not sure. I didn't care deeply for Bill. I thought he paraded his formal education. He was out of Duke, you know, and he used to correct the grammar of other ballplayers. There were things about Bill that didn't enchant me.

In 1939 the Reds were in the World Series—that was the year the Yankees won in four straight and when big Ernie Lombardi wound up sprawled out at the plate. When we got to Cincinnati for the third game I went down to the bench before the game, and my old friend Paul Derringer said, "Hello, Red, you know Bill Werber, don't you?"

And Werber said, "Yes, I know the son of a bitch."

It went on, a tiny few exchanges like that, and then he said, "Get off this bench! Get out of the dugout!"

I said, "No, I'm a guest here."

And he got up and shouldered me out of the dugout, just kind of strong-armed me out. I had my portable and I was strongly tempted to let him have it—with the typewriter. But I somehow didn't feel like doing that on the field before the first World Series game in Cincinnati and so I left.

I remember Charlie Dexter coming along behind me and he said, "What are you going to do? Are you going to protest to the Baseball Writers Association?"

And I said, "No, Charlie, the player doesn't like me."

I didn't speak to him again. And then one day I was in Washington, in the National Press Building. I was on the elevator going to the Press Club and a most successful-looking insurance salesman carrying a briefcase, well dressed, got aboard and said, "Hello, Susie," to the elevator operator.

And I said, "Hello, Bill," and we shook hands. It had been at least ten years.

When Curt Flood sued baseball, Bill wrote me a letter. He was absolutely against Flood's suit and wrote disagreeing with something I had written in a column. Bill said that Curt Flood, with his limited education, was doing better than he had any right to expect.

I wrote back one letter saying that Flood had more ability and character than a great many educated men. I was trying to put Bill down. But he quickly responded with further argument which I didn't bother to answer. I didn't want to become his pen pal.

I won't deny that the heavy majority of sportswriters, myself included, have been and still are guilty of puffing up the people they write about. I remember one time when Stanley Woodward, my beloved leader, was on the point of sending me a wire during spring training, saying, "Will you stop Godding up those ballplayers?" I didn't realize what I had been doing. I thought I had been writing pleasant little spring training columns about ballplayers.

If we've made heroes out of them, and we have, then we must also lay a whole set of false values at the doorsteps of historians and biographers. Not only has the athlete been blown up larger than life, but so have the politicians and celebrities in all fields, including rock singers and movie stars.

When you go through Westminster Abbey you'll find that excepting for that little Poets' Corner almost all of the statues and memorials are to killers. To generals and admirals who won battles, whose specialty was human slaughter. I don't think they're such glorious heroes.

I've tried not to exaggerate the glory of athletes. I'd rather, if I could, preserve a sense of proportion, to write about them as excellent ballplayers, first-rate players. But I'm sure I have contributed to false values—as Stanley Woodward said, "Godding up those ballplayers."

1.

Olympics

KINGS GET IN FREE

LONDON, 1948
England's biggest track meet in forty years opened this afternoon with a pageant of nationalism, an orgy of oratory and a paroxysm of symbolism but no running, jumping, or bulging of the biceps. The recorded casualties were a half-dozen Boy Scouts and Sea Scouts who fainted under the malevolent sun which beat upon Wembley Stadium with padded brutality.

King George VI, perspiring royally in his gold-braided sailor suit, and his missus, Queen Elizabeth, in some yards of pale blue fluff with a large, floppy hat to match, got in on passes (no tax or service charge). About 82,000 cash customers paid up to two guineas apiece ($8.40) to watch the stately and magnificent rinky-dink that set off the games of the fourteenth Olympiad.

The King earned his free ticket, though. The gentry and the costers who bought theirs had only to sit and swelter in the great, steaming, concrete cauldron. His Majesty had to stand at rigid, humid attention for fifty minutes, which is the equivalent of clutching a strap on the East Side subway from Parkchester to 14th Street; he had to salute the flags of fifty-nine nations carried past the royal box. He had to make a sixteen-word speech. Never were the hardships of the monarch business more amply demonstrated although, admittedly, the hours and salary are usually very good.

Besides sitting and sweltering, the cash trade beat sweaty palms red, yowled and chanted and waved flags as the musclemen of their countries marched by. For let there be no mistake about it, these Olympics are the amateur sporting world's clearest expression of nationalism.

It was the desire of the games' founder, it says here in the program, that "the spirit of international comity be advanced by the celebration of chivalrous and peaceful contests," and Lord Burghley, the reformed Olympic hurdler who is chairman of the Organizing Committee which runs these games, spoke of "kindling a torch of that ageless and heartfelt prayer of mankind for peace and good will among men." But when their teams marched in, partisans hollered just as fight fans do for Rocky Graziano, who is no career torch-kindler.

They made clear the sound and healthy point that in the carnival of international competition which the ensuing fortnight will see, the idea is going to be, as it should be, to knock the spots off the other guy.

Wembley Stadium at two o'clock was a cooked gaboon of concrete, its gray slopes packed, its currycombed infield a vivid green encircled by a track of bright red clay. In one section of seats, the massed bands of His Majesty's Brigade of Guards blared and oompahed. Across the arena, about two-fifteen, a great covey of Olympic brass lined up in the sweaty elegance of silk hats and frock coats.

At two forty-five exactly (in the king-and-emperor business, punctuality is of the essence) His Majesty came hiking out of a tunnel under the stands, shook hands with Burghley and the president of the International Olympic Committee, a silk-hatted Swede named J. Sigfrid Edstrom. With these two trailing him, the King then strolled the length of the waxworks, pumping hands with each exhibit. Amid a moderate patter of handclapping, he walked up to the royal box and sat at his spouse's left, directly under the tote board for Wembley's dog races.

Out of a runway at the east end of the oval came a Boy Scout with bare knees and a sign reading "Greece." Being the original Olympic nation, Greece's team led the march. The Greeks in the front ranks were all bald, obviously committeemen, caterers, and coaches. Their big silken flag, a white cross on a blue field, dipped as it passed the royal box. The King, standing, snapped to salute.

Thereafter, he remained standing as the flags passed in alphabetical order, never once shifting to relieve the heat on his royal bunions, saluting even those flags which were not dipped. About a half-dozen standards were not lowered, either because of national rules, or because their bearers hadn't been sufficiently rehearsed, or as a form of political criticism. Ireland's flag was half-dipped; grudgingly might be an accurate adverb. Colombia's didn't go down, but its bearer snapped into a majestic goose-step as he passed. By and large, the teams marched better than baseball squads do at the flag-raising on opening day.

The first wholehearted burst of applause came for Australia, first of the United Kingdom affiliates to show. However, the loudest enthusiasm manifested between A and E was inspired by the Danish team, whose claque set off a volley of yells and upped with a regular flurry of red Danish flags with their white crosses. Subsequently, this section boisterously hailed all Scandinavians—the Finns, Norwegians, Swedes, and even Iceland's team. As each such group appeared, the rooters gave off a chant that sounded, from this seat, like "Yale, Yale, Yale."

There were big teams and little. Panama was represented by one guy in a Panama hat, not Lloyd LaBeach, the sprinter. India's team wore baby-blue burnooses. New Zealand's had what looked like smoking jackets. The Swiss wore caps like lady softball players. The United States got a restrained hand; the last man in our ranks halted to snap the King's picture.

Well, the King finally got to sit down. He looked on while trumpeters trumpeted, speakers spoke, and attendants released a great mess of caged pigeons, which zoomed and swooped over 82,000 unprotected skulls. The billing promised 7,000 pigeons, or one for every twelfth head, but it looked like maybe 2,000. Chances are the brass didn't dare turn loose that many squab in this hungry nation. Almost immediately twenty-one guns boomed. Sounded like first day of the duck season off Little Tail Point in Green Bay, Wisconsin.

Now a tall young blond in his underwear burst through the entrance and circled the track, bearing aloft the Olympic torch, a blinding magnesium sparkler which hurt the eyes. Theoretically, the torch had been lighted on Mt. Olympus and delivered by Western Union boys running in relays across Europe, with a Ford truck following with a spare torch in case the real McCoy went out. Actually, the torch that appeared here was a ringer, a special oversize job carried on the last relay from a suburb like Bay Ridge.

The torchbearer dashed up into the stands, brandished his torch on high and dropped it into a tall concrete bird bath—from which red flame arose. That flame will burn throughout these games.

The crowd made with the tonsils. It was hokum. It was pure Hollywood. But it was good. You had to like it.

VICTORY SPELLED BACKWARDS

LONDON, 1948

And now, the Royal Air Force band must return to the desolate, forsaken field of Wembley Stadium and unplay "God Save the King." Blighty's only track victory in the Olympics, which was presented to Britain last Saturday under the Marshall Plan, fell under the terms of reverse lend-lease today and was restored to the United States, the original copyright holders. It was the most sensational reversal since Serutan.

At 4:00 P.M. on Saturday, the American team of Barney Ewell, Lorenzo Wright, Harrison Dillard and Mel Patton—identified locally as three cups of coffee with the cream on top—fled home first in the 400-meter relay by seven or eight yards.

Five minutes later a vigilante committee of judges ruled that Ewell, after running the first hundred meters, had bootlegged the baton to Wright in a sinister black-market deal consummated outside the legal zone. The United States was disqualified; England was declared the winner; the Union Jack flapped from the victor's flagpole; the British Lion looked up from his lunch of cold mutton and cheese and roared his triumph to the skies.

But they had reckoned without J. Arthur Rank and his magic lantern. Today Mr. Rank brought out his stereopticon machine and pictures of the race were shown to the American, the Frenchman, the Finn, the Dutchman, the Czech, and the two Britons composing an International Jury of Appeal. The slides proved, beyond possible cavil, that the baton-snatch had been engineered in strict obedience to the laws of God and man.

The jury thereupon declared the Americans undisqualified. The decision came shortly after 12:30 P.M. Thus the United States triumph was accomplished in 68 hours 37 minutes 40.6 seconds. This is not an Olympic record.

Gold, silver, and bronze medals for first, second, and third place were, of course, awarded last Saturday to Great Britain, Italy, and Hungary, whose runners now are required to disgorge, yield up, surrender, and relinquish the hardware. Chances are that before these twelve gimcracks reach their rightful owners, Scotland Yard will have to comb every hock shop in London.

Thus history was made today, both in international athletics and in the film industry. It was not only the first reversal of a decision involving victory in any Olympic competition; it was also one of the few times within living memory that the movies definitely settled a disputed point in any sport. In the past, it has almost invariably turned out that the cameraman was ogling a blond when the deed was done.

Before these pictures were shown to the jury, they were viewed by Castleton Knight, producer of Mr. Rank's sweaty epic. He gave it as his inexpert opinion that the camera had caught the Americans red-handed and the disqualification would stand. The London press quoted Mr. Knight to this effect, unaware that he didn't happen to know what he was talking about.

This was, nevertheless, a great day for the flicker industry. All through the games, there have been approximately as many cameramen as athletes on the field, creating the impression that this struggle for world supremacy was mere window-dressing for a J. Arthur Rank production. That impression has been gloriously confirmed. Eighty-two thousand cash customers saw a race last Saturday. Now they've got to go to a theater to see the offiical contest.

Half an hour after the jury's decision, the films were run off for the press. Agreement was unanimous that Ewell and Wright had swapped the stick well over on the alkaline side of the white stripe marking the limit of the legal zone. The only argument concerned their margin of safety.

"Three feet," said Mr. Knight.

The assembled experts jeered.

Twelve feet, they insisted. Ten, anyway. Two full strides, someone estimated. Another counted three. Somebody else guessed four.

"Aw," said somebody, "give 'em three steps."

"Coo," said a small voice, " 'aven't we given 'em enough already?"

As if things weren't tough enough for the bandsmen, having to learn the anthems of fifty-nine nations, including Liechtenstein, now they've got to play "The Star-Spangled Banner" backward.

"O, Yas Nac Uoy Ees . . . ?"

GOOD, CLEAN FUN

HELSINKI, 1952

The Lady of the Bath glanced up without curiosity when four gents tottered out of the steam room of the sauna, all naked as jaybirds and broiled like proper sirloins, charred on the outside, medium rare in the middle. The Lady of the Bath, an old doll wearing spectacles and a long rubber apron, was busy soaping and scrubbing the tract of masculine meat on her pine-board table, and the newcomers represented more work on an already crowded day.

The sauna (pronounced *sowna*) is a Finnish bath, and a great deal more. It is a sacred rite, a form of human sacrifice in which the victim is boiled like a missionary in the cannibal islands, then baked to a turn, then beaten with sticks until he flees into the icy sea, then lathered and honed and kneaded and pummeled by the high priestess of this purgatorial pit.

Nothing relaxes a Finn like this ritual of fire worship, water worship, and soap worship. It is an ancient folk custom dating from forgotten times, and it explains why Finland produces so many great marathon runners. Anybody who can survive a sauna can run twenty-six miles barefoot over broken beer bottles.

The most gracious gesture of hospitality a Finn can make is to bathe with his guest. From an American host, a suggestion that everybody go get washed might imply that the guest was getting a trifle gamy, but Americans don't know everything. Lots of them haven't been bathed by a doll since they were six.

"A foreigner," says a pamphlet on the subject, "who leaves Finland without the intimate acquaintance of a sauna cannot boast of having got into the grips with the Finnish mentality. Through it the creature of civilization is enabled to get in touch with the primal forces of nature—earth, fire and water."

Curious about primal forces, three Americans and Kai Koskimies, their Finnish keeper, had taxied out to Waskiniemi, on the outskirts of Helsinki, where a birch forest meets the blue waters of the Gulf of Finland. There they stripped to the buff, bowed cordially to the Lady of the Bath, and entered the steam room.

In a murky, low-ceilinged cubicle recognizable by anybody who ever read Dante, several other lost souls attired in sweat sat on benches with faces buried in their hands. The room was heated—an understatement, as ever was—by a sort of Dutch oven in which cobblestones are cooked over a fire of birch logs. A thermometer registered only 130 degrees Fahrenheit, and Kai, making a snoot of disapproval, scooped water onto the hot rocks to get up a head of steam.

The visitors were destined to discover the differences between dry heat and the steamy coziness of this inferno. The steam room is the simple, ancient type of sauna, which is part of the humblest Finnish home. There are 400,000 of them in Finland, one for every ten people. "The air gives off a slight but exhilarating aroma of smoke," says the pamphlet. "The effect of the open fireplace feels strong to sensitive people."

Four sensitive people stood it as long as any hickory-smoked ham could have done. Then they oozed out of the cell like melted tallow, and Kai led the way to another room, providing dry heat. There the thermometer outraged him. It registered only 176 degrees, not even warm enough to boil an egg. The sauna proprietor agreed that this was ridiculous.

"This is no sauna," he said, and did something with the fireplace. "In one, two, three minutes it will be warm." In one, two, three minutes the thermometer raced up to 219 degrees. Missionaries are fricasseed at 212.

Bundles of leafy birch branches were provided as knouts so the bathers could beat themselves. Kai splashed water around to cool the wooden floor and benches, but it evaporated instantly. Even with the insulation of a folded Turkish towel, the seats were like stove lids.

Relaxing Finnish-style, everybody sat rocking from cheek to cheek to avoid being fried outright. At the same time, all laid about with the birch, flogging themselves like flagellants. After that came a refreshing dip in the sea.

The Gulf of Finland is colder than an Eskimo spinster. All feeling, however, had been left behind in the stew pot. The instant a guy hit the water he turned numb; he suffered no more than a corpse.

Cleanliness was next on the schedule, and the Lady of the Bath was the babe to provide it. She starts with a shampoo, then works on the subject in sections—just as one eats a lobster, cleaning up one claw, laying it aside, and picking up another. Her powerful fingers probe deep, finding muscles the doctors never have charted. She is skillful, efficient, and thorough. She scrapes the hull with a rough wet towel. The combination massage and scouring process is genuinely relaxing, easing muscles, untying knotted nerves.

That's all there is to a sauna, except for one technicality. The technicality is that as soon as you're finished, you do it all over—the heat, the swim, and the shower. In the winter, when the sea drops two degrees in temperature and freezes over, you can't swim. You go outdoors and roll in the snow instead. On the second time around, the temperature in the dry oven had got satisfactorily cozy. It was slightly over 269 degrees. This created some excitement around the sauna. They said it was a world record.

When it's all over, you get a diploma testifying that you are alive and clean. This is partly true.

CZECH AND DOUBLE CZECH

HELSINKI, 1952

In the morning there was a headline in a paper from Paris reading: *"La Finale du 5000 Mètres? Ce Sera la Bombe Atomique des Jeux!* (This will be the atomic bomb of the games.)" In the afternoon there was thin sunshine, turned on specially for the occasion by the Finns, to whom nothing is impossible when it involves entertaining the thieves of time and destroyers of distance in congress here from all the nations of the world.

The steep slopes of the stadium were peopled with the greatest crowd yet drawn for Olympic competition here. Thousands of athletes not engaged on the day's card sat among the cash customers, taking time off from their rehearsals to see the *bombe atomique* go off.

Even on the field there was uncommon congestion. Judges scurried in flight as whirling hammer throwers flung hardware about the huge playpen. Guy Butler, an old English Olympian now turned journalist-photographer, was stooping to dig into his equipment case when something hissed through the air and landed—kerchok!—just short of his unprotected flank. He whirled and saw, quivering in the real estate, the javelin of a Russian broad (the term is purely descriptive, not ungallant).

On the fifth day of boisterous combat, this conclave of gristle had achieved a climax with the second bid for a gold medal by the comical contortionist Emil Zatopek. Four years ago, this gaunt and grimacing Czech with the running form of a zombie had made himself the pin-up boy of the London games. Witnesses who have long since forgotten the other events still wake up screaming in the dark when Emil the Terrible goes writhing through their dreams, gasping, groaning, clawing at his abdomen in horrible extremities of pain. In the most frightful horror spectacle since *Frankenstein,* Zatopek set an Olympic record for 10,000 meters in London and barely failed to win the 5,000 from Belgium's Gaston Reiff. This year he broke his own records for both speed and human suffering at 10,000, and two days ago he created a minor sensation in his 5,000-meter heat. Leading on the last lap, he made the only political gesture yet seen on this playground, slowing up and beckoning to his Communist cousin, Russia's Aleksandr Anoufriev, to come on and win the heat.

Now he was back in the 5,000 final, trying for a distance double that had defied every mortal save Finland's Hannes Kolehmainen, who won these two tests in 1912. To the Finns, these are the races that count; anything shorter is for children.

For example, an old gaffer around here overheard mention of Andy Stanfield, the Jersey City sprinter, and asked: "Stanfield? Who is he?"

"The American champion," he was told. He blinked.

"How can he be champion to run two hundred meters?" the old guy said. "He should run anyway five kilometers."

That's what Zatopek was doing, along with Reiff; Alain Mimoun, the French Algerian schoolmaster; Herbert Schade, the German favorite, and Chris Chataway, the Oxford blue. These five were the leaders from the start, and they made up a sort of gentlemen's club on the front end, some distance removed from the ten other starters. Then Reiff quit the lodge, giving up on the eleventh turn around the track, with a lap and a half to go.

All through the race, Zatopek had commanded the rapt attention of spectators, and with every agonized step he had rewarded them. Bobbing, weaving, staggering, gyrating, clutching his torso, flinging supplicating glances toward the heavens, he ran like a man with a noose about his neck. With half a mile to go, Schade and Chataway passed him. He seemed on the verge of strangulation; his hatchet face was crimson, his tongue lolled out. A quarter-mile left, and he went threshing to the front again, but as they turned into the backstretch for the last time, he was passed by Schade, then Chataway, then Mimoun.

Now he was surely finished, a tortured wreck three yards back of the three leaders who ran in a tight little cluster into the last turn.

Suddenly, midway of the turn, there was a flash of red on the outside. Four times in front and four times overtaken, that madman was rushing into the lead with his fifth and final spurt. He went barreling past the rest in an unbelievable charge. There was a jam on the inside, and Chataway sprawled over the curb into the infield.

Mimoun took out after Zatopek. The little Algerian made a fine run, as fruitless as it was game. He tailed Zatopek home as he had at 10,000 meters. Even Schade, in third place, broke Reiff's Olympic record, and Chataway, who got to finish fifth alongside his countryman Gordon Pirie, was only four-tenths of a second off the London time.

A little later in the day, Mrs. Zatopek won the javelin throw in the women's department. Czech and double Czech.

THE SIX O'CLOCK SWILL

MELBOURNE, 1956

This is written after a conscientious and coldly scientific survey of Melbourne's most celebrated institution—the six o'clock swill. The Olympic Games will spawn bigger headlines in the world press, but the press of this troubled world is not noted for its sense of proportion. Take a bottle-scarred researcher's word for it, the Olympic marathon will produce no gamer competitors or pluckier stayers than the legions who rush the growler six evenings a week in Melbourne's pubs. The six o'clock swill is a charming folk custom sired by a law which requires saloons to stop serving at six P.M. This creates a challenge which no Aussie worth his malt will take lying down, or at least not as long as he can stand. Most offices close at five, most shops at five-thirty. It isn't easy to make your load in one hour, much less thirty minutes, but these people come from pioneer stock.

In a recent referendum a proposal to keep bars open until ten o'clock was defeated by an odd coalition, not to say an unholy one. Marshaled against the bill were the outright prohibitionists, the saloonkeepers, and the housewives. The first group wants the joints closed as early as possible, the proprietors are happy with the roaring business they do and don't want working hours extended and labor costs increased. The wives just want their husbands.

"When my Joe comes home," the suburban ladies concede, "he's generally tiddly and sometimes rotten. But he does get home for supper."

Briefed on these simple, sordid facts, an exploring party set out at five P.M. guided by a Melbourne taxpayer whose feeling for the six o'clock swill is one of warm appreciation. "There's bound to be jostling," he said, "and you're odds on to slop some beer on another bloke. You say 'Sorry.' When you've spilled enough beer on him you're friends for life. Makes it a quite decent social do, if you know what I mean."

First stop was the pub in Hosie's Hotel, an old place lately rebuilt, rather shiny with blond paneling. It's a fairly sizable room with two bars forming an L down the lefthand wall and across the back. Drinkers weren't three deep as they are in a good New York saloon in rush hours. They simply packed the joint from wall to wall, laborers, clerks, businessmen, truckers, here and there a sailor or soldier. All were males. "The women," the guide said, "are breaking down the barriers. It's only in the last five or six months that they've been showing up in pubs. By the time the games are over, I think it will be broken down altogether, except in a blood house like this. Toss that off and we'll go along."

He led the way down the street to the Port Philip Club Hotel, a long arcade with bars in the arcade proper and bars in rooms branching off to right and left. The place was jammed with sailors. When you ordered a beer, the barman didn't carry your glass to a tap. He carried a pistol-shaped spigot hitched to a long tube and squirted your glass full where you stood.

"For mass production," the guide said, "Detroit couldn't beat this. Would you call it Willow Run? Let's go meet Chloe."

Chloe is a gilt-framed blob of pink loveliness in Young and Jackson's pub a few doors down the street. She hangs on a battered, scaly wall, gloriously nude and internationally famous. She was painted in 1875 from a model—legend says—named Marie, a lively lady of Paris. The tale is told that one night Marie gathered all her friends for a lavish feast, wined them and dined them and sent them away, then boiled match heads into a poisonous potion and gulped it down.

It was getting on toward six o'clock and the jam in Young and Jackson's several bars was beyond describing. More than a few customers had heavy-looking satchels full of bottled beer that they would take home, the guide said. Six o'clock struck and a voice of dire warning came howling out of loudspeakers. Some drinkers lined up three or four glasses, for they would have fifteen minutes to empty them and clear out. A minute after six, men were pleading for one more and bartenders were opening the taps from which beer no longer flowed.

Downstairs somebody had shut off a master valve.

"SKULLDUGGERY" EXPOSED

NEW YORK, 1956

Well, the sordid truth is out, and from now on Allen Dulles will keep his snooping beak away from here if the miserable reprobate knows what's good for him. He and his whole Central Intelligence Agency might as well be told right out what they can do with their flamin' cloaks and daggers.

A Russian periodical called *Literary Gazette* has revealed that when we were all in Melbourne for the Olympics last fall, Dulles had a stable of shapely dolls on call to corrupt the Soviet athletes.

How about that for discrimination? Our own agents skulking around Olympic Village plying Bolsheviks named Tcherniavski and Bachlykov with dainty viands and toothsome blonds, and who consoles the flower of the loyal American press along Flinders and Swanston Streets? Avery Brundage, that's who. As they say Down Under, well ecktually!

It's all clear enough now that *Literary Gazette* has blown the whistle, but it is humiliating to realize that scores of the busiest ferrets in American journalism could be on the scene and fail to see what was going on under their twitching noses.

A fellow thinks back to Olympic Village now and recalls scenes in the Recreation Center which seemed innocent enough at the time. It was bright, airy and a generally merry place where kids of all nations frolicked in their spare time. During the day you might see Andy Stanfield, the sprinter, beating a Russian hurdler at chess. Others would be whacking a ping-pong ball around or writing letters or playing cards while the walls trembled under the impact of a rock-and-roll record.

In the evening Mrs. Earlene Brown would take over, and then the joint started jumping. Earlene was the belle of the ball, the darling of the international set. She is a jolly Negro woman out of Los Angeles, 226 tireless pounds, a smasher on the dance floor.

Not only Russians, but Afghans, Turks, Slavs and Finns learned rock-and-roll from Earlene. Who'd ever suspect that this jovial Mata Hari's dark purpose was to wean Soviet music lovers away from Tchaikovsky and Shostakovich into the imperialist camp of Elvis Presley?

Yes, and under cover of Elvis' bawling, manly Muscovite hammer throwers would be out strolling beneath the Southern Cross, murmuring state secrets to Allen Dulles' "flopsies," to use the solicitous Australian term.

Allen must have swiped a leaf from Jim Norris' book and signed all available talent to exclusive service contracts, for downtown Melbourne after dark reminded hardly anybody of the Casbah.

It was downright pitiful to see dashing correspondents of the romantic Richard Harding Davis type languishing in the International Press Bar of the Melbourne Cricket Ground with no better way to pass the evening than a celibate game of ricki-ticky for the bartender's shillings.

Only once were traces of rouge and lipstick detected on Melbourne's sternly Puritan face. A chunk of the American Navy sailed in one day about noon. Within an hour, the streets swarmed with gobs and every blessed one of them had a bit of fluff on his arm.

The Games were pretty well along when the fleet arrived. By that time, no doubt, the last Russian broadjumper had been brainwashed and Mr. Dulles had turned his delectable operatives out to pasture.

American agents, *Literary Gazette* reports, "tried to palm off 'secret documents' on our girls and boys. They tried to give them photographs of military objectives in order to convict them later of espionage." It is mortifying to realize that a lot of us saw that happening and thought it was only a cuddly camaraderie characteristic of childish games.

In the opening ceremonies, the big U.S.S.R. team followed the big U.S.A. delegation into the Stadium and the two groups lined up side by side on the infield. Pretty soon they broke ranks and mingled, indistinguishable in their white jackets except for a trace of tattletale gray in the Soviet uniform.

American women took off their shoes and wiggled their toes in the grass. Men swapped lapel badges for souvenirs. American women traded white gloves for the Soviets' red breast-pocket handkerchiefs. Who could have known there was microfilm in every glove?

Literary Gazette says sneak thievery went on, and blames American spies. Melbourne hotel owners who applied the time-honored Kentucky Derby gouge will properly resent that. Since the days of the immortal robber, Ned Kelly, the home-grown Australian bandit has been the equal of any.

WHEN IN ROME

ROME, 1960

This town was raised on wolf milk, as any friend of Romulus and Remus could tell you, and the critter is regarded as more or less sacred here. When a guy is a wolf, Romans don't dignify him by calling him that. They call him a parakeet, presumably for the way he whistles.

A parakeet sidled up to Mrs. Olga Fikotova Connolly and made signs indicating that he deemed her a right tasty dish. Olga, defending Olympic discus champion, married the Boston strongboy, Harold Connolly, after winning the Gold Medal for Czechoslovakia in Melbourne. She now is competing for the United States while her mate defends his championship in the hammer throw.

"Husband," Olga said, scaling the language barrier like Lee Calhoun clearing a hurdle, "hammer . . . boing!"

When last seen, the parakeet was headed down the Appian Way, lengthening stride at every jump. The moral seems to be that things haven't changed much around here since J. Caesar was making passes at Cleopatra.

There always are minor changes, of course, one of which will be noted tonight when the Romans jump the gun on custom and bring the Olympic torch into the city a day ahead of the opening of the Seventeenth Games.

Ordinarily this hallowed Roman candle, lighted in Olympia and hauled from Greece to the site of the games by steamship, Ford truck, and boy scouts in running pants, travels on a schedule calculated to bring it into the main arena just at the climax of the opening ceremonies. There a runner flings it into a big birdbath full of benzene, which bursts into flame and is kept blazing until the last weary marathon runner has tottered through his last paces three weeks hence.

Rome, however, figures that she's learned a thing or two in the last 2,500 years about putting on a circus. The torch will make its scheduled appearance in Stadio Olimpico Thursday afternoon, but before that it will have been carried ceremoniously up the steep stairs to the Capitol itself, heart of this ancient city. Passing through Naples tonight, the torch will reach the Appian Way at evening tomorrow, come blazing through the darkness under the triumphal Arch of Constantine and arrive about nine P.M. in the Campidoglio, the lofty little piazza designed by Michelangelo.

It is revealing no secret to observe that the Latins are an emotional race, flaky about melodrama. This characteristic is reflected everywhere, in the dress that the whole city has put on for the carnival, in the way the organizing committee has managed to blend the antique and modern in the stage settings.

There isn't a street that is not festooned with flags and banners—the red, white, and green flag of Italy, the burgundy and gold of Rome, the white Olympic flag with its five interlocking rings. Olympic posters appear on building fronts everywhere, especially those marked *affissione vietata*, meaning post no bills.

While runners and cyclists and soccer players and fighters and swimmers are competing in magnificent new stadia and arenas—built for this festival with $70,000,000 of gambling profits from the national football lottery—rasslers will be writhing and gymnasts gyrating in some of the most ancient monuments of the civilized world.

Mats will be spread under the mighty arches of the Basilica di Massenzio, built by Maxentius in A.D. 306 at the end of the Roman Forum, and the grunts of the rasslers will be heard where other crowds heard the roars of lions. Among the arches, pillars, and crumbling walls of the Baths of Caracalla, gymnasts will fling themselves about in premises that were devoted to physical culture 1,700 years ago.

Not since 1896 in Athens have any games of the modern Olympic era had a setting to compare with this, yet antiquity hasn't taken charge altogether.

Bravely holding the fort for the modern view is Flaming Mamie, a splendid new statue executed for this show, that stands outside the glaringly modern Palazzo dello Sport, the boxing and basketball arena.

Mamie is a tall marble broad wearing a union suit and holding a torch aloft. She is knock-kneed and flat-chested, but the most striking feature is her abdomen.

It may be art, but any respectable obstetrician would take another view.

WINNERS TELL JOKES

ROME, 1960

Thirty-seven soft-shoe shufflers in their underwear crowded up to the starting line for the 20,000-meter walk—a sprint of about twelve and a half miles—and a guy in the press box said: "Did I ever tell you about my Uncle George? He was disqualified from the Olympics for beating the gun three times in the 50,000-meter walk."

The hikers went wriggling and squirming away like night crawlers after a rain, elbows pumping, shoulders shrugging, hips swinging, and laughter followed them around the brick-red track and out onto the baking streets. Last one through the gate was a Tunisian named Naoui Zlassi, wearing a pillowcase on his nob. About an hour and three-quarters later he would get back last, with his headgear missing and sunset rays lighting his glistening scalp the way the sunset lights Mount Rainier.

"As a chart-caller would put it," a guy said, "he raced evenly," and this was pretty hilarious, too, for as they say around the poker table, the winners tell funny stories and the losers say, "Deal."

This was on Friday, when American hearts were light and gay for the first time in the Seventeenth Olympic Games. In the morning faces had been longer than the Appian Way, for on the afternoon before, John Thomas of Cambridge, Massachusetts, had lost to two Russians the high jump he couldn't possibly lose and Ray Norton, considered the world's greatest sprinter, had run last in the 100 meters. Now, though, it was a bright new day, and the band kept whomping away at a truncated version of "The Star-Spangled Banner," and the banner itself kept creeping up the flagpole, and chauvinistic kissers gleamed with broad Yankee grins.

In the morning there'd been guys around ready to horsewhip Thomas because, after shattering every high-jump record ever set by man and making "seven feet" a dirty pair of words, he had been, on one day of his young life, unable to clear more than 7 feet ¼ inch. Fact is, he had more excuses than anybody needs, and nobody who jumps seven feet needs any.

After a bout with the popular tourist disorder called the Tyrrhenian two-step, he came up to the biggest day of his nineteen years feeling plumb peaked. He was second-guessed severely for passing his turn when the bar was at the Olympic record of 6 feet 11½ inches. This was a tactical decision. He felt he had one good jump left in him, and he made it, and this day it wasn't good enough.

Though he didn't mean to, he demonstrated why Olympic records seldom match world records. All around the globe there are guys shooting at world records every week of the year. An Olympian gets one chance in four years to surpass the best that the greatest have accomplished under ideal circumstances.

"It isn't everybody can win a bronze medal in the Olympics," young Thomas said afterward, consoling himself.

He was dead right, but in their disappointment a lot of Americans failed to recognize this until the next day, when the Yanks came on like gang busters.

First the American hurdlers "ran the table," as we say around the poolroom. On the little chopping block where the medalists get their hardware, Glenn Davis, Cliff Cushman, and Dickie Howard took their places. The self-possessed Davis, Olympic and world champion, bent low to let England's old Olympian, Lord David Burghley, hang the gold medal around his neck, waved to the crowd, grabbed Lord David's elbow with a companionable clutch, and shook hands. Cushman grinned like a blond billiken getting his silver bauble. Hands folded as in prayer, Howard bowed his neck as though for the guillotine.

Then Wilma Rudolph, a leggy doll from Clarksville, Tennessee, ripped three-tenths of a second off the world record for females at 100 meters. The record won't go into the books because of a following wind that blew one gasp harder than the legal limit, but she smashed her field and up went the flag again.

Here came Earlene Brown to pick up a bronze medal for third place in the distaff shot put, and then the interminable business in the men's broad jump soared to a climax.

The broad-jump record has been a track-and-field freak, the only one to withstand the assault of postwar legions. Jesse Owens set the world record of 26 feet 8¼ inches in Ann Arbor, Michigan, in 1935, and it stood alone as the oldest in the books until Ralph Boston beat it this year by three inches. When these Games opened, no Olympic jumper had ever matched Owens' leap of 26 feet 5¼ inches in Berlin in 1936.

Halfway through Friday's round, Boston did 26 feet 7¾ inches. It wiped Owens' Olympic mark off the books and virtually assured America of another gold medal. At this point Bo Roberson, a reformed halfback from Cornell, was second, but in his last try Russia's Igor Ter-Ovanesyan moved ahead of him, and then the German Manfred Steinbach hurled himself into third place.

Roberson had one jump left, last of the whole field. He teetered at the starting mark, a great big rubberized corset binding his damaged left thigh. Then he took off—and took the silver medal with a spring of 26 feet 7½ inches.

"I feel like a father watching his children do well," said Jesse, beaming.

MULTIPLE MOM

No doubt about it, said a guy in the Winter Olympics press center, a story had to go with this. He had heard that on the Swiss *luge* team there was a forty-two-year-old mother of five whose maternal duties did not deter her from swooshing down Alps in mile-a-minute lunges through a twisting trough of sheer ice while stretched supine on a toy sled.

The guy had been told that her fifth child was born only four months after she won the world championship three years ago. So apparently she'd had a stowaway aboard, although there is no doubles event for gals in *luge* racing.

If this was true and if there was anything to that theory about prenatal influence, then the chances were that by now mom's littlest darling would be faster on a sled than Kris Kringle with all his bloody reindeer.

Obviously, this called for investigation, not in a prying spirit but only to advance the science of eugenics. After all, in the Kentucky bluegrass horsemen breed for speed.

Well, sir, it was a pity. The story had everything except the virtue of truth.

Run to earth in Olympic Village, Elisabeth Nagele turned out to be a hausfrau, all right, but a hausfrau of thirty, not forty-two, a dewy and tasty thirty. She is a compact Swiss bonbon only five-feet-two with green eyes, rose-petal skin, a shy, sweet smile and long auburn hair clasped at the back and just allowed to ripple.

Wrapped from throat to shapely ankle in a snowsuit of fire-engine red, she looked like something under the tree on Christmas morning.

With one of the girl guides they have around here interpreting, the question about junior's prenatal competition was put as discreetly as possible.

Nein, said Frau Nagele, sweetly but firmly. She won the world championship in February 1961. The baby wasn't born until December.

Ah, well. The conversation continued on less clinical grounds.

Frau Nagele's husband, Robert, is coach of the Swiss *luge* team, or *rodelbund.* Growing up in the village of Schiers, Elisabeth went belly-flopping on these devilish contraptions as all Alpine kids do, but she didn't see competition until 1955 when she married and moved to the winter sports resort of Davos.

She dug the racket, which proves there is no accounting for a lady's tastes.

The *luge* racer, new to the Olympics this year, stretches himself spine down and feet foremost on his tiny steel-shod sled. Zooming and clattering down the chute, he steers by dropping a shoulder to shift his weight.

The sled leaps and bucks and plunges, bashing his crash helmet against the ice. He wears thickly padded gloves. If he should graze the wall without this protection it would be look, ma, no fingers.

It was on one of these infernal things that a member of the British team was killed before the Games started.

Still, little Mrs. Nagele loves it. Six years after her first ride down a racing course she was champion of the world. Her eldest daughter —there are three girls and two boys, aged two to eight—is already first-rate.

Four times Frau Nagele went tearing through the hairpin turns on the lower slopes of Patscherkofel to finish twelfth in the first Olympic competition.

"Nicht gut," she said.

She rolled up her right sleeve to show technicolor bruises along the inner side of the elbow. A few days ago, she said, the muscles were swollen clear out to here. She had mashed the arm on a practice run and the pain handicapped her. Made her, she was afraid, a mite too cautious in competition.

"What did the coach say about your twelfth place?"

"He is not satisfied," Frau Nagele said. She made a wifely little snoot.

SAYONARA

TOKYO, 1964

Now the sacred Olympic smudge smolders out, sending its last column of oily smoke into the drizzling smog, and it is Sayonara, Tokyo, farewell, land of peach blossom and raw fish with the eye left in, good-bye, O gracious, giggling hosts, and banzai to the kamikaze taxi jocks, so brave, so misdirected.

The great global festival of sinew and sweat shuts down, and the departing guest can only hope that those who elevated the production to a level of magnificence never approached before may yet lay hands on that perfidious salesman of soda water and so avoid the alternative of falling on their swords.

The sordid details of the Japanese Organizing Committee's lone defeat in the games of this XVIII Olympiad have been suppressed, but this is the tale being told as the athletes in Orympic Virrage—to use the local pronunciation—pack their spiked shoes and barbells.

It seems that in the bustle and confusion of the clambake's opening, one imposter squirmed through security regulations and got himself accredited as a bona fide correspondent representing, he said, a newspaper called *France West*. Subsequently it was discovered that he was a Gallic One-Eye Connolly whose real occupation was peddling Evian mineral water, that excellent French product which all experienced tourists mix with their Scotch in Paris.

For the Organizing Committee it was an appalling loss of face. Ever since the foul deception was uncovered, agents have been tearing around town asking, "Would you happen to know where I can buy a shipload of Evian water?" in the hope of apprehending the miscreant. No success so far. Hara-kiri may be the only solution.

Ah so, it was a busy time and a good one. Visitors who found leisure to investigate entertainment after dark report that the lid was on the Ginza and little was to be seen of the ladies whose profession is, in the enchanting Japanese expression, "selling springtime."

Still, there must have been some nocturnal attractions, for on the elevator one noon a man was heard to ask his American companion: "Where were you rast night, so rate?"

And then there was the guy in charge of keeping newspaper stiffs off the press buses returning to town from the Toda rowing course after Philadelphia's Vesper Club had brought off its smasher in the eight-oared race. He said he had "lesponsibilities" and seemed chagrined when it turned out that not all seats were taken.

"I find," he said reluctantly, "we have ress number. You may lide."

Finally, there was splendorous cocktail party tossed by the Seiko Watch people, who provided the timing instruments for all Olympic events.

It was charming, with sushi as flavorful as raw fish can get, the tempura as delectable as deep-fried shrimp can be, and the premises festooned with small, exquisite creatures in gorgeous kimonos doing the hostess bit with incomparable grace.

There was also a platoon of dolls playing the koto, an instrument that looks like a dugout canoe with strings on it. As favors, guests received a Japanese watercolor with this printed message over the signature of Tokii Akimoto, mama-san of the koto troupe:

Well come to our performance today. Of course you may had many good times since visited japan, just we supposed.

but Especially this time, we presented with "Harmony of KOTO-tone" for you. KOTO is representation of typical japanese musical instrument, just like harp. How do you like it? Are you satisfied with this? We played the melody of SAKURA, ROKU-DAN, CHILDORI, and the other few concert, as well as we can. We hope to comfort your tiredness travel with our KOTO-performance.

but We are very afraid what do you feel about it. Do you Vanish Out your discomfort travel? If we can be of any service to you, we shall be veryglad. Please, remember what magnificent splendid meny japanese KIMONO ladys playing KOTO even after you'd return home. How's your opinion and impression about it. Answer us Please, in after days, we'll wait it. Then Thank You for your appreciation and cooperation, today. finally, we'll present with great pleasure a piece of "SHIKISHI-picture" in memory of this entertainment.

Please Take it with one of your souvenirs from japan. The sign is mine, The Illustration is printed with KIYOKO TASTUKE (very famous artist of Nippon-GAFU in japan) by shes hand.

T. akimoto.

THE BLACK BERETS

MEXICO CITY, 1968

The 400-meter race was over and in the catacombs of Estadio Olimpico Doug Roby, president of the United States Olympic Committee, was telling newspapermen that he had warned America's runners against making any demonstration if they should get to the victory stand. A fanfare of trumpets interrupted him.

In stiff single file, the three black Americans marched across the track. All of them—Lee Evans, the winner; Larry James, second, and Ron Freeman, third—had broken the recognized world record. Rain had fallen after the finish and, although it was abating now, the runners wore the official sweatsuits of the United States team, plus unofficial black berets which may or may not have been symbolic.

Each stopped to enable John J. Garland, an American member of the International Olympic Committee, to hang the medal about his neck. Then each straightened and waved a clenched fist aloft. It wasn't quite the same gesture meaning, "We shall overcome," which Tommie Smith and John Carlos had employed on the same stand after the 200-meter final.

Lord David Burghley, the Marquis of Exeter who is president of the International Amateur Athletic Federation, shook hands with each, and they removed the berets, standing at attention facing the flagpole as the colors ascended and the band played "The Star-Spangled Banner." Smith and Carlos had refused to look at the flag, standing with heads bowed and black-gloved fists upraised.

Evans, James, and Freeman stepped down, and out from under every stuffed shirt in the Olympic organization whistled a mighty sigh of relief. The waxworks had been spared from compounding the boobery which had created the biggest, most avoidable flap in these quadrennial muscle dances since Eleanor Holm was flung off the 1936 swimming team for guzzling champagne aboard ship.

The 400-meter race was run Friday, about 48 hours after Smith and Carlos put on their act and 12 hours after the United States officials lent significance to their performance by firing them from the team. The simple little demonstration by Smith and Carlos had been a protest of the sort every black man in the United States had a right to make. It was intended to call attention to the inequities the Negro suffers, and without the aid of the Olympic brass might have done this in a small way.

By throwing a fit over the incident, suspending the young men and ordering them out of Mexico, the badgers multiplied the impact of the protest a hundredfold. They added dignity to the protestants and made boobies of themselves.

"One of the basic principles of the Olympic games," read the first flatulent communiqué from on high, "is that politics play no part whatsoever in them. . . . Yesterday United States athletes in a victory ceremony deliberately violated this universally accepted principle by using the occasion to advertise their domestic political views."

Not content with this confession that they can't distinguish between human rights and politics, the playground directors put their pointed heads together and came up with this gem:

"The discourtesy displayed violated the standards of sportsmanship and good manners. . . . We feel it was an isolated incident, but any further repetition of such incidents would be a willful disregard of Olympic principles and would be met with severest penalties."

The action, Roby said, was demanded by the International Olympic Committee, including Avery Brundage, president, and by the Mexican Organizing Committee. They are, as Mark Anthony observed on another occasion, all honorable men who consider children's games more sacred than human decency.

Soon after the committee acted, a bedsheet was hung from a sixth-floor window of the apartment house in Olympic Village where Carlos has been living. On it were the letters: "Down with Brundage."

There were, of course, mixed feelings on the United States team. Lee Evans was especially upset, but when asked whether he intended to run as scheduled, he would only reply, "Wait and see."

"I had no intention of running this race," he said over the air after taking the 400, "but this morning Carlos asked me to run and win."

Said Carlos: "The next man that puts a camera in my face, I'll stomp him."

AMATEUR AMITY

1968

Baron Pierre de Coubertin was a little twerp standing 5-foot-3, a dropout from the French military academy of St. Cyr who specialized in political science and education. He cultivated a mustache that could shelter a covey of quail and a notion that international rivalry in sports would promote international amity in everything else. Toward this end he revived the Olympic Games, that sweaty love-in whose latest renewal has produced the following tidbits:

1. Hans Gunnar Liljenvall, a member of Sweden's modern pentathlon team, flunks his drunkometer test and the Swedes, who finished third, are ordered to return their bronze medals.

2. S. Collard, masseur to Dutch cyclists, gets the bum's rush for flipping vitamin pills to his bike riders.

3. Tom Evans, coach of the United States free-style wrestlers, says rasslers for other countries dumped matches on orders from their coaches, who made deals to protect one another in different weight classes.

"I don't mind bad decisions or inferior refereeing," says the broad-minded Evans, "but throwing matches is too much."

4. The United States Olympic Committee is investigating reports that some of our amateurs are on the payroll of sporting goods manu-facturers, and Dan Ferris of the Amateur Athletic Union says athletes from virtually every country have been getting from $500 to $6,000 in payola.

5. Two American foot racers demonstrate silently for human rights, and are blackguarded by the United States brass for "advertis-ing their domestic political views," and kicked out of Mexico.

6. Harry Edwards, leader of the aborted Negro boycott of the games, scatters vague charges in Washington implying misuse of funds by American officials and says "payoffs to coaching staffs" should be investigated.

It should not, however, be inferred that the hoedown south of the border has been totally devoid of the sweetness and light which the dear little Baron yearned for. In a gush of loving chauvinism, a manu-facturer in Prague's garment center promised a lace dress to every Czechoslovak cupcake who won a medal.

The modern pentathlon is a military event combining riding, fenc-ing, pistol shooting, swimming and cross-country running over five consecutive days. Theoretically, the contestant is a soldier who, finding himself in enemy territory, fights loose with sword and pistol and makes his way to freedom on horseback, afoot, and by swimming a river.

You'd think a guy who's going to be fighting and fleeing for five days would be entitled to a few belts of schnapps beforehand, espe-cially if he's a Swede. As the poet wrote about Minnesota:

> Across the plains where once there roamed
> The Indian and the Scout,
> The Swede with alcoholic breath
> Sets rows of cabbage out.

Sweden's Olympic delegates swore that none of their guys had more than a beer before the competition, but the medical committee hollered copper when its hydrometer showed Liljenvall's radiator protected to 20 below zero. Out he went.

As for payola, the Olympic gospel declares that "an amateur is one who participates solely for pleasure and for the physical, mental, and social benefits he derives therefrom, and to whom participation is nothing more than recreation without material gain of any kind, direct or indirect."

Nothing could be sweeter than that, or sillier in today's economy. If the groundhogs who administer amateur athletics could face reality, they would discard such tumescent definitions for a simple yardstick: an athlete is a professional if he makes his living at the game; otherwise he is an amateur.

Except in American colleges and a few countries like Russia, a man can't make a living running 200 meters. If by padding expense accounts and endorsing spiked shoes he can raise the price of a few beers, he injures nobody. And anybody who thinks payola is something new should consult *The Story of the Olympic Games,* by John Kieran and Arthur Daley. He will read:

> They (the games) lost the spirit of the older days. . . . Winners were no longer contented with a simple olive wreath as a prize. They sought gifts and money. . . . The games were finally halted by decree of Emperor Theodosius I of Rome in 394 A.D.

AVERY IN WONDERLAND

1972

"Let the jury consider their verdict," the King said, for about the twentieth time that day.

"No, no!" said the Queen. "Sentence first—verdict afterwards."

"Stuff and nonsense!" said Alice loudly. "The idea of having the sentence first!"

Without a hearing, without a defense and without appeal, Karl Schranz of Austria has had his buttons cut off and been drummed off the ski slopes of Sapporo, Japan, by the self-appointed, self-perpetuating kangaroo court that calls itself the International Olympic Committee. Never has that clutch of overripe playground directors brought off a more transparent exercise in face-saving and never in all his years as Defender of the Faith has Avery Brundage, the noblest badger of them all, been in finer form.

Schranz, at thirty-three the senior member of Austria's alpine ski team, ranks third in the world this winter in the art of sliding downhill, which makes him a national hero. His crime was cashing in on his fame by endorsing ski equipment. This puts him in a class with ladies of the peerage who advertise that they wash their faces with a certain soap, movie stars who shill for deodorants on television, and practically every other schussboomer who ever cracked a fibula.

Indeed, Brundage, doubling as chief justice and prosecutor, went into the star chamber with a list of about forty skiers whom he considered guilty of violating the amateur code. Had the I.O.C. cast them all into outer darkness, the millions Japan spent getting ready for the Winter Games would have gone down the drain and the slopes would have been stained by the blood of National Broadcasting Company vice presidents falling on their Scout knives.

Quailing from such a responsibility, the vestals of the Olympic flame made an example of Schranz and found all other defendants without sin. Brundage said the Austrian was singled out because he was "the most blatant and verbose," which is pretty bad, and also "disrespectful of the Olympic movement," which is unforgivable.

Schranz, it seems, wasn't content merely to sell his name and photograph to advertisers. He compounded his misbehavior by denouncing the Olympic fathers to the Associated Press for their "nineteenth-century attitudes" and charging that they favored "rich competitors over poor ones."

Brundage characterized these remarks as "very ill-advised," and he was right. Schranz should have said eighteenth century.

Avery Brundage is both the president and symbol of the I.O.C. He is a rich and righteous anachronism, at eighty-four a vestigial remnant of an economy that supported a leisure class that could compete in athletics for fun alone. His wrath is the more terrible because it is so sincere and unenlightened.

It goes without saying that Karl Schranz is a professional. So are all the state-supported athletes of many countries; so are the American kids who are hired to play games for colleges; so are all those Olympic runners who took bribes from manufacturers of track shoes during the 1968 games in Mexico City.

Several years ago the custodians of amateur morals in United States skiing circles decided that the way to keep athletes pure was to beat them to the loot. A firm of agents was employed to sell official endorsements for every item of winter sports equipment from thermal underwear to skis. Price lists were drawn up for manufacturers wishing to advertise that the United States ski team used their mittens or boots or goggles.

An interesting rationale operates here. If a manufacturer pays an individual skier for using his product, it is dirty money. If the same manufacturer pays off the national association, the swag is as clean as new powder.

The simple truth is that the whole concept of amateurism is archaic, as the dear old doyens of lawn tennis came reluctantly to admit at long last. Brundage is not the only hardshell who refuses to recognize this. He is just the godliest, the most intransigent and the loudest. He isn't going to change, but perhaps one of these days younger and more flexible minds will reject the outmoded ideal of the gentleman sportsman and come around to the realization that open competition is the only kind that is practicable today in any sport.

A man is not unclean because he earns his living with his muscles.

MURDER IN MUNICH

MUNICH, 1972

Olympic Village was under siege. Two men lay murdered and eight others were held at gunpoint in imminent peril of their lives. Still the games went on. Canoeists paddled through their races. Fencers thrust and parried in make-believe duels. Boxers scuffled. Basketball players scampered across the floor like happy children. Walled off in their dream world, appallingly unaware of the realities of life and death, the aging playground directors who conduct this quadrennial muscle dance ruled that a little bloodshed must not be permitted to interrupt play.

It was 4:30 A.M. when Palestinian terrorists invaded the housing complex where athletes from twelve nations live, and shot their way into the Israeli quarters.

More than five hours later, word came down from Avery Brundage, retiring president of the International Olympic Committee, that sport would proceed as scheduled. Canoe racing had already begun. Wrestling started an hour later. Before long competition was being held in eleven of the twenty-two sports on the Olympic calendar.

Not until 4:00 P.M. did some belated sense of decency dictate suspension of the obscene activity, and even then exception was made for games already in progress. They went on and on while hasty plans were laid for a memorial service.

The men who run the Olympics are not evil men. Their shocking lack of awareness can't be due to callousness. It has to be stupidity.

Four years ago in Mexico City when American sprinters stood on the victory stand with fists uplifted in symbolic protest against injustice to blacks, the brass of the United States Olympic Committee couldn't distinguish between politics and human rights. Declaring that the athletes had violated the Olympic spirit by injecting "partisan politics" into the festival, the waxworks lifted the young men's credentials and ordered them out of Mexico, blowing up a simple, silent gesture into an international incident.

When African nations and other blacks threatened to boycott the current games if the white supremacist government of Rhodesia were represented here, Brundage thundered that the action was politically motivated, although it was only through a transparent political expedient that Rhodesia had been invited in the first place. Rhodesia and Brundage were voted down not on moral grounds but to avoid having an all-white carnival.

On past performances, it must be assumed that in Avery's view Arab-Israeli warfare, hijacking, kidnapping, and killing all constitute partisan politics not to be tolerated in the Olympics.

"And anyway," went the bitter joke today, "these are professional killers; Avery doesn't recognize them."

The fact is, these global clambakes have come to have an irresistible attraction as forums for ideological, social, or racial expression. For this reason, they may have outgrown their britches. Perhaps in the future it will be advisable to substitute separate world championships in swimming, track and field, and so on, which could be conducted in a less hysterical climate.

In the past, athletes from totalitarian countries have seized upon the Olympics as an opportunity to defect. During the Pan-American Games last summer in Cali, Colombia, a number of Cubans defected and a trainer jumped, fell, or was pushed to his death from the roof of the Cuban team's dormitory.

Never, of course, has there been anything like today's terror. Once those gunmen climbed the wire fence around Olympic Village and shot Moshe Weinberg, the Israeli wrestling coach, all the fun and games lost meaning. Mark Spitz and his seven gold medals seemed curiously unimportant. The fact that the American heavyweight, Duane Bobick, got slugged stupid by Cuba's Teofilo Stevenson mattered to few besides Bobick.

Even the disqualification of sixteen-year-old Rick De Mont from the 1,500-meter freestyle swimming, in which he has shattered the world record, slipped into the background. This may be unfortunate, for it appears that the boy was undone through the misfeasance of American team officials and if this is so the facts should be made public.

The United States party includes 168 coaches, trainers and other functionaries, which seems like enough to take care of 447 athletes. It wasn't enough, however, to get two world-record sprinters to the starting blocks for the 100-meter dash, and it wasn't enough to reconcile young De Mont's asthma treatments with Olympic rules on drugs.

After the boy won the 400-meter freestyle, a urinalysis showed a trace of ephedrine, a medicine that helps clear nasal passages. A list of forbidden drugs, released before the Games, includes ephedrine. The fact that De Mont uses it for his asthma appears on his application sheet for the Games.

Why didn't the American medical staff pick this up and make sure there would be no violation? Efforts to get an answer today were unavailing. Dr. Winston P. Riehl, the chief physician, couldn't be reached. Dr. Harvey O'Phelan declined to talk.

THE GREEKS HAD A WORD FOR IT

MONTREAL, 1976

A guy from Germany said he was taking a poll and needed an American opinion: would the Olympic Games survive or collapse? Would there be another carnival four years hence in Moscow and if so, what about 1984? If the American had to bet, would he bet that Olympics would take place in 1984? The American said he sometimes bet on horses and even guessed right on rare occasions, but that was the limit of his imbecility. To bet on people would be stupid; trying to predict how politicians and playground directors would behave four or eight years hence would be sheer madness.

The Jeux de la XXIe Olympiade are a week old, and nobody is surprised that two dozen nations have walked out in protest, that a fencer was caught cheating and sent away in disgrace, that some judges are incompetent and some less than perfectly impartial, that conflicting ideologies have collided head-on and there have been quarrels and clashes and charges of unsportsmanlike conduct. The big news is that competition has reached the halfway point in spite of these distractions.

"We had the first of the daily elevator breakdowns about ten minutes ago," said Tim Horgan of Boston this morning. "If you thought you were in Hook and Ladder Company No. 2, that was the emergency call bells."

Excitable is the word for the Hotel Meridien's self-service elevators. But Montreal's newest hotel provides creature comforts, courteous service and excellent food. Partly because the accredited press outnumbers competitors by a thousand or so and partly because of security measures made indispensable by the massacre of Israelis in Munich four years ago, interviewing athletes can be difficult, but the Olympics in ancient Greece had an official corps of whip-bearers to keep order, and it is said a master threatened a slave with a trip to Olympia as punishment for disobedience.

"But some unpleasant and hard things happen in life," wrote the first century stoic Epictetus. "And do they not happen at Olympia? Do you not swelter? Are you not cramped and crowded? Do you not bathe badly? Are you not drenched whenever it rains? Do you not have your fill of tumult and shouting and other annoyances? But I fancy that you bear and endure it all by balancing it off against the memorable character of the spectacle."

Epictetus is quoted by M. I. Finley and H. W. Pleket in their new book, *The Olympic Games: The First Thousand Years,* and if anybody thinks the troubles besetting Montreal's big show are a modern development, he ought to check with these scholars.

The games that started in 776 B.C. on the plain of Olympia beside the Alpheus River in the district of Elis were dedicated to Zeus, and athletes swore by the boss god that they would obey the rules. In the museum at Olympia is a bronze statuette of Zeus hurling a thunderbolt at some bum who violated his oath, but not even that prospect discouraged the cheaters. The first of these in the records was Eupolus of Thessaly, who bribed three boxers to go in the water for him in 388 B.C. He was fined and the money was used to erect a statue of Zeus to appease the god and to warn other crooks. In time there was a long file of these statues, called zanes, outside the stadium, each bearing on its base a description of the offense.

The Soviet water polo team created a flap here by calling in sick when it was supposed to play Cuba. Well, in A.D. 93, Apollonius, a boxer from Alexandria, was late for the 218th Olympics and said he had been delayed by headwinds in the Aegean. Heraclides, a teammate from Alexandria, said nuts, the breeze had been favorable but Apollonius had used up his travel time fighting for money in Asia Minor. When they gave the wreath to Heraclides, Apollonius slugged him and got fined.

Then there was the case of Lichas, the ringer. He was a Spartan diplomat, and when Sparta was barred from the games in 420 B.C. because she was at war with Elis, Lichas entered the chariot race posing as a Boeotian. He was caught and flogged.

Cheating, faking, using the Olympics for political gain, cashing in on athletic renown—the Greeks had words for it all. Even the ancient judges caught hell. In 396 B.C. they gave a sprinter from Elis a 2-1 decision over a runner from Ambracia. The Olympic Council reversed them and fined the two chauvinists.

Small wonder that the Roman Emperor Theodosius abolished the games in A.D. 394. Will that happen again? Should it? The thing has grown so big it may collapse of its own weight. It commands such attention that it offers an irresistible temptation as a forum for any individual or group with a statement to make. It is a carnival of nationalism that repels some.

Drastic changes are needed. Americans, Russians, Chinese, Indians should march under the Olympic flag and no other. Eliminate national anthems and national colors. Play the Olympic hymn and raise the Olympic flag at victory ceremonies. Discontinue all team sports. Forget the nonsense about amateurism and professionalism.

Olympic athletes were pros 2,500 years ago and they are pros today. Knock off the hypocrisy, stop telling kids what an honor it is to represent their country and give them a chance to play games for the fun of it. Maybe it would work.

FIELDS OF FRIENDLY STRIFE

MONTREAL, 1976

The Games of the XXI Olympiad end tomorrow, and not a moment too soon. Another day or so of camaraderie and good will on the fields of friendly strife and somebody would wind up with a knife between his ribs. Up to now, this sweaty carnival has run smooth as the course of true love, if you don't count the angry withdrawal of thirty nations, cheating disqualifications, rumors of attempted bribery, political and ideological clashes, threats, bluffs, defections, charges of kidnapping and the use of forbidden steroids.

It won't be easy to wait four long years to see them do it all over again in Moscow.

Grantland Rice wrote a poem saying in effect that "wars are made by old men, but oh, how young they are where all the crosses stand." With occasional exceptions, the world's finest athletes who meet in these Games like and respect one another; it is their leaders who stir up trouble.

The party here began with the Canadian government of Pierre Elliott Trudeau breaking its word to the International Olympic Committee. Although the government had promised that if Montreal got the Games, all teams recognized by the I.O.C. would be welcome, Canada yielded to pressure from Peking and refused to accept Taiwan as the Republic of China, the name accredited by the I.O.C. When the I.O.C. didn't have the guts to hold Canada to its promise, Taiwan withdrew.

Black African nations demanded that New Zealand be kicked out because a Kiwi rugby team had played in South Africa, the land of apartheid. The I.O.C. replied that rugby wasn't an Olympic sport, so twenty-nine countries walked out—removing one of the five rings, each representing a continent, that make up the Olympic symbol.

In addition to the usual complaints of incompetent or prejudiced judges and rumors that this athlete or that team was high on drugs, discovery that a Soviet fencer had his sword wired illegally and disqualification of an American, a Czech and a Pole for using anabolic steroids enlivened the fortnight of competition. There was also a report that a death threat had caused the withdrawal of the Soviet sprinter, Valery Borzov, from the 200-meter dash.

Up to now, however, no male ringer masquerading as a woman has flunked the sex test.

Meanwhile, two Rumanian athletes and one from the Soviet Union sought political asylum in Canada. This brought no official response from Rumanian authorities but Vitaly Smirnov, the boss Russian here, hollered that Sergei Nemtsanov, a seventeen-year-old diver, had been "kidnapped." Smirnov said last night that if the kid wasn't returned immediately to Olympic Village, the Soviets would pull out of today's competition and tomorrow's closing ceremonies.

However, after meeting with the I.O.C. this morning, the Soviets withdrew that threat. It was explained euphemistically that the I.O.C. had "requested them not to take extreme measures." What probably happened is that the I.O.C. said in effect: "You pull out now, and we'll pull the 1980 Games out of Moscow."

Admittedly, that would require a form reversal by the I.O.C., which is not noted for displaying the courage of its convictions. If the I.O.C. sat still when a continent walked out of the show entirely, where would it get the backbone to take firm action about one country quitting a day or so ahead of schedule?

One answer may be that if the nation that has been awarded the next carnival were to pick up its toys and go home now, it would do more than embarrass its host. It would throw the whole Olympic movement into turmoil, threatening survival of the Games. With a ready-made club to use in this emergency, the worms might turn.

Though they didn't go home, the Soviets didn't give Canada absolution for harboring defectors. Mihail Efimov, press officer, told Neil Amdur of *The New York Times* today that the U.S.S.R. still "reserved the right to make some solution in the future."

Did this mean Russia might boycott next September's Canada Cup, an open hockey tournament among Canada, the United States, Czechoslovakia, Finland, Sweden and the U.S.S.R.?

"Maybe," Efimov said.

Up to now there has been no official word as to young Nemtsanov's whereabouts or his motives for defecting. There is a rumor that he is sweet on a girl he met on an earlier visit. However, he isn't the first athlete from beyond the Iron Curtain to defect during international competitions, and love isn't always the spur.

As the story here goes, John Naber, America's top swimmer, invited his chief rival from East Germany, Roland Matthes, out to dinner, and after consulting his leaders Matthes returned with a long face. "They won't let me go," he is supposed to have said. People can get plumb sick of that sort of thing.

BOYCOTT THE MOSCOW OLYMPICS

1980

Neville Trotter is as right as two martinis at lunch. He is the Conservative member of the British Parliament who has asked the Prime Minister, Margaret Thatcher, to lead a worldwide boycott of the Olympics in Moscow to protest the Soviet invasion of Afghanistan.

"Another venue should be found," Mr. Trotter says, "and if necessary the games should be postponed for a year. This is the one lever we have to show our outrage at this naked aggression by Russia. We should do all we can to reduce the Moscow Olympics to a shambles."

The boycott movement hasn't gained much momentum as yet. It was discussed as a possibility at a meeting of the North Atlantic Treaty Organization nations in Brussels. On the *MacNeil/Lehrer Report* on television, Senator Carl Levin of Michigan said a boycott should be considered and Senator Richard G. Lugar of Indiana said it would be "small potatoes."

At the International Olympic Committee headquarters in Lausanne, Switzerland, Lord Killanin, president of the I.O.C., declared the games would go on and pleaded for politicians to stay out of Olympic affairs. If horses ran as true to form as the Olympic oligarchy, the favorite would never lose. Ever since they learned to speak with heads buried in sand, the badgers have been saying that politics has no place in the Olympic movement, and as long as any of them can remember, the games have been a stage for political discord and social protest.

The official—and inflexible—position of the Olympic brass on these matters was enunciated almost half a century ago by the noblest badger of them all, the late Avery Brundage. In 1935 there was strong sentiment in this country against participation in the 1936 Olympics in Berlin, on the grounds that sending a team to that carnival of Nazism would be tantamount to endorsing Hitler.

"Frankly," said Brundage, then president of the United States Olympic Committee, "I don't think we have any business to meddle in this question. We are a sports group, organized and pledged to promote clean competition and sportsmanship. When we let politics, racial questions or social disputes creep into our actions, we're in for trouble."

The boycott movement was defeated, and Avery in victory was even franker than before. "Certain Jews must now understand," he wrote, "that they cannot use these games as a weapon in their boycott against the Nazis."

Hitler's anti-Semitism eventually led to the unspeakable Holocaust, but in 1935 the only known fatality was the suicide of Fritz Rosenfelder after his expulsion from an athletic club in Württemberg.

When Americans look back to the 1936 Olympics, they take pleasure only in the memory of Jesse Owens' four gold medals, in the discomfiture of Joseph Goebbels at the success of America's "black auxiliaries." Except for that, we are ashamed at having been guests at Adolf Hitler's big party.

We should have known better. As early as 1933, Julius Streicher's *Der Stürmer* had carried this comment on Rosenfelder's suicide: "We need waste no words here. Jews are Jews and there is no place for them in German sports. Germany is the Fatherland of Germans and not Jews, and the Germans have the right to do what they want in their own country."

We didn't know better, and we were painfully slow to learn. General Charles E. Sherrill, an American member of the I.O.C., asked that Helene Mayer be invited to compete for Germany to prove that Jews would not be discriminated against. Daughter of a Christian mother and a Jewish father, she was a champion fencer who had represented Germany in the 1928 and 1932 Olympics. On his return to America, General Sherrill said: "I went to Germany for the purpose of getting at least one Jew on the German Olympic team, and I feel that my job is finished. As for obstacles placed in the way of Jewish athletes or any others in trying to reach Olympic ability, I would have no more business discussing that in Germany than if the Germans attempted to discuss the Negro situation in the American South or the treatment of the Japanese in California."

Jews were barred from swimming facilities in Germany, from the ski resort of Garmisch-Partenkirchen and from all private and public practice fields, and of course they were not permitted to compete in Olympic tryouts. Yet Frederick W. Rubein, secretary of the United States Olympic Committee, said: "Germans are not discriminating against Jews in their Olympic tryouts. The Jews are eliminated because they are not good enough as athletes. Why, there are not a dozen Jews in the world of Olympic caliber."

Said General Sherrill: "There was never a prominent Jewish athlete in history."

The Olympic brass won that time. We did not meddle in the internal affairs of Germany.

The games went on in Australia almost immediately after Soviet tanks crushed a revolt in Hungary, though blood flowed when Hungarians met Russians in water polo. The games went on in Mexico City two weeks after Army machine guns massacred more than thirty students in the Plaza of the Three Cultures. The games went on in Munich while Arab terrorists were murdering eleven members of the Israeli delegation. On that occasion, though, they took time out for a memorial service that Avery Brundage turned into a pep rally.

"We have only the strength of a great ideal," Avery said. "I am sure the public will agree that we cannot allow a handful of terrorists to destroy this nucleus of international cooperation and good will we have in the Olympic movement. The games must go on."

That day it was written here: "The men who run the Olympics are not evil men. Their shocking lack of awareness can't be due to callousness. It has to be stupidity."

ON PLAYING IN IVAN'S YARD

1980

President Carter has warned that the United States might withdraw from the Moscow Olympics if the Soviet Union's aggression in Afghanistan continues. Some voices have seconded the motion, Saudi Arabia has already pulled out, and sentiment in favor of a boycott will spread as Soviet tanks and troops press on with their bloody work.

It is unthinkable that in the present circumstances we could go play games with Ivan in Ivan's yard. The United States should lead a walkout now, making it clear to the Russians that even if the shooting ends and the invading forces go home, the rape of a neighbor will not be quickly forgotten. With their parades and flags and anthems and the daily count of medals won, the Olympic Games are a carnival of nationalism. The festival is a showcase for the host nation to display its brightest face to the world. It is inconceivable that we should lend our presence to a pageant of Soviet might.

Dispatches from Moscow tell of an "Olympic purge" already under way to present the Communist society as an ideal surpassing even the dazzled view that Lincoln Steffens got. ("I have been over into the future, and it works.") To scrub up the capital for an anticipated 300,000 visitors, "undesirables" will be sent out of the city and contact with foreigners will be discouraged. Dissidents, drunkards, psychotics and Jews who have applied for emigration are undesirable. School children will be sent to summer camps. Kevin Klose, the *Washington Post* correspondent, reports that some teachers are telling their pupils that American tourists will offer them poisoned chewing gum.

Unofficial sources, Klose writes, "sardonically use the Russian word *chistka* or 'cleaning' to describe what is going on. It is a word with dread connotations for Soviets because it is the term used in designating the Stalinist purges that swept millions to their death in slave labor camps beginning in the late 1930s."

All of this hints at how important the Olympics are to the government. Diminishing their vast propaganda show or possibly causing its cancelation would be a sterner measure than many might think. And the millions of tourist rubles involved are no small matter.

It was inevitable that as soon as the President mentioned the possibility of a boycott, the stuffed shirts in the Olympic movement would revive the threadbare argument that politics should not be injected into the Olympics—as if the games ever had been free of politics, as if the Olympic movement itself weren't shot with politics. Not that the playground directors have a monopoly on unrealistic thinking or fatuous speech. Consider the statement of Gerhart Baum, West Germany's Interior Minister:

"In the opinion of the government, sports cannot be used as a means for political ends. Sports cannot solve problems whose solution can only be achieved politically."

In 1956, Egypt, Lebanon, and Iraq withdrew from the Melbourne Olympics to protest an Israeli invasion of the Sinai and the Gaza strip. Spain, Switzerland and the Netherlands walked out to protest the Soviet march into Hungary. In 1976 the entire African continent boycotted the Montreal games because of the presence of New Zealand, which countenanced athletic relations with South Africa. The quadrennial quarrel over the two Chinas remains unresolved.

And still the Olympic brass clings to the fantasy that these are contests for individuals, not nations. Then after each contest they raise the winner's national flag and play his national anthem. Between games, Olympic fund raisers beg for contributions to help beat the Russians.

Aside from the garbage about politics, the only argument against withdrawal is that it would penalize American kids who have endured the drudgery of training for four years or more with their dreams fixed on this one opportunity for international competition.

It would, indeed, be a disappointment, perhaps not their first and surely not the last they will ever experience. But any measures taken against Soviet aggression will demand sacrifices from someone. As Mary McGrory observed in her *Washington Post* column, if we got into war, those kids are the ones who would do the fighting.

Chances are the savants who write editorials in *The New York Times* today weren't even reading that page in 1936, but the paper opposed American participation in the Nazi Olympics of that year. When the Nazis "deliberately and arrogantly offend against our common humanity," the *Times* said, "sport does not 'transcend all political and racial considerations.' "

"Deliberately and arrogantly" sound like the words Jimmy Carter used last week. Considering the provocation, they are mild. The Soviets invaded an independent nation—which happens, incidentally, to be a member of the Olympic family—executed the leader of that nation's government and then said the government had invited them in.

In ancient Greece, wars were suspended when the Olympics rolled around. It says here the Olympics should be suspended when the caissons roll.

2.

Racing

GODLY GAMBLING HELL

The pastor at St. Peter's announced the annual fuel collection. By old local custom, this announcement is scheduled for this weekend in August when the godly horseplayers are in town holding enough of the folding money to defray the cost of heating church and school, rectory and convent through Saratoga's long winter when the snow lies deep on the racetrack and visitors have forsaken the mineral springs and health baths.

"I heard it said," the priest said, "that Saratoga and the racetrack especially have been enjoying their best season in history. More people have been attending the races and more money has been going through the mutuel machines than ever before.

"I understand that yesterday the daily double windows were kept open longer than usual and when they closed there were still lines waiting and 150 people were turned away. If any of those people are here this morning, we will cheerfully accept those bets, in the collection basket."

The cheerful words came pleasantly from the pulpit. Maybe there are churches where tolerant mention of gambling would seem out of place, but not in Saratoga, where racing remains a recreation first and a business enterprise last. It has often seemed here that there is a happy affinity between horse playing and piety, and it is an established fact of theology that men who live on the racetrack live long and do good deeds.

"Last Sunday," the priest said, "I told you about Archbishop Cushing taking up the collection in a little church in Scituate, a village on the south shore of Massachusetts. I told you the collection came to $17,000—that the people in the pews contributed $7,000 and just afterward a man came in and gave the Archbishop a check for $10,000.

"Later a man said to me, 'That was a pretty good story, Father, but you didn't identify the guy who gave you $10,000.' He thought he had me stuck, but I said, "I'll tell you who that man is. It is Mr. Perini, owner of the Milwaukee Braves.'

"Mr. Perini is a highly successful contractor and his team is leading the National League and last night they played to 43,000 people and the night before there were 44,000 in Milwaukee Stadium, so we know Mr. Perini can afford to be generous. I understand he gives $10,000 every year to the Archbishop's charities.

"Because of his generosity, we are happy that a man like that has his team at the top of the National League."

This was pretty early, before breakfast for some, but priests rise early and have time to scan the sports page before mass. It was gratifying to be brought up to date on the baseball and racing news, including attendance figures. For some reason not altogether obscure, memory recalled a Sunday morning in Edgartown, on Martha's Vineyard, when a visiting priest was making a pitch for the foreign missions.

He was a tall, rangy, lean-muscled young man you would peg on sight as South Boston Irish. You could imagine him playing plenty of first base for Boston College or Holy Cross. He was talking about how you can't possibly lose doing charity, how true generosity inevitably repays itself:

"My father," he said, "ran a trolley car in Boston and I don't have to tell you that things weren't easy for him financially. One day two Sisters of Charity got on his car, and when they were about to get off he handed each one a dollar.

" 'Sisters,' he told them, 'I'd like you to take this, please, and use it for whatever purpose you think best.' "

For a moment the quiet voice ceased. Then it went on: "This was true charity," the priest said, "because two dollars meant a great deal to my father, but this was a gift from the heart.

"It was charity that must be rewarded, and that same afternoon— that very afternoon—my father hit the daily double at Suffolk Downs, and he got plenty."

Thus for the sermon for the first Sunday after the Travers Stakes.

MR. FITZ

1963

This is about Mr. Fitz. Not James E. Fitzsimmons, the great trainer of racehorses, but Mr. Fitz, the great man. Mr. Fitz has decided the first eighty-nine years are the hardest. When he starts his ninetieth year on July 23 he'll be in retirement, he says. You can get bets.

Officially and technically, Mr. Fitz will retire in June. After that, when the yellow and purple silks of Wheatley Stable or Ogden Phipps' cherry and black appear on the track, Mr. Fitz's name no longer will be printed on the righthand side of the program. When the alarm clock shows 5:30 A.M., there will be nothing to call him out of the sack.

Mr. Fitz says he won't mind that, especially on raw mornings or rainy ones. A fellow has to wonder, though. What's he going to do with all that bustling energy, all that sparkling enthusiasm for living, all that affection for people? How about the bright mornings in the Hialeah Stable area and the soft afternoons under the old elms of Saratoga?

Evenings he can still watch a good shoot-'em-up on television and then, before retiring, make the breakfast batter for the family—half buckwheat, half pancake flour with a little molasses for extra flavor. When there's a party he'll still bake the patty shells for canapés because his are the lightest and flakiest. Still, it is hard to believe that will fill the hours for a man who has had almost no empty ones since the day Grover Cleveland took oath as President.

When they write about Mr. Fitz they write about Gallant Fox and Omaha and Johnstown, Dark Secret and Faireno and Nashua, Bold Ruler and Misty Morn and High Voltage—all horses. About the man —well, there was a morning at Hialeah when everybody was talking about the behavior of a jockey who seemed to be getting too big for his britches.

Mr. Fitz sat listening to the arguments pro and con, taking no part until his opinion was sought directly.

"There are two groups in racing whose rights should be considered," he said then. "There are people who furnish the actors for the show, the owners with the costly stables. And there is the public that furnishes the money. Both of them got to lose, no chance in the world to break even.

"All the rest of us—jockeys, trainers, grooms, everybody—we make our living off this game them other people support and it's up to us to do as we're told."

The best part of greatness, and perhaps the biggest part, is humility.

Every August for some years now, one Sunday has been given over to a party at Fitzsimmonsville, the cottage colony on Lake Desolation where Mr. Fitz and his remarkable tribe live during the Saratoga meeting. The first time it was proposed, Mr. Fitz took a dim view.

"A party?" he said. "Who'd ever want to come?"

Outnumbered and overruled, he gave reluctant consent, but as the day approached he fretted and stewed, nervous as a bride. Chances are nobody knows whether there were 100 guests or 250, for who was counting? But it was a howling success, as it had to be, and Mr. Fitz was delighted.

"Kathie," he told his granddaughter—he was only about eighty then, "Kathie, if the good Lord spares you, we'll do it again." The good Lord has, and they have.

Even more recently than that, Mr. Fitz was still driving his own car. He's hardly big enough to see over the wheel sitting bolt upright, and he is too bowed to sit up. It was something to see him peeking up through the spokes of the wheel, especially with his friend Jonesy at his side. Jonesy was hard of hearing.

"See anything coming, Jonesy?" Mr. Fitz would say approaching an intersection.

"Hah?" Jonesy would shout, cupping an ear. "How? Whatzat again?"

Jonesy was "with" Mr. Fitz. Probably his title was stable cook or something, but there have always been men "with" Mr. Fitz, not always in a clearly defined capacity. Jonesy got the blame for everything.

Mr. Fitz says pancakes taste better if you make the batter the night before. When he has mixed up a big bowl and stashed it in the refrigerator, the kitchen doesn't necessarily look like a hospital corridor. This has occasionally elicited comments from the distaff side.

In a store Kathleen Fitzsimmons was reminded of her grandfather's hotcakes when she saw a tall plastic pitcher with a snap-down lid. She brought it home late that night after a date, transferred the batter from the bowl and set the pitcher on the top shelf of the refrigerator, the narrow one up beside the freezing unit. Then she washed out the bowl, tidied the mess and retired.

Down early the next morning, she found her grandfather in a rage. What was the matter? Why, that blasted Jonesy, wherever he was, must have stolen the batter. It was right here—

"What's this?" Kathie said, reaching for the pitcher.

How the hell did you expect me to see it way up there?" Mr. Fitz snapped.

SECRETARIAT'S FAREWELL

1973

In Secretariat's mail was a postcard signed Fiji. It read: "I can't wait." Fiji is a broodmare owned by Walter Salmon's Mereworth Farm, one of thirty-odd mares that will be dating Secretariat next year when the celebrated sex symbol takes up his role as a lover, bestowing his favors at $190,000 each.

Preparing for his new career, the best horse of his time formally closed up shop on the race trade yesterday with a ceremonious farewell to his New York public.

It was a nippy day of sunshine and clouds, and if the big red colt didn't draw children from their play and old men from the chimney corner, he did at least prompt thousands among Aqueduct's election day crowd to put aside their past performance charts and venture out into the gusty chill for one last look.

"He doesn't know what to do," said Mrs. John Tweedy, the mistress of Meadow Stable, as her champion posed in the winner's circle under a blue-and-white blanket. "He's not run, he's not tired and he's not won."

"Eddie," called Henny Hoeffner, Lucien Laurin's assistant trainer, when Edward Sweat, the groom, was leading the horse away, "go right back to the truck. He doesn't need anything. He doesn't know what he's doing with all this applause."

It was Secretariat's seventeenth visit to the winner's circle and the only time he ever got there without working for it. This reminded some of the older crocks present of the day twenty-four years ago when Stymie made a similar valedictory at old Jamaica, then a stately pleasure dome affectionately known as Footsore Downs and now a housing development about three miles from Aqueduct.

Stymie was a showy chestnut like Secretariat, and although television had not discovered horse racing in his day, he was as dearly beloved by his following of thousands as Secretariat has been among TV's millions.

Like his public at Footsore Downs, Stymie was common folks, a refugee from the claiming races, which became a millionaire by honest effort. It took the three-year-old Secretariat only twenty races to make a million dollars; Stymie faced the starter 131 times, running until the end of his eighth year.

For his farewell, Hirsch Jacobs had Stymie ponied down the homestretch to the paddock instead of coming the shorter way around the clubhouse turn. He was unidentified by silks or bridle number, yet the horse players recognized him instantly and waves of applause followed him from the far end of the grandstand to the clubhouse. Saddled in the paddock, he returned to the track, but flatly refused to enter the winner's circle.

He had got there thirty-five times on merit and Stymie took favors from nobody.

New York has had a number of these little ceremonies since Stymie's day—Native Dancer, Tom Fool, Nashua, Kelso and the mare Shuvee were saluted in this fashion—and never was more genuine warmth displayed than yesterday. Secretariat looked magnificent as always, Ron Turcotte was properly turned out in Meadow Stable's blue-and-white blocks, and Edward Sweat was resplendent. A puffy new cap had replaced the groom's porkpie hat. He had a mod jacket, burgundy slacks and two-toned shoes.

Mrs. Tweedy got a big bouquet of red roses and an assortment of mementoes including a silver scroll inscribed with the colt's racing record and the words: "From a grateful New York Racing Association whose fans thrilled to his matchless heroics for two years of an historic career, on the occasion of Secretariat's final racetrack appearance."

An agreeable extra touch was the presentation of wrist watches to Eddie Sweat and Charley Davis, the exercise rider, who was mounted on Billy Silver, the stable pony.

All this happened after the third race. By the time the field lined up for the sixth race Secretariat was back in his barn at Belmont where he will await shipment to Claiborne farm, in Paris, Kentucky. In the sixth race was a three-year-old gelding named Master Achiever. On July 4 last year, Master Achiever got second money when Secretariat finished fourth in his first start. Next time they met, Secretariat won by six lengths. Yesterday Master Achiever was sixth.

For yesterday's seventh, the field included Angle Light, which beat Secretariat in the Wood Memorial last spring. This time Angle Light was second. They are still working for a living, steeds like Master Achiever and Angle Light. For the big horse, it's all fun now.

THE GRAY HORSE

SARATOGA SPRINGS, 1952

A man with half an eye—which is all anybody could be expected to have open at that hour of the morning—could have seen that this was Alfred Vanderbilt's stable, for the black kitten playing with a tuft of thistledown in the barnyard wore a cerise collar with white diamonds. Corroborative evidence was furnished by the presence of Squire Vanderbilt and his trainer, Bill Winfrey, drinking coffee in the stable office.

"There is a horse in this barn," a visitor said, "name of Native Dancer. I've read that he can run, so don't tell me about that. Tell me what he's like personally."

"He has heard about Cousin," Winfrey said. "And he's trying to make up for him by being just the opposite. I can't fault him anywhere."

Cousin is the Vanderbilt three-year-old that considers horse racing a sinful occupation. Vanderbilt and Winfrey pleaded with Cousin to win the Kentucky Derby this year, but he said the hell with it and went off to sulk on Sagamore Farm in Maryland. Native Dancer, a two-year-old, has demolished all opposition in his five races, and if he doesn't put his earnings over $100,000 in the Hopeful on Saturday, they'll be combing bodies out of the infield lake until next August.

"He's full of play," Winfrey said, "and always ready to do his work. I can't fault him at all."

"What do the boys in the stable call him?"

"Native Dancer," the trainer said.

"Sometimes," Vanderbilt said, "in a burst of originality, they call him 'the gray horse.'"

There is a turf writer here who saw Native Dancer win his maiden race on Wood Memorial Day at Jamaica last April and then canter by six lengths in the Youthful Stakes two weeks later. Although the colt came out of the Youthful with bucked shins and subsequently developed a splint, this man went around betting that Native Dancer would come back and win his next five starts. He still has two races to go, but the man has been haunting the sales of Grand Union Hotel furnishings, pricing *objets d'art.*

"We painted the bucked shins," Winfrey said, "and fired him for the splint, and he hasn't given us any trouble since."

"Who named him?" Vanderbilt was asked.

"I think I did," he said. "He's by Polynesian out of Geisha, you know. He's Geisha's second foal. The first one was by Questionnaire and I wanted to call him Wrong Slant, but I settled for Orientation. He wasn't much, ran for about $3,500, and we sold him.

"It isn't easy getting names approved. Take my mare Pansy. I just name her foals for the sires and ignore the dam. She produced a foal by Shut Out, so we called him Social Outcast, and another by Questionnaire that we named Query.

"Back about 1938 I bought a mare named Miyako from H. A. Waterman, for $15,000, I think. I assumed Miyako was a Japanese name, so when she had a filly by Discovery I called it Geisha. Why did I buy Miyako? Mostly because Waterman was selling her, I guess. She was a sister of El Chico, the unbeaten two-year-old of 1938, and she had won a stakes, the Autumn Day at Empire City.

"Geisha wasn't too sound. She won two or three races and we didn't want her claimed and she couldn't move up, so we retired her. Of course, a horse that won three races for me in those days was practically the same as Man o' War. That's B.W.—before Winfrey."

"How did you happen to send Geisha to Polynesian?"

Alfred grinned. "I didn't look the whole country over and decide this was the mating that would produce a champion. Since Polynesian went to stud I've booked two mares to him each year, and though I was asked to reduce it to one, I don't want to, because I think he's going to be an outstanding sire.

"Geisha has a full sister of Native Dancer that's a weanling, and she has a yearling by Amphitheatre. The way to get a good horse is to breed a Discovery mare to something."

A moment of respectful silence was observed following this thickly veiled commercial for Discovery, the Sagamore Farm's presiding

stallion. Then Native Dancer was led out for his work, bucking ebulli-
ently at the end of a shank.

The gray horse is a strapping colt, big as a three-year-old, with a
white star. Bernie Eversole got up on him, and Winfrey told him to
work three quarters with First Glance. While trainer and owner
walked to the grandstand to watch, the pair jogged, broke at the top
of the back stretch, and came around together. Native Dancer
doesn't run, he flows.

"Does he have the look of eagles in his eyes?" Mr. Vanderbilt was
asked.

"Where else?" the owner said.

DEAD SEA DOWNS

JERICHO, OCCUPIED JORDAN, 1967

The lowest gambling hell in the world lies hard by the shore of the
Dead Sea, 1,291 feet below sea level. Nowhere on the face of the earth
can you get lower, not at Charles Town or Suffolk Downs, not even
at Aqueduct on a Tuesday in November.

The gambling hell has no official name. Call it Dead Sea Downs or
Qumran Park. It is a little Shoeless Joe of a racetrack on the desert,
at present a casualty of last June's six-day war but in its time a center
of cheerful debauchery in a region where sin isn't exactly an innova-
tion. (After all, when Joshua brought the walls of Jericho tumbling
down, the only house in town left standing was that of Rahab, the
harlot.)

Dead Sea Downs sits beside the highway leading south from Jericho. A faded wooden sign over the gate shows a running horse with
a jockey in silks, and squiggly Arabic lettering identifies it as the
"course for horses Arabian."

The track is a one-mile oval of sand crusted with little white drifts
of salt, overgrown now with clumps of thorny burnet called netish,
meaning "scratcher." Except for a panel or two of fence at the finish
line, the inside rail consists of rusty oil drums set on end, and a low
ridge of sand substitutes for an outside rail.

What's left of the grandstand looks out across the saltiest puddle
in creation, steely under the fierce sun, to the Moab Mountains on
the east shore. Behind the stand a rude fence encloses the paddock
walking ring, and behind that rise stark cliffs pitted with caves where
the Dead Sea Scrolls lay hidden for two thousand years.

Today the grandstand is just a grand place to stand, a roofed platform like the New Haven station platform at Rye or Greenwich.
Before the war it had chairs for the beauty and chivalry of Jordan,

who gathered each winter Sunday to play the ponies and the camel race that concluded each program. Everybody says the Bedouin jockeys pulled their camels.

In the spring, racing moved across the Jordan River to Amman, the capital, so Dead Sea Downs was idle when the war came. Now that Israel occupies this West Bank territory, neither the horses nor the horseplayers are welcome back.

At its peak, Dead Sea Downs must have been something, but not much, like Saratoga when the games were running at Canfield's or Riley's or Piping Rock. A player who tapped out at the track could repair to the Dead Sea Hotel on the lake shore where Sharif Ben Nasser provided an opportunity to recoup at baccarat or roulette.

Ben Nasser, uncle of King Hussein and formerly Jordan's prime minister, is an Arabic version of James Cox Brady, president of the New York Racing Association, and Ogden Phipps, chairman of the Jockey Club. His huge racing string is the Middle Eastern equivalent of the Phipps family's Wheatley Stable, and last month, when the Shah of Iran threw a coronation for himself, Sharif sent his gaudiest steeds to dress up the show.

Ben Nasser is a tycoon of many parts, though some of his most profitable enterprises might not appeal to the Messrs. Cox and Phipps. His Dead Sea Hotel was an embarrassment to the king because things went on there which might be all right in other seashore resorts like Sodom or Atlantic City but, in the opinion of local Bedouins, tended to give this neighborhood a bad name.

Twenty-one centuries ago this land was occupied by the Essene sect, an extraordinarily strict religious body, some of whose puritanism seems to have survived. At any rate, Uncle Ben's casino finally was shut down, ostensibly because of illegal gambling, which was the least of its pleasures.

In a way it's too bad that there is no racing here now, for this is where it all started. There is a legend that when Mohammed was wheeling and dealing, he turned loose a herd of horses on the desert within sight of water. As they raced to drink, a trumpeter sounded recall. Most of the steeds ran on but those that wheeled back in obedience became the foundation for Mohammed's breeding operation.

That's how the expression, "improvement of the breed," began, but of course horses had been used for cavalry earlier. In the Maccabean war about 170 B.C., Lydias led a force of 100,000 foot-soldiers, 20,000 horses, and 32 elephants to subdue the Jews. The campaign was bad for Eleazer, brother of Lydias. He got hit on the head with a falling elephant and snuffed it.

As history goes in these parts, all this is modern. Archaeologists have established there were people here in the Mesolithic era, at least ten thousand years ago, and everybody knows that where you have people you have horseplayers, except maybe in Appleton, Wisconsin. Not even Max Hirsch goes back that far.

A VERY PIOUS STORY

1948

At the Derby, Walter Haight, a well-fed horse author from Washington, told it this way.

There's this horseplayer and he can't win a bet. He's got patches in his pants from the way even odds-on favorites run up the alley when he's backing them and the slump goes on until he's utterly desperate. He's ready to listen to any advice when a friend tells him: "No wonder you don't have any luck, you don't live right. Nobody could do any good the way you live. Why, you don't even go to church. Why don't you get yourself straightened out and try to be a decent citizen and just see then if things don't get a lot better for you?"

Now, the guy has never exactly liked to bother heaven with his troubles. Isn't even sure whether they have horse racing up there and would understand his difficulties. But he's reached a state where steps simply have to be taken. So, the next day being Sunday, he does go to church and sits attentively through the whole service and joins in the hymn-singing and says "Amen" at the proper times and puts his buck on the collection plate.

All that night he lies awake waiting for a sign that things are going to get better; nothing happens. Next day he gets up and goes to the track, but this time he doesn't buy a racing form or scratch sheet or Jack Green's Card or anything. Just gets his program and sits in the stands studying the field for the first race and waiting for a sign. None comes, so he passes up the race. He waits for the second race and concentrates on the names of the horses for that one, and again there's no inspiration. So again he doesn't bet. Then, when he's looking them over for the third, something seems to tell him to bet on a horse named Number 4.

"Lord, I'll do it," he says, and he goes down and puts the last fifty dollars he'll ever be able to borrow on Number 4 to win. Then he goes back to his seat and waits until the horses come onto the track.

Number 4 is a little fractious in the parade, and the guy says, "Lord, please quiet him down. Don't let him get himself hurt." The horse settles down immediately and walks calmly into the starting gate.

"Thank you, Lord," says the guy. "Now please get him off clean. He don't have to break on top, but get him away safe without getting slammed or anything, please." The gate comes open and Number 4 is off well, close up in fifth place and saving ground going to the first turn. There he begins to move up a trifle on the rail and for an instant it looks as though he might be in close quarters.

"Let him through, Lord," the guy says. "Please make them horses open up a little for him." The horse ahead moves out just enough to let Number 4 through safely.

"Thank you, Lord," says the guy, "but let's not have no more trouble like that. Have the boy take him outside." Sure enough, as they go down the backstretch the jockey steers Number 4 outside, where he's lying fourth.

They're going to the far turn when the guy gets agitated. "Don't let that boy use up the horse," he says. "Don't let the kid get panicky, Lord. Tell him to rate the horse awhile." The rider reaches down and takes a couple of wraps on the horse and keeps him running kind, just cooking on the outside around the turn.

Wheeling into the stretch, Number 4 is still lying fourth. "Now, Lord," the guy says. "Now we move. Tell that kid to go to the stick." The boy outs with his bat and, as Ted Atkinson says, he really "scouges" the horse. Number 4 lays his ears back and gets to running.

He's up to third. He closes the gap ahead and now he's lapped on the second horse and now he's at his throat latch and now he's past him. He's moving on the leader and everything behind him is good and cooked. He closes ground stride by stride with the boy working on him for all he's worth and the kid up front putting his horse to a drive.

"Please, Lord," the guy says. "Let him get out in front. Give me one call on the top end, anyway."

Number 4 keeps coming. At the eighth pole he's got the leader collared. He's past him. He's got the lead by two lengths.

"Thank you, Lord," the guy says, "I'll take him from here. Come on, you son of a bitch!"

STEVE CAUTHEN'S "PERFECT RIDE"

LOUISVILLE, 1978

The way Laz Barrera planned it, Steve Cauthen would take Affirmed out of the gate briskly and then tuck him back behind the pace. There could be no loitering at the start because Affirmed was in the second stall with Raymond Earl, a speed horse, at his left. If he didn't get out of there in a hurry, the whole Kentucky Derby field would be running over him.

The colt and the kid obeyed the trainer exactly. Coming past

Churchill Downs' seething stands the first time, Cauthen kept glancing to his right in search of Sensitive Prince. He knew that the unbeaten front-runner, breaking from the outside post, would be along as soon as he could get clear of the others. The kid was right about that, and as they reached the clubhouse turn, Sensitive Prince came sailing across his bow to take the lead from Raymond Earl.

Cauthen steadied Affirmed in third place, precisely where Barrera wanted him. Then the rider started looking back for Alydar, Affirmed's most persistent rival. He couldn't find him, however, for Alydar had beaten only two horses to the first turn and Jorge Velasquez couldn't get him running.

"I was looking back for him most of the whole race," Cauthen said later.

"Steve Cauthen rode that horse perfect," Barrera said. "He rode like he rode this race a hundred years ago and came back to ride this one at eighteen years old. Do you believe in renaissance (reincarnation)?"

Barrera told Cauthen to come into the homestretch fairly well out in the track so that Alydar, who prefers to wait and make one big move, would have to come through on the inside or go wastefully wide around him. Laz didn't want Alydar blasting past him on the outside as he had done in the Champagne Stakes last year.

He needn't have worried. Afterward, Velasquez suggested that the track may have been too hard for Alydar's taste. He said the favorite only ran a little in the last eighth of a mile.

Affirmed, still going on his own, had put Sensitive Prince away on the last turn and Cauthen didn't have to ask him for anything until Believe It ranged up and thrust his head in front with a quarter-mile to go. Then Steve moved, and Affirmed drew two lengths clear without apparent effort.

"Then he started pricking his ears like he always does," the kid said. "So I started hitting him."

Still looking back for Alydar, he gave his mount six stout licks on the right rump. At last Alydar showed up, too late. For just a moment, those in the crowd of 131,004 who could see anything but sunburned necks had a notion that the favorite might get there. They were wrong by a length and a half.

Alydar was $1.20 to $1.00 in the mutuels, Affirmed $1.80. That margin was reflected at the wire, in reverse. It was a marvelously formful finish with all of those who had seemed to have a chance represented in alphabetical order—Affirmed, Alydar, Believe It, Darby Creek Road, Esops Foibles, Sensitive Prince.

After days of raw rain, the weather had turned spectacularly clear, and as the track dried, management rolled it. It was fast enough for a mile and a quarter in 2 minutes, 11/5 seconds, which was faster than the Derby record that Whirlaway held for more than 20 years, but no threat to Secretariat's 1:59 2/5.

Inevitably, somebody asked Barrera to compare his horse with Secretariat, the glamour horse in all young memories.

"I got an opinion," the trainer said, "and it'll be proved the day we find a horse that can make him run fast."

"Were you disappointed in the time?" another deep thinker asked.

Barrera's round, expressive Latin face was a study.

"When you get $180,000 to win a race," he said, shrugging off $6,900 of the purse, "how can you be disappointed in time?"

He had insisted that Affirmed was in hand throughout the race and had plenty left at the end. This inspired a trenchant question that was put to Cauthen:

"Do you think he could have run a better race, Steve?"

This was the first Derby ride for the eighteen-year-old from Walton, Kentucky, but he had seen five earlier runnings. His mother Myra started bringing him over for the race when he was three. She and her husband Tex were watching yesterday along with Steve's young brothers, Doug and Kerry. They had a better view than Steve, who needed a rear-view mirror.

Now he stared at the source of the last bright question.

"What do you want?" he said.

SPECTACULAR BID'S BIRTH

VERSAILLES, KENTUCKY, 1979

The 17th of February, 1976, was mild for that time of year with temperatures in the fifties, and although there were occasional showers the horses on Buck Pond Farm were out in the fields as they always are when weather permits. Two or three broodmares were getting close to their time and the foaling barn was being prepared for them when, at 8:25 A.M., somebody saw the six-year-old gray, Spectacular, lying down just beyond the farm manager's cottage. About eleven months earlier Spectacular had had her first date, traveling over to Gainesway Farm near Lexington to meet a stallion named Bold Bidder. Sometimes a mare's first delivery can be difficult, but by the time they got to Spectacular she already had her baby. "Good, big, strong colt," Victor Heerman, Jr, wrote in the foaling records. "Shows quality."

"I've been in this business thirty years," Vic Heerman said today, "and I like to think I've had some success in it. I always hoped for a horse like this and I thought that if I ever got one I might command some respect as a horseman. So now that I planned this mating and bred the colt and raised him, everybody says, 'If he knew anything about what he was doing he never would have sold the horse.' "

Vic Heerman speaks quietly in even, precise tones with just the trace of a smile on his lips.

"When we sell a yearling," he said, "we hope the buyer has good luck with it, but I never dreamed this one might have 15 or 20 million dollars' worth of luck."

That's the sort of luck Spectacular's baby son might represent if he wins the 105th Kentucky Derby Saturday and goes on to become the champion his trainer believes he will be. As the Derby favorite, Spectacular Bid has been insured for more than $14 million by Harry Meyerhoff, his wife, Teresa, and his son Tom. They paid $37,000 for him at the Keeneland yearling auction in the fall of 1977.

Spectacular Bid's birthplace is on Payne's Mill Road near here about a mile off the Versailles Pike. There are showier places in the blue grass country and more elaborate breeding establishments but none richer in history. It was founded in 1783 by Colonel Thomas Marshall, the father of Chief Justice John Marshall and a hero of the Battle of Brandywine who shared that Delaware River rowboat with George Washington. After the Revolution, when what is now Kentucky's Fayette County was part of Virginia, Washington appointed Colonel Marshall surveyor general for this area, which was to be assigned in land grants to officers of the Virginia State Line Regiment. He chose for himself this tract about ten miles west of Lexington. The gracious home that Colonel Marshall built is occupied now by Dr. and Mrs. George Proskauer. In 1973 the three hundred rolling acres were bought by Mrs. Proskauer in partnership with Vic Heerman, who sold his interest to her three years later. It was he who planned the mating that produced Spectacular Bid.

"I had worked for Bill Gilmore of Gilmore Steel in California," said Heerman, who now lives in Lexington, "and I knew his family. When I was at Buck Pond, his daughter, Mrs. William M. Jason, sent me this little mare to be bred to a proven stallion. I say little, but what I really mean is light, an Arabic type. Bill Gilmore was active in racing in northern California and his daughter thought it would please him if she got into racing on her own, so she and a friend, Bill Linfoot, a veterinarian, bought a mare named Stop on Red. They agreed to breed her for the sales and they set a minimum sales price of $20,000. If a yearling didn't bring that much, they would take it out of the sale.

"Stop on Red had a filly by Promised Land that Mrs. Jason took a fancy to and she bid it in for $20,500. Bill Linfoot got $10,250 for his half and Mrs. Jason's mother bought a half-interest for that amount.

The two women raced the filly, Spectacular, just around northern California. She had speed but wasn't highly competitive. She won four of her ten races but wasn't greatly interested in racing.

"This was the mare they sent to Buck Pond. It was the only mare they owned. Because she wasn't the robust type, I felt she should be bred to a big, strong son of Bold Ruler and at the top of my list in that respect was Bold Bidder. He was a strong horse who could get a mile and a quarter, something not all Bold Rulers could do. Mrs. Jason asked about the double cross to To Market, who sired the dams of both horses, and I said I thought it might be helpful, that it might have a coarsening effect that would add substance to the foal.

"It has been written that Spectacular Bid was sent to the Keeneland summer sale, the big one, didn't draw a bid and was returned. Not so. I nominated the colt for the summer sale and he was turned down on his breeding. Now Keeneland can't wait to get his half-brother next July, so I guess his pedigree has improved.

"We were disappointed when the colt went for only $37,000 at the fall sale. I had another gray in the sale, by Al Hattab, and he sold for $40,000. They were stabled quite far from the sales ring where not many buyers went to look at them. Jim Hill, the vet who recommended that Mickey Taylor buy Seattle Slew, looked at him three times and twice he brought Mickey along, so I knew he was interested. But at the sale Jim wasn't a bidder.

"Later I asked him why and he said, 'I just don't know. Maybe I went to the bathroom. Maybe somebody asked me out for a drink and I forgot there was a horse I wanted to bid on.'"

At Buck Pond, the present farm manager, Ed Caswell, had said: "I came to work here about forty-five days before Spectacular Bid left the farm. He was a nice-looking colt, intelligent acting. He didn't do anything wrong. He lived up in that paddock where he could go in that run-in shed if he wanted to."

Now Heerman drove to Wimbledon Farm No. 2 outside Lexington, where he has kept his stock since leaving Buck Pond. "The colt lived in that field," he said, pointing, "until he went to the sale. He and his mother were moved here in September and he was weaned in October. There's his mother, we'll walk over to her."

Flanked by two other mares, Spectacular walked toward the visitors. Her gray coat is as light as her son's is dark. She is dappled and lop-eared and lovely and friendly as a puppy.

"All right, girls," Heerman said, dismissing them. "Spectacular has a two-year-old filly by Crimson Satan that Robert Sangster has bought. She'll race in England and Ireland with Vincent O'Brien as trainer. Then there's a yearling colt by Crimson Satan who'll go to the Keeneland sales in July. Last spring we were told Spectacular was in foal to Bold Bidder but she came up empty.

"Sangster has bought a half-interest in the mare. He is the football pool man in England who has been winning all the races over there. He and the ladies will take alternate foals. He wanted his first foal to be by Alleged, who won the Arc de Triomphe for him twice, so Spectacular was bred to Alleged March 28 and we're told she is in foal."

Sangster is reported to have paid in the neighborhood of $900,000 for his interest in the mare.

"Mrs. Jason told me she had promised not to announce the price," Heerman said, "but I understand it was phenomenal for half of a barren mare."

A VOTE FOR TA WEE

1970

Betty Friedan, stay as sweet as you are, don't take any wooden nickels, and may 1971 be the year you'll run all chauvinist male pigs back to the dishpan where they belong. And, dear, if you're uncertain where to hit first with your troops from Women's Lib, you might consider the offices of the Thoroughbred Racing Association, the Triangle Publications, *Turf and Sport Digest,* and *Newsweek.*

These are the strongholds of the misogynists who perpetrated the grossest injustice of 1970 upon a member of the deadlier sex. They denied little Ta Wee the title of Horse of the Year, a distinction she deserved as richly as they deserve a dainty shoe in the blouse of the breeches.

There were wide differences of opinion among the electorate who voted in the annual polls to designate racing champions in 1970. The TRA poll picked out Personality as the boss hoss. Staff members of Triangle Publications—the *Daily Racing Form* and the *Morning Telegraph*—chose Fort Marcy. So did *Turf and Sport Digest.* Pete Axthelm, sports editor of *Newsweek,* went for Personality.

Pooh. The perspicacious Mike Casale, the perceptive Dave Alexander of the *Thoroughbred Record, The New York Times*'s discerning James Pilkington Roach, and the pertinacious Red Smith say Ta Wee.

Let us compare credentials.

Fort Marcy was beyond question the best grass horse of the year. He had no peer on this continent, and he polished off a picked field from abroad in the Washington, D.C. International at Laurel. This was his third straight victory in a $100,000 stakes, following scores in the United Nations and the Man O'War.

He has more than a million dollars in the bank, less than his owner, Paul Mellon, but more than his trainer, the gifted Elliott Burch.

However, Fort Marcy was not a standout on dirt, and that is the surface for all but a few major races in the United States. In the view of Pete Axthelm and others who plumped for Personality, that disqualified Fort Marcy.

Personality ran on skinned tracks and his eight victories included scores in the Preakness, the Wood Memorial, the Jersey Derby, the Jim Dandy, and the Woodward.

Bred by the late Hirsch Jacobs, he is a versatile son of the brilliant Hail to Reason and Affectionately, the Jacobs family's pet mare. Hirsch Jacobs considered Personality the finest horse he ever bred but did not live to see the colt succeed. John Jacobs, Hirsch's son, trained the horse and his stablemate, High Echelon. When Personality caught the sniffles a few days before the Belmont Stakes, John Jacobs sent High Echelon out to win that mile-and-a-half climax of the Triple Crown series.

Hirsch Jacobs was America's leading trainer over many years, but he never had a winner of the Kentucky Derby, the Preakness, or the Belmont, which make up the Triple Crown. John Jacobs won two of the three, and had two different three-year-olds fit enough to collaborate on the job.

That made him trainer of the year in this book, but Personality was only the best three-year-old. Neither he nor any other colt could carry Ta Wee's shoes.

Five times a winner and twice second in seven starts, the lady was unmatched for consistency. However, it was neither the number of races won nor the times she registered on the clock that puts her in a class by herself. She is simply the greatest weight-carrying filly of our time and one of the two best on this continent in any time.

The legendary Pan Zareta, whose owners ran her to death for $39,000 in purses half a century ago, is the only name in American racing history fit to be bracketed with Ta Wee's. Pan Zareta won a race in Juarez, Mexico, carrying 146 pounds.

In the Correction Handicap, which was Ta Wee's first start of 1970, she won under 131 pounds. Never again did they let her go to the post with only the kitchen stove on her back. They kept piling on the furniture until Tartan Stable entered her against colts in the Fall Highweight Handicap at Belmont. Tommy Trotter gave her 140 pounds, something the New York racing secretary had never in his life done to a girl. She won, so when she rejoined the ladies for the Interborough Handicap, he gave her 142. She won.

In more than three hundred years of New York racing, no filly or mare had ever lugged such a load on the flat. In a sense the voters were right. She isn't Horse of the Year. She's the Horse of Three Centuries.

CLOCKERS ARE LITTLE MEN

1948

According to the best traditions, sunrise on a spring morning is supposed to make a guy glad to be alive. But at sunrise, how can a guy tell he's alive? There is a law in the benighted state of New York which bars children from racetracks in the afternoon, the archaic theory being that frequenting a gambling hell is an occasion of sin for minors. Wherefore a small boy, if he is to be reared properly, must be taken to the track for the morning works.

There were only a few sets on the training track at Belmont when the small boy got out of the car and walked along the outside rail toward the glass-fronted shed which is supposed to furnish shelter to frostbitten trainers, but is always filled with clockers. It had been explained what a clocker was, how highly skilled his job, which demands that he recognize any one of maybe a thousand horses that will be working unidentified by silks.

"Why don't they call 'em timekeepers?" the boy asked.

There was a Palomino pony with one of the sets on the track, and the boy pointed him out joyfully.

"Look!" he said. "He looks just like Trigger!"

A horse working alone galloped by.

"Black Beauty!" the small boy said. Might have been, too.

A stable swipe came walking along the rail with his head down. He passed the small boy just as a horse drove by working nice, reaching out and grabbing ground.

"Lookit 'im go!" the boy said.

"He ain't goin' so fast," the swipe said without lifting his head or breaking his stride. "About thirteen and a half."

The clockers were all standing down in front of the little house, because by this time the sun was warm on their shoulders. They were swapping notes and telling lies. The small boy stood a little way off from them and watched. After a while he said:

"Clockers are all little men. Look, there's even a midget."

"They don't have to be big," he was told.

"Just have good eyes," he said.

Big Jim Healey was there watching his horses. Not the same Healey the man was telling a story about, how he raced his string one meeting in New Orleans and, on returning, was asked how it had gone.

"It was all right," this other Healey said, this having been his first visit to the home of Antoine and Arnaud and Galatoire and Broussard and oysters Rockefeller and *pompano en papillote*.

"It was all right," this other Healey said, "but there wasn't any good place to eat."

"I found a place just before I left," he said. "If you're ever down there, try it. Morrissey's Cafeteria."

A. G. Robertson, the trainer, was there. A man asked him which was the most improved three-year-old he'd seen.

"The only three-year-old I've seen," Robbie said, "is Citation. The rest are all eight years old."

"How about Coaltown?"

Robbie sighed. "There's nothing can catch that Coaltown. I wish I had something like him and nobody else in the world knew about him but me."

The small boy, who'd been sitting in the house to rest, came out and said it was colder in there than outside. Sammy Smith, who is called Dude Smith, nodded. He said it seemed like spring, but there was always a cold wind this time of year at Belmont.

"There was a clocker died here a few months ago," he said. "Guys used to say spring was here and it would seem like it was. That clocker would take a walk out in the infield and he'd come back shaking his head. No, he'd say, it wasn't here. Every day he'd take a walk out in the infield. Finally he'd come back and say, 'Spring is here.' He'd write it down on the rail here, 'Spring is here.' And it would be. It might be late, but spring wouldn't be here to stay till that day the clocker wrote it down on the rail here. He'd wait till he found blackberry bushes broke out in the infield, and then he'd know."

By now Ed Christmas had a set working that included Escadru, his Kentucky Derby prospect. The clockers came to attention when Escadru worked with a stablemate. One of them made like Freddy Capposella, giving it a call: "That's Escadru behind—Escadru moving up—he takes the lead—Escadru is doing some running, boys, I'll give you a tip."

The rider pulled Escadru up and the small boy walked back toward the car, passing Ed Christmas, who'd been off by himself watching his horse work.

"The clockers got excited," a man told Mr. Christmas.

"What did they catch 'im in?" Ed asked.

"They didn't say."

"This your boy?" Ed asked. Not exactly changing the subject, you understand.

A GOLD CUP

1951

When the train from Louisville pulled into Penn Station, a great big man got off, watching his step as nervously as a man carrying a bowl of goldfish across Times Square. This man was carrying a polished mahogany case about two and a half feet tall. With him was a little, grinny guy almost exactly the size of the magnum of champagne which the porter held cradled in his arms. There was a rush of feet and a boy and girl plunged down the station stairs and hurled themselves on the big man.

"Look out!" Jack Amiel warned his son and daughter. "Don't scratch it."

"Is this it?" the kids asked. "Honest?" They stood off and regarded the gleaming box. Jack Amiel, who owns Count Turf, and Conn McCreary, who rode the colt in the seventy-seventh Kentucky Derby, stood off and regarded them. The case held the Derby Gold Cup, which the kids had ordered by telephone Friday night.

"We've got the place for it all picked out," they had told their father. Now their eyes were shining the way Amiel's and McCreary's had shone the night before.

The night before—Saturday evening—the only two men in the world who had truly believed in Count Turf had got aboard the train, got settled in a bedroom, and then removed the cup from its case and its swaddling of tissue and soft flannel. They had pulled a folding chair into the middle of the room and set the cup on its green marble base, both steadying it with anxious hands. Then they sat back and gazed with pious eyes.

A long while later they put the cup away, got out a deck of cards, and started to play gin rummy.

"What do you want to play for?" McCreary asked. "Tenth of a cent? Penny a point? Dollar?"

"Anything," Amiel said, "I'll play for anything."

Rakish mischief crept into the jockey's grin. "Let's play for the Gold Cup," he said softly.

His employer howled as though hit with a battery.

Whenever visitors came into the room, the cup was taken out again, set up, admired, and tenderly returned to its case. Once, gazing at it, McCreary said a curious thing.

"It seems to me," the little harp said, hesitantly as though the idea embarrassed him slightly, "that the Derby has come to be a kind of religious thing. Like for people that don't have any Confession."

There'll never be another night like that for Jack Amiel, the Broadway restaurateur—not if he wins a dozen Derbies. For this was his first. It was McCreary's second—he won on Pensive in 1944 and was eighth, fifth, third, and fifth in four others—but none was like this for him, either. This one was his answer to the guys who had said he was washed up, and to Amiel, who had vowed he wasn't.

"How did you happen to buy the horse?" Amiel was asked.

"I was crazy about Count Fleet," he said. "I used to see him race and I thought he was great. Well, I always buy a few yearlings at Saratoga, and when I saw this one in the ring, the muscling of his chest and shoulders impressed me. I thought he looked just like his sire, and later John Hertz, who owns Count Fleet, told me this was the first Count Fleet he ever saw that looked like the sire. I figured the yearling would bring $14,000 to $16,000 and he'd be worth it. But I got him for $4,500. Anyhow," he said, "his breeder, Dr. Porter Miller, called me before the race to wish us luck. I thought it was the nicest thing. I told him: 'You let this horse go so cheap, I hope you get the $2,500 award for breeding the winner.' "

McCreary told how he had sat in the jockeys' room plotting silently while other riders talked. "I know my orders will be to lay back and wait," one kid said, and then another and another said the same thing and Conn thought: well, if all but three or four would be waiting with their horses, he'd be better off close behind the leaders, ahead of the heavy traffic.

So as soon as he could, he tucked in behind the three pacemakers, "letting them run interference." When a horse started to move outside of him, he moved to avoid being shut off, passing everything but Repertoire.

"Repertoire bumped me," he said, "and I yelled: 'Hey, none of that!' and bumped him back. Then I was in front. I knew I had it."

The chart had Count Turf eighteenth at the start, eleventh at the half-mile, sixth at three-quarters, and fourth at the mile. "Actually," Conn said, "Count Turf got his nose in front at the three-eighths pole. That's seven-eights of a mile from the start. I could have gone to the front any time after a half."

Another visitor had arrived and the cup came out again. McCreary eyed it. "I wish they'd give a little one for the jockey," he said. "I'd rather have it than the money."

He meant it. His 10 percent of the purse is $9,800 and, as a gift from the owner, there'll be a $1,000 bond for each of McCreary's four kids. But Conn meant what he said. When he said it, anyway.

HOIST THE FLAG

"I guess he just put his foot down wrong," said Sidney Watters, Jr., and in those nine words there was more heartburn than some men suffer in a lifetime.

Watters was talking about Hoist the Flag, the even-money favorite for the Kentucky Derby, who broke a leg in a workout Wednesday. Sidney Watters had saddled the colt for six races and seen him finish first six times without ever being extended, and not even the trainer knew how great the horse might be. Now nobody will ever know.

Hoist the Flag ran four times within a month last fall, and his two races this year were eight days apart. Thus he had less than six weeks in competition, yet already he was becoming a legend. Then in a fraction of a second it was all over.

Every safety precaution that could be taken had been taken. The colt worked on a track that had been narrowed to perfection, without a soft spot or a pebble on it. He was handled by Jean Cruguet, a thoroughly competent jockey who had ridden him in all his races and knew him well. The workout was perfect, and then—

"Hoist the Flag," said Dr. Michael Gerard, "has suffered a comminuted fracture of the first phalanx of the right hind leg and he also has a fracture of the cannon bone in the same area. The prognosis is very guarded and at this point it is impossible to be optimistic."

The phalanx is the great pastern bone and "comminuted" means pulverized. Serious though the injury is, an operation was performed intended to save the colt for breeding.

"I can't believe it really happened," Sidney Watters said. "I deliberately waited until the harrows came on the training track (at Belmont). We broke him off at the mile pole where there was virtually no traffic, and worked him around the three-eighths pole. He did just what we wanted him to do—five-eighths of a mile in 1:02.

"He had done his work and was pulling up at the quarter pole when I saw Jean trying to pull him up. I sensed that something was wrong because we had intended to gallop him out to the finish line.

"It was a perfect strip. A horse hadn't been on it (since the harrows). I guess he just put his foot down wrong."

A son of Tom Rolfe and the War Admiral mare, Wavy Navy, Hoist the Flag was bred in Kentucky by John M. Schiff, who sent him to the 1969 yearling sales at Saratoga because that was a "tax year" when Schiff had to show a cash return from his breeding operations. Sonny Whitney authorized George Poole, who trains some of his horses, to bid up to $35,000. George went $1,000 higher on his own authority, then backed off, and Mrs. Stephen C. Clark, Jr., got the colt for $37,000.

Months before they got to the races, Sidney Watters recognized signs of exceptional quality in the colt. Now in his early thirties, Watters is so tall you'd never pick him out as a former rider, but he's a reformed steeplechase jock out of Monkton, Maryland, who has never lived away from horses except for four years in the Pacific Theater. During World War II when he somehow folded his lanky silhouette into the tail-gun turret of a B-24, where Eddie Arcaro couldn't have breathed.

Hoist the Flag had usual ailments of the young, including tender shins that kept him away from the races until last September 11. That day he won a six-furlong maiden race at Belmont by two and a half lengths. Twelve days later he went six and a half furlongs and won by five lengths. On October 1 he beat Executioner, Limit to Reason and other top two-year-olds in the Cowdin Stakes at seven furlongs.

Possibly his shins hurt in the Cowdin, for he bore in on Executioner, but the claim of foul was not allowed. Nine days later he finished the one-mile Champagne Stakes three lengths ahead of his field but was disqualified for crowding early in the race. The ruling cost his owner $145,025.

After a stop at Middleburg, Virginia, where his shins were treated, the colt wintered in Camden, South Carolina. In one month he had so impressed Tommy Trotter that the New York racing secretary ranked him best of the two-year-olds, giving him top weight of 126 pounds in his experimental handicap. But if he was as impressive in the fall, he was an absolute smasher when he came back to the races three weeks ago.

He had grown into a strikingly handsome bay more than sixteen hands tall, fairly crackling with power. Going six furlongs at Bowie, he won by fifteen lengths in the excellent time of 1:10 3/5. Eight days later he won the Bay Shore Handicap at Aqueduct by seven lengths. Cruguet flicked him once with the whip and he flashed home in 1:21, the fastest seven furlongs ever run by a three-year-old in New York.

Even without the loot from the Champagne Stakes, he had won $78,145, more than double his purchase price. Watters planned to send him a mile in Saturday's Gotham Stakes and a mile and an eighth in the Wood Memorial two weeks hence, then head for Kentucky and the Triple Crown races.

With all his future ahead of him, there was no telling how many millions he might have accumulated on the track and as a syndicated stallion. That's only money. More important to some, everything about him spelled class. Now it's all gone. The harrowing uncertainty of the turf.

JOHN NERUD DAY AT BELMONT

1979

First they ran a flag up the staff at Belmont Park. Red letters on a green background, representing the racing colors of Tartan Farm, read: "John Nerud Day." Then a chestnut colt named Sofiysk, a son of Dr. Fager bred by John Nerud for Tartan Farm and trained by John's son Jan, won the second race and paid $11.80 for $2. It was a $15,000 purse, with $9,000 for the winner.

"Can you imagine getting $9,000 for a horse to break his maiden?" John asked Ted Atkinson, who used to ride for him. "But then, back in 1938 did you imagine you and I would be here today?"

They were at lunch in the directors' room—John and Charlotte Nerud, Ted and Martha Atkinson who had come in from their home in Virginia, Everett and Petey Clay who were up from Miami, Pat and Jeannie O'Brien, and other friends. John Nerud, who made the Racing Hall of Fame as a trainer, retired from that dodge this year and now, as general manager of Tartan Farm, supervises the breeding and racing operations of that establishment in Florida, Kentucky, New York and California. In his youth, John left his native Nebraska with a horse and a little money.

"When the sharpies got through with me," he has said, "I had neither. So I took a job as groom and then as a jockey's agent." One of the jockeys whose "book" he handled was Ted Atkinson.

"I made enough money with Ted to buy a few horses," he said at lunch. "Ted won a race for me in New England with a horse named Bit o' Green and that night I told Charlotte, 'We're going to get rich. When they start giving $800 purses, there's no way we can miss getting rich.' After that I went into the Navy and Ted went to New York."

"The winter you left me in Havana," Atkinson said, "I rode races for $5 and $15—$5 to ride and $15 for a winner."

"When I started racing in the bushes," John said, "we ran for $60 purses and had to work to get them."

John Nerud trained winners of nine different national championships. Dr. Fager was sprint champion of 1967, he was the champion sprinter, champion handicapper, champion grass horse and the horse of the year in 1968. Ta Wee was sprint champion in 1969 and 1970. Dr. Patches was sprint champion last year. Dr. Fager still holds the world record of 1:32 1/5 for a mile, which he set carrying 134 pounds at Arlington Park eleven years ago.

"Records are set to be broken," John said. "Horses are getting bigger and faster all the time. I believe, though, that Dr. Fager's time

is going to be hard to beat until a faster artificial track is developed."
John was responsible for developing the Tartan all-weather surface
in use at Calder Park in Miami.

"There never was a horse as strong as Dr. Fager," he said, "or one
that could do what he could do. Man o' War was the best of maybe
5,000 foals of 1917. Dr. Fager was the best of 25,000 in 1964."

John recognized a man across the room. "Cyrus Austin," he said.
"I trained for him twenty-five years ago." He walked over to shake
hands. While he was gone, Everett Clay quoted some Nerudisms.

About judging a horse's ability: "Don't tell me who a horse is by.
Tell me who he can run by. Unless a foal is born with two heads or
three legs, there's no way of knowing that he's no-account when the
farm turns him over to the trainer."

About Gallant Man before John saddled him to win the 1957 Belmont Stakes: "The one that beats him ain't gonna enjoy his supper
none."

About the price of yearlings the year a son of Secretariat brought
$1.5 million: "A horse is worth $50 and what the traffic will bear."

How to win races: "The time to run a horse is when he is ready.
The secret of success in racing is to make the right mistakes."

About his seventeen years with the late William L. McKnight, one
of the world's richest men, who founded Tartan Farm: "The reason
I stayed with him as long as I did, he was the only man who could
afford me."

About a man he didn't admire: "He'll have to grow a hell of a lot
to get as big as his mouth."

About a duck he had as stable pet: "He don't even know he's a
duck. When it rains, he takes off for the nearest shed. And he sleeps
with the dogs and cats."

About a horseman who wound up a meeting with nothing but a
couple of slow horses and a stack of feed bills: "I know that feeling.
You sleep all day to keep from thinking of eating and walk all night
to keep from thinking of sleeping."

There are more, not all suitable for a family newspaper.

THIS FILLY RAN ALL THE WAY

LOUISVILLE, 1980

In the year of Rosie Ruiz, a lovely filly named Genuine Risk struck
a blow for the distaff side today. Running every step of the mile and
a quarter—and there are films to prove it—she beat ten colts and
two geldings in the 106th Kentucky Derby, a race that no member

of her sex had been able to win in sixty-five years.

As sometimes happens with fillies in the spring, Genuine Risk had been "horsing" in the last few days, but if she had her mind on love yesterday, she put frivolous matters aside when the field began the first run down the Churchill Downs homestretch.

Jacinto Vasquez, the little guy from Panama who won the 1975 Derby for Genuine Risk's trainer, LeRoy Jolley, had the filly comfortably placed behind the leaders around the clubhouse turn, saving ground on the rail thereafter until they approached the far turn. There he eased her back and took her outside moving up swiftly as the two favorites, Rockhill Native and Plugged Nickle, raced each other into defeat.

With three-sixteenths to go she was in front, and now Vasquez went to work in earnest. He whipped her once with the stick in his right hand, switched to his left and fetched her six more whacks as she drew out.

The California colt Rumbo, closing fastest of all, still had a length to make up when he reached the wire in second place. Behind him came two others from the West Coast, Jaklin Klugman, who was bred out there, and Super Moment, a Kentuckian who had run all but one of his races in California.

It has been suspected all along that the current crop of three-year-olds had somewhat less quality than others of the recent past, but Genuine Risk ran a fine and honest race under a splendid rider. Her time of 2:02 was altogether respectable—faster than Spectacular Bid's clocking last year, faster than Seattle Slew's in 1977 and just the same as the time Foolish Pleasure made for Vasquez and Jolley five years ago.

There was class in her performance and poetic justice in the fact that she produced it so soon after the flap about Rosie Ruiz's finish in the Boston Marathon. Rosie got a laurel wreath for leading all other women home in Boston, but she was suspected of joining those runners late in the race and she was disqualified.

There is nothing suspect about the filly's credentials. Until she ran third to Plugged Nickle in the Wood Memorial, she was undefeated, with six races and six victories. In those events, however, she had been opposed only by members of her own sex, and going a mile and a quarter against colts this early in life is considered a daunting task for a filly.

Over 105 years, only thirty had even started in the Derby. Only one —Harry Payne Whitney's Regret in 1915—had won the race and none had tried since Whitney's son, C. V. Whitney, got fifth with Silver Spoon in 1959.

Genuine Risk's defeat in the Wood convinced her trainer that she would be wise to rejoin the ladies. "I found out what I wanted to learn yesterday," Jolley said the next day. "There's no sense shipping her a thousand miles to find it out again."

After that, however, there were discussions with Bertram and Diana Firestone, the filly's owners. Except for some bad luck in the Wood, she might have finished second. Vasquez thought she could have got back no more than a half-length behind Plugged Nickle. As it was, she was beaten only a length and a half. So plans were changed. Jolley abandoned his notion of pointing her for the filly Triple Crown—the Acorn, the Mother Goose and the Coaching Club American Oaks. She was given her shot at making history.

Now the question is whether she will be asked to try for the unisex Triple Crown by going in the Preakness two weeks from now and the Belmont Stakes three weeks after that. It is a difficult chore for a robust colt. Before the Derby, Jolley and the Firestones had seemed to indicate that they would pass up the Preakness, though she has been nominated for that stakes and the Belmont. Asked about the Preakness after today's score, Mrs. Firestone hesitated.

"I don't know," she said.

Vasquez had fewer doubts. Asked whether he thought Genuine Risk could go the Belmont distance of a mile and a half, he said: "With this competition, she can go two miles."

As a matter of fact, the jockey's faith in the filly was no sometime thing. He rode her last year in her first three starts, and when she won at a mile in her third outing, he told Jolley, "Boss, I think you have a chance to win the Derby."

Jolley took Vasquez off Genuine Risk for her fourth race—"There was something between us," the jockey said—and rode Lafitt Pincay. She won that one by a nose over Smart Angle, who wound up the year with the Eclipse Award as the nation's top two-year-old filly.

Since then, Jacinto has had the mount, and things have gone swimmingly.

A DAY AT ASCOT

ASCOT, ENGLAND, 1960
Inside the brick wall surrounding Ascot Heath stands a sentry box with a sign promising that a ring official will visit this point after each race to assist with regard to any dispute which may arise between bookmakers and backers. The first race was just over but there was no official on the spot, nor any bookmakers, backers, or signs of

dispute. Half the Royal Family was on the premises, and horse players were being so polite their teeth hurt.

In the royal box at the front of the members' stand were Queen Elizabeth in pink and the Queen Mother. Meandering about on the clipped green turf near the walking ring were Princess Margaret in blue and her squire, Antony Armstrong-Jones, sans camera. There was no sign of the Queen's consort, Prince Philip, who leaves the family gambling to his womenfolk.

A slightly bewildered Yank plodded among innumerable brick structures asking gate guards in iron hats hard questions like how to get to the press room. "Afraid I don't quite know, sir," was the standard reply. "Suppose you try that chap over there."

Memory recaptured a day at Belmont when Alfred Vanderbilt was encountered frowning over the page in the program giving location of change and information windows. There was a list of windows providing both change and information, then at the bottom: "For change only, window 22, ground floor, clubhouse."

"What do you make of this guy in 22?" Alfred asked. "Do you suppose he is just an ignorant slob?"

Ultimately the Yank found himself at the rail in front of the members' stand, where he didn't belong. To his right were the shouting bookmakers in front of crowded stands extending down to the "silver ring," where the costers get in for $1.40 instead of $5.60, the grandstand price. To the left and behind were the paddock and level green walking ring with mutuel windows taking bets of fifty-six cents.

The main event, third in a program of six races, was the King George VI and Queen Elizabeth Stakes, for entire horses and mares of three and older at a mile and a half, worth $65,366 to the winner. This is one of England's great races, which frequently produces a candidate for the Washington, D.C. International at Laurel. Everybody knew it would go to Petite Etoile, the young Aga Khan's four-year-old, who has been regarded as the finest of her sex in this land since Pretty Polly, winner of the Oaks in 1904.

"It must be Petite Etoile," read the headline in one morning newspaper. "Petite Etoile can set seal on great career," declared the conservative *Daily Telegraph*. "Big Ascot prize should go to Petite Etoile," announced the *Times*. Forty of forty-two handicappers published in the *Sporting Chronicle* picked Petite Etoile. She had won nine races in a row, including the 1,000 Guineas, the Oaks, the Champion Stakes, and the Coronation Cup, and today's prize would give her a bankroll of $230,642, a record for the English turf.

Petite Etoile is a handsome Amazon with the iron-gray coat of Native Dancer, a silver face, and silvery tail. Sir Harold Wernher's Aggressor was in a nervous lather. He is a big bay five-year-old that trounced Parthia, last year's Epsom Derby winner, in the Hardwicke Stakes here last month, but he carried only 130 pounds then against Parthia's 136. Today both would have 133 like the other males of four or older. Petite Etoile had a three-pound sex allowance, and the three-year-olds Flores III, His Story, and Kythnos had 119.

The field started in front of a background of trees and ran clockwise, the wrong way for American tracks. De Voos, a speed horse from France, rushed away in front as expected, with Flores III second and Parthia next. Petite Etoile and Kythnos brought up the rear.

They flashed into view on the backstretch, disappeared, and the public address caller said De Voos led for a mile, then was caught by Flores III. Parthia was still third, Petite Etoile and Kythnos still seventh and eighth.

Coming down the green homestretch, Jimmy Lindley moved Aggressor to the front, but with 200 yards to go Lester Piggott had Petite Etoile coming hard at him on the outside. The filly didn't get there. "That's the boy, Jimmy," a man at the rail said, and his voice sounded loud in the hushed English crowd as Aggressor flashed in with Petite Etoile second and Kythnos third.

Lindley rode back to unsaddle, slapping his mount affectionately on the stern, grinning back at the polite applause. Piggott was solemnly expressionless on the beaten favorite.

Some horse players started home, down a roofed walk to the railway station. Somebody had been ahead of them with a piece of chalk. Scrawled on the wall of the tunnel was a name: ELVIS PRESLEY.

NAMESAKE IN THE RAIN

1968

W. W. Smith is a dark bay gelding with one white hind foot, a long, plain face, and a name of rare distinction.

"Kind of a rangy dude," said his trainer, Steve Demas. "Not much to look at, as horses go."

"Oh, well," somebody said, "neither is his namesake, even as horses go."

This was a rainy evening at Roosevelt Raceway, a night for planting mud-spattered shoes under a table in the clubhouse dining room, for prodding sluggish corpuscles into action with a touch of the craythur, for a whirl of lighthearted gambling over the chicken chow mein. Perhaps there are pleasanter ways to spend a rainy evening in New York, but they are not recommended by the clergy.

The rain had held off until about seven o'clock and when it did start, it was hesitant, almost apologetic, so that by the time it began to fall in earnest about 27,000 horse players were safely under cover within point-blank range of the mutuel windows. Down on the flood-lit track, horses had water in their ears and the climate dripped clammily down drivers' necks, but all was cozy up where the glassed-in sinful dwell.

Chief purpose of the visit was to meet W. W. Smith face to face, an encounter that had been too long delayed. Five years had passed since Delvin Miller named the horse, believing that this yearling son of Thorpe Hanover and Beatrice Adios, a daughter of Del's great stallion Adios, would prove worthy of the distinction.

To Del's aching embarrassment, this beautifully bred pacer flatly refused to pace. After everything else had failed, Miller had the colt gelded, though he hated to do it because complete horses named Smith are so rare. Even that did no good, and in desperation Del sold him.

W. W. Smith was two or three then. Not until he was four did he show any evidence of quality. His owners had him up at Saratoga in the summer of 1966 when—whoosh—he started going in world record time.

He had a smashing season as a four-year-old. He tapered off last year when he won only three of twenty starts, but one of these three was a mile in 1:58 1/5 at Vernon Downs.

This year, with Steve Demas training him for Alice and Herman Picard of Voorheesville, New York, W. W. Smith has been pacing and winning. On several occasions Roosevelt's Joey Goldstein called to say, "W. W. Smith is going tomorrow night, can you come out?" But something always got in the way until the other evening. By that time the horse's record for the year was eight victories, two seconds, and two thirds—twelve times in the money in twenty-two races for earnings of $47,525.

Now he was going in a $15,000 open handicap, and in the judgment of Roosevelt's racing secretary he was only fourth-best in the field of seven. Rated ahead of him were Romulus Hanover, winner of the first Adios Pace at The Meadows near Washington, Pennsylvania; Hodgen Special, another member of the Demas stable who would be coupled with W. W. Smith as a betting entry; and the five-year-old Deputy Hanover.

Romulus Hanover was everybody's best bet, not without reason. A four-year-old, he has won just short of half a million in spite of a gimpy leg that took him out of training for six months this year. This was to be the second race of his comeback; in his first a week earlier, he'd been beaten only three quarters of a length as Overcall won by a head with W. W. Smith and Meadow Paige in a dead heat for second.

This time Meadow Paige, coupled with Romulus in the betting, went right to the front, led the first time around and was still on top entering the homestretch. Usually Lucien Fontaine drives W. W. Smith, but Lucien owns Hodgen Special, so he had the reins on that one and was keeping him just off the pace, within striking distance.

W. W. Smith, with Carmine Abbatiello in the sulky, was sixth into the stretch, leading only the odds-on favorite, Romulus. At the finish Romulus was sixth and W. W. Smith last.

Witnesses who had invested their savings on W.W. for what might be termed sentimental reasons, watched with quivering lip as Abbatiello's red and gold silks receded. Then, out of the corner of the eye, they spotted the number on the winner. He was Hodgen Special, stablemate of W.W., scoring for the entry at $11.80 for $2.00— and how sweet that is.

But why, Steve Demas was asked in the moist paddock while W.W. cooled out under a red blanket, why had the old boy finished last? Steve smiled fondly.

"He's never been sound," he said. "He's temperamental. He's kind of homely, and when one drop of rain falls he can't handle the wet track. The rest of the time he's beautiful."

WILLIE SHOEMAKER

1970

It was March of 1952 and a couple of guys in the walking ring at Santa Anita bumped into their equestrian friend, Eddie Arcaro, accompanied by a bat-eared wisp of a kid in silks.

"Meet the new champ," Eddie said, and William Lee Shoemaker acknowledged the introduction with a tiny, twisted grin.

In 1952 Arcaro had been riding races for more than twenty years. Only two men in the world—Sir Gordon Richards and Johnny Longden—had brought home more winners. In about six weeks he would ride his fifth Kentucky Derby winner. He was rich and famous and destined to go on as top man in his field for another decade, yet he was cheerfully abdicating his title to a twenty-year-old only recently sprung from apprentice ranks.

Gifted with the class of the true champion himself, Arcaro could recognize class in another. Before he was through, Eddie would ride winners of $30 million, but if somebody had asked him to name the jockey likeliest to break that and all other records for success on horseback, he would without hesitation have named the painfully bashful, almost wordless Shoe.

Last Monday Bill Shoemaker won the fourth race at Del Mar aboard a horse named Dares J. It was Shoe's 6,033rd visit to the winner's circle, an all-time record. Characteristically, he explained that he had profited from opportunities that weren't enjoyed by Johnny Longden, whose record he had broken.

"I had a lot more mounts early in my career than Longden did," he said. "He didn't ride many horses in his first ten years. When I came along there were more racetracks and more racing."

That is true, but it took Longden forty years and more than 32,000 races to get 6,032 winners. Shoe did it with 25,000 in twenty-two seasons.

Opportunity has no great value without the talent to capitalize on it. When Shoe was a sixteen-year-old working horses for a man in California, his boss told him he'd never make a race rider and turned him loose, keeping another exercise boy whom he deemed more promising. The other boy hasn't won a race yet, though once he came close. Put up on a horse that was pounds the best, he came into the homestretch leading by six lengths, turned to look back, and fell off.

At seventeen Shoe was a winner. At eighteen he tied Joe Culmone for the national championship with 388 winning rides. At nineteen he led the country with purses of $1,329,890. At twenty-one he rode 485 winners for a world record.

His mounts have brought back $41 million. If he received only the standard fee of 10 percent, he has earned more than $4 million in the saddle. No other performer in any sport ever collected that much directly out of competition.

And that isn't counting what the little bandit takes from large, muscular golfers who simply will not believe that this imperturbable scamp can go on scoring in the early 70's round after round and even outhit them from the tee when he's in the mood.

If Bill Shoemaker were six feet tall and weighed 200 pounds he could beat anybody in any sport. Standing less than five feet and weighing around 100, he beats everybody at what he does. Pound for pound, he's got to be the greatest living athlete.

He hadn't been around long before horsemen had to discard a belief that had been handed down for generations. It was an article of faith that "live" weight was easier on a horse than "dead" weight; a man whose horse had drawn a heavy load from the handicappers shopped around for a big jockey who needed no ballast.

Then along came Shoe weighing well under 100 pounds with all his tack. With enough lead in the saddle pockets to sink a battleship, he won every stake in sight, and that took care of that old husband's tale.

Not that Shoe was out to prove anything. That isn't his style. He goes along quietly doing his thing and if he kicks one for an error, as we all do, he cops no plea. It can't give him any pleasure to remember the 1957 Kentucky Derby that he lost with Gallant Man because he misjudged the finish line and eased his horse too soon. Yet because Ralph Lowe, who owned Gallant Man, took defeat like a gentleman, Shoe endowed a Ralph Lowe Trophy to be presented annually to a racing man distinguished for sportsmanship.

Instead of hiding out and hoping people would forget his mistake, Shoe puts up his own money to remind people of it every year. The word for that is class.

3.

Football

VINCE LOMBARDI

After lunch the players lounged about the hotel patio watching the surf fling white plumes high against the darkening sky. Clouds were piling up in the west, moving against the wind which came whipping in from the Gulf Stream. Vince Lombardi frowned.

"Could be a nor'easter," he said, "and that's trouble. When you've lived on the coast as many years as I did, you know. This wind could be worse than the cold."

The coach of the Green Bay Packers is a stout fellow who insists that humans can play outdoor games competently in weather as frightful as the 13 below zero which punished the Packers and Cowboys in Wisconsin December 31. In fact he wanted a spot of winter for the National Football League championship game, reasoning that his troops were better acclimated than the Dallas delegation.

"I figure Lombardi got on his knees to pray for cold weather," said Henry Jordan, the tackle, after the Green Bay game, "and stayed down too long."

But Vince fears high winds make every forward pass a gamble. To Vincent T. Lombardi gambling on a football field is a crime against nature.

"Everybody loves a gambler," he has said, "until he loses."

Jerry Kramer, the indestructible guard, strolled by. "I feel fine," he said. "Just getting out of that cold makes everything fine."

"Did you come up with frostbite like Ray Nitschke?" The Green Bay linebacker is still limping on his frozen toes.

"I got a pretty uncomfortable chest congestion," Kramer said. "It's just clearing up."

The defending champions of the universe seem relaxed and confident about Sunday's Stupor Bowl rumble with the Oakland Raiders, champions of the American Football League. Lombardi says it's hard to judge a team's frame of mind, but he'll be watching his mercenaries sharply in their final full dress workout, and if he spots any traces of complacency they'll hear about it.

A winner's purse of $15,000 a man is wonderfully relaxing. Don Chandler, the place-kicker, says his $23,000 loot from last year's league championship and Stupor Bowl exceeded his post-season total for seven preceding seasons with the Packers and Giants.

The coach respects the Raiders. At least he says he does. He has a set pattern which he employs in his daily press conferences. It begins with praise of Daryle Lamonica, the Oakland quarterback, and it's all honeyed applause of the pass receivers, the defense, the runners, the American League as a whole.

Last year he was accused of low-rating the Kansas City Chiefs after the Packers squashed them. Now he says they brought that on themselves by saying some pretty brash things before the game.

"They do more things defensively," he was saying about the Raiders, "than a lot of teams in our league." Asked to elaborate, he explained: "They use three variations of the odd defense. Most of us use the even defense—that is, with men head-on against the guards. But they'll space linemen in the gaps and they do a lot of stunting. They'll slant the linemen one way and the linebackers the other way, all three linebackers. The Bears do a lot of that sort of thing. The Oakland defense is a good deal like the Bears'."

"So it's up to Bart Starr to catch 'em slanting or stunting the wrong way?"

"Right. But if they guess right against you, you're in for a very bad day, coach."

When they had to play the Los Angeles Rams for the Western Conference championship two weeks after the Rams beat 'em, the Packers felt the pressure keenly and rose to the challenge like kamikaze pilots. They were cooler about the Dallas game and wondered whether they were "high" enough. They were.

"I never go into any game," the coach said, "without feeling we can win. And I go into every one scared. I'll go into this one scared."

"But," he was asked, "have you ever played against mustaches?" (The Raiders' Ben Davidson springs from ambush behind shrubbery that could house a whole colony of starlings.)

"The last mustache I ever had to deal with was my father's," Vince said. "He's eighty-one and I still can't beat him."

THE GUY WHO STARTED IT ALL

NOTRE DAME, INDIANA, 1947

The guy who started the fight thirty-four years ago is around here today to see it finished. He is a big, twinkling old free-style cusser with a plainsman's face, weathered to a bright terra-cotta shade, under a cattleman's soft gray hat. His name is Jesse Harper, and it was he who united Notre Dame and Army in the holy bonds of football, which will be put asunder here day after tomorrow.

Jesse Harper is, as he has been for a good many years, a cattle baron operating out of a ranch in southwestern Kansas. In 1913 he was coach of a lot of guys named Knute Rockne and Gus Dorais and Ray Eichenlaub and Fred Gushurst here at Notre Dame. There've been some towering yarns spun about the origin of the series with the Army, but the way Harper told it today was just simple enough to be the real story.

"I wrote 'em a letter," he said.

Notre Dame wasn't altogether unknown in football in 1913. In Midwestern football that is. The Irish had been playing since 1887 and had beaten some tolerably celebrated opponents, including Michigan. But their fame hadn't reached the East.

"In those days," Harper recalled, "we usually got to work on the next fall's schedule along about February. We wanted an Eastern game, so I wrote a letter to Army and they happened to have an open date and took us on. Why did I pick Army? I don't know. It was a good game and good games weren't easy to get. Maybe it's true, as the old stories go, that Army was looking for a Midwestern opponent that wouldn't be too tough when they got my letter. But as far as I know, my letter was all there was to it."

It is revealing no secret to report that Army took a brief lead of 13 to 7 and did not score again while Eichenlaub's furious plunges and Dorais' forward passes to Rockne and Gushurst were bringing five touchdowns and a Notre Dame victory, 35 to 13. Throwing to receivers "as far as thirty-five yards away," Dorais worked the new-fangled pass successfully thirteen times in seventeen attempts for gains of 243 yards.

"After the game," Harper said, "I went in to see Charley Daly, the Army coach, and Major Graves, and off in a corner I saw an officer who really was giving his wife hell. Being a married man, I sidled over to get an earful. Well, he was telling her, well, you've been hollering about why we don't play some decent opposition. Now, dammit, are you satisfied?

"That winter I ran into a fellow from Annapolis who climbed all over me. 'We expected to beat Army,' he told me, 'but they came along with that forward pass you showed 'em and blew our brains out.' "

Harper sat in today's press conference. It must have been a rewarding experience for him to see three dozen newspaper men from all over the nation solemnly scribbling notes as Moose Krause, Frank Leahy's assistant, and Jack Lavelle, the king-size scout, dropped pearls of wisdom on the thick rug of the lounge in Rockne Memorial Field House.

In Harper's day, a Notre Dame–Army game stirred somewhat less journalistic commotion. When he took that 1913 team to New York the players grabbed eagerly for newspapers to see their names immortalized in headlines. They had to comb the columns before Dorais found an obscure paragraph in the *Times.*

"The Notre Dame football team," the lead said, "which has come all the way from South Bend, Illinois—"

Dorais crumpled the paper in his hands.

"Why, the fatheads! They don't even know what state we're from!"

There was, of course, no admission charge for the spectators who lined the unfenced field on the plains of West Point. Notre Dame's guarantee was a thousand dollars and, Harper said with justifiable pride, the trip produced a net profit of eighty-three dollars. By 1919 expenses were somewhat higher. The earliest Army game expense account still preserved here shows the following items in Rockne's hand for the West Point game of November 8, 1919:

"Receipts, $1,000. Railroad, $1,381.35; meals, $184; ferry, $6.90; tips to porters, $6; tips to waiters $12 [this was first written as $6 then changed to $12]; trip to Chicago to get shoes, $10.58; transfer of trunks, $3. Total expense, $1,603.83. Loss $603.83."

It is worthy of note that Rock drew an advance of $1,600 from the treasurer and reported expenses of $3.83 more than that, even as a touring sportswriter of 1947.

BACHELORS III

1969

Joe Willie Namath, a saloonkeeper from Beaver Falls, Pennsylvania, was in Santa Monica, California, Sunday night presenting an Emmy award on television. It must have been a nerve-wracking evening for Bill Cosby and Merv Griffin, who appeared on the show with him, and for Columbia Broadcasting System which televised it. For all they knew, they would wake up Monday morning and find they had all been ex-communicated by Pete Rozelle. Guilt by association.

Ambrose Bierce, a livelier lexicographer than Webster but not so widely advertised, defines impartiality as "inability to perceive any promise of personal advantage from espousing either side of a controversy or adopting either of two conflicting opinions." That's for the white-livered who won't take either side, but how about the fellow that takes both sides?

Obviously, there are two sides to the Namath affair, and the disposition here is to take both. It is difficult to see how Pete Rozelle, discovering that the fuzz was taking an unflattering interest in the Namath grog shop called Bachelors III, could do less than direct Joe Willie to get out of the gin mill or out of football.

Off his established form, it is impossible to picture Namath meekly accepting this ultimatum as long as he felt, and Rozelle publicly concurred, that he had done no wrong. After all, the Securities and Exchange Commission had raised no objections when four stockbrokers ran the same pothouse under the name Margin Call.

On one side, there is the fact that for years professional football has maintained a list of joints which were off-limits for players because the clientele in these traps included characters not considered desirable companions. "Remember," players are told before a trip to Chicago or Miami or New Orleans, "if you're seen in one of these places, you're out of this game."

Nobody has ever seriously disputed the view that professional athletes must be more particular about the company they keep than sportswriters, Senators, or Supreme Court justices.

On the other hand, if Joe Willie Namath can't let a friendly bookmaker use his telephone once in a while, how can Art Rooney own the Pittsburgh Steelers? Art Rooney, who was guest of honor along with Namath at the pro football writers' banquet last week, is respected as one of the gamest gamblers of our time. The tale is told that Art once bet $10,000 on a horse at 60 to 1 and, after the horse finished first, sat quietly while a foul claim was argued.

The story goes that when the stewards took the horse's number down, costing Rooney $600,000, his comment was "who do you like in the next?" Strength to that man, but what about Joe Willie, who only sells rye to bookies?

Bert Bell, who was Pete Rozelle's predecessor and the chief architect of pro football's monstrous boom, was an enthusiastic gambler whose wide acquaintance with pros in that field kept him au courant with all irregularities in the betting pattern. This was applauded as a safeguard for football.

Obviously, there is a double standard here. To be sure, there always has been, and the argument that a football player must be like Caesar's wife only confirms this. That "Caesar's wife" bit refers to Pompeia, Big Julie's second spouse, whom he divorced for playing house with one Publius Claudius. Meanwhile, Julie himself got married three times and had a son with Cleopatra on the side.

Paul Hornung and Alex Karras admitted betting on football, not dishonestly and not for important money, but improperly under the rules. In Namath's case there has been no admission of wrongdoing or any suspicion of same.

Up to now, the worst that has been charged against Namath is that he is a part owner of a watering hole where some of the animals who come down to drink are unappetizing. If there are graver reasons for "law enforcement agencies" to stake out the joint, Joe and his fans are entitled to hear about them.

Many football players have pieces of restaurants that own liquor licenses. Namath's teammate, Gerry Philbin, opened one the other night in Amityville, Long Island. The Packers' Max McGee and Fuzzy Thurston have been running a string of steak houses around Green Bay for years.

It may be tough to find unsavory characters around Amityville, but if there are any such in the Fox River Valley of Wisconsin, they undoubtedly patronize Max and Fuzzy, because Max and Fuzzy serve the best food in the area.

Who among the patrons of Bachelors III, Toots Shor's, 21, and Jilly's is savory and who unsavory? There is a crying need for a bill of particulars.

WHAT NOW, MR. PRESIDENT?

NEW ORLEANS, 1972

On the Miami Dolphins' eighth play from scrimmage, Paul Dryden Warfield ran a down-and-in pattern from his wide flanker position, and history quivered in the throes of creation. Lee Roy Jordan, the Dallas Cowboys' middle linebacker, was helping Mel Renfro cover Miami's gifted receiver as Bob Griese cocked his throwing arm. The pass was high. Warfield leapt, but could only wave at the ball.

At least one fan, sitting in statesman-like comfort far from the bitter chill of Tulane Stadium, must have regarded the television screen with a disappointed frown.

"I think you can hit Warfield on a down-and-in pattern," the fan named Richard M. Nixon had told Don Shula, the Miami coach, after the Dolphins qualified to represent the American Conference in the playoff for the professional football championship of this mercenary world. Now it turned out that the fan could be mistaken like anybody else.

Indeed, it turned out that the fan had erred in more than one respect. He had not told Shula what to do about Roger Staubach, the Cowboy with the squirrel-rifle arm. He had set up no adequate defense against the rushes of Duane Thomas, Walt Garrison and Calvin Hill, who operated like infuriated beer trucks. He had prescribed no antidote for the violence of the Dallas offensive linemen, who charged like wounded water buffalo all afternoon, blasting avenues through the Miami defenses.

Due in part to these errors of omission, Super Bowl VI was a sorry letdown for at least half of the 81,023 witnesses present. Most of them —sharing the mistaken notion of Pete Rozelle, pro football's supreme being, that New Orleans was in the "warm weather"—had come poorly prepared for this day's windy 39 degrees. Physically miserable, they were not warmed spiritually by the competition, for as the game progressed it became almost as unhappy a mismatch as the Joe Frazier–Terry Daniels fist fight here last night.

Coming through at last after making a five-year career of failure in the big games, the Cowboys led all the way in this 24–3 romp, setting Super Bowl records with rushing gains of 252 yards and 23 first downs.

Not only did they muffle Coach Nixon's big weapon; they turned another of his favorite tactics to their own use.

During the regular season, the White House strategist urged George Allen, coach of the Washington Redskins, to use Roy Jefferson on a flanker reverse, sometimes described as the end-around play. Allen did, and Jefferson lost thirteen yards. Today with the Cowboys leading, 10–3, Staubach used his wide receiver, Bob Hayes, on precisely that play, and Hayes swept sixteen yards to the Miami six-yard line. Two plays later Thomas raced on a stuttering slant into the end zone, and the game was out of the Dolphins' reach.

In the Dolphins' nomenclature, there is no such thing as a down-and-in pattern, but they do have two passes answering that description. On one, which they call simply a "slant," the receiver runs straight downfield 8 or 10 yards, then breaks toward the middle. On the other, called a "post pattern," the receiver goes deep and angles toward the goalposts.

Presumably it was the latter which the Machiavelli of Pennsylvania Avenue had in mind. The Dolphins never did make it work with Warfield.

That incomplete pass for Miami's eighth play was on the short slant pattern from Warfield's usual position far out on the left flank. The next time Griese threw his way, Warfield had started downfield and veered out toward the sideline. That pass was too high also, which was just as well politically. Herb Klein, of the White House staff, observed in a speech in Hot Springs, Arkansas, yesterday that no politician sensitive to economic issues would ever call a down-and-out.

Warfield went back to the short slant toward the middle, and for the third time the pass was too high for him. Not until his fourth attempt did he catch the ball, and that was out in the flat zone for a five-yard gain.

Late in the second quarter Warfield lined up in "slot left" formation (five yards inside the wide receiver). He raced downfield, threw in a little sidestep, and clutched a pass on the Dallas 24. The gain put the Dolphins in position for their only score, on Garo Yepremian's field goal.

Minutes after the game ended, the telephone rang in the winners' dressing room. It was Washington calling. "He commented on every phase of the game," said Tom Landry, the Dallas coach. "He singled out our offensive line for praise. He said we played almost a perfect game."

How about the down-and-in pattern?

"He didn't mention it," Landry said.

GOOD OL' BOY WOODY HAYES

1979

People keep saying that Woody Hayes is a great football coach who overstayed his time. This implies that there was a time when slugging a member of the opposing team was proper coachly deportment.

Let's face it, throwing a punch at Charlie Bauman of Clemson was only the last degrading incident in a pattern of behavior that had long distinguished the Ohio State coach. For years, Hayes had been throwing tantrums, screaming abuse and striking out at anyone within reach when his team was losing. His employers shrugged off these embarrassments, his idolators chuckled over them and agreed that there was good ol' Woody for you, and the objects of his spleen turned the other cheek. After he shoved a camera into the face of a *Los Angeles Times* photographer while Southern California was horsewhipping Ohio State in the 1973 Rose Bowl, the photographer was persuaded to drop charges; when Hayes punched Mike Friedman, a cameraman for ABC, after an Ohio State fumble in a 14–6 defeat by Michigan, that admirable network stood up for its man by saying ABC wasn't going to make trouble because ABC would have to do business with Woody in the future.

Evidently nobody in authority realized that a full-grown man who attached such importance to a game was, at best, immature, not to say a case of arrested development. The saddest part of the whole affair is that nobody at Ohio State saw the denouement approaching and protected Hayes from himself.

The only way to protect him would have been to ease him into retirement, and he would have resisted that. Still, it would have been infinitely preferable to what happened. By procrastinating, the Ohio State brass invited a situation where it became necessary to throw Hayes out on his ear after twenty-eight years of service. The college wound up looking as bad as the coach.

College football began as a recreation for undergraduates, but it outgrew that role many years ago. Not many thoughtful persons, aware of the abuses that accompanied it, would argue that it had been an altogether healthy growth. Indeed, some might wonder how far the cause of higher education was advanced by shipping a consignment of scholar-athletes from Columbus, Ohio, to Jacksonville, Florida, during their Christmas holidays to lose in the Gator Bowl to scholar-athletes from Clemson, South Carolina.

"I don't think it's possible to be too intent on winning," Woody Hayes has said. "If we played for any other reason, we would be totally dishonest. This country is built on winning and on that alone. Winning is still the most honorable thing a man can do."

Woody and his scholar-athletes were trying to win in the closing moments of last Friday night's game, when Charlie Bauman intercepted a pass and went out of bounds right where the Ohio State coach stood. That architect of young manhood laid hold of Bauman and fetched him a roundhouse right to the chops. Fists flailing, he tried to charge onto the field, but his own scholar-athletes, already bruised and bleeding from their pursuit of culture, overpowered him.

Curiously, although all this was visible to a national television audience, it escaped the attention of the ABC broadcasters in Jacksonville. There was neither comment nor replay. For that matter, there was no kickoff in ABC's version of the Sugar Bowl game later in the weekend. When that game between Penn State and Alabama started, a commercial was on the screen.

"No alumni and nobody else, not even you members of the press, fire the coach," Hayes has said. "The players fire the coach and as long as I'm on the same wavelength with them, I can coach as long as I want to."

It didn't work out exactly that way, for the comments of Ohio State players, published after Hayes had been dismissed, indicated that most of them remained loyal to him. Comments from other college coaches were generally sympathetic to Woody, too.

"I think you ought to take into consideration the enormous pressure of coaching football today," said Bo Schembechler of Michigan. The authorities at Ohio State had been taking that into consideration for twenty-eight years in Woody's case. They had to take it into consideration before Hayes arrived, for there was pressure on Wes Fesler, Carroll Widdoes, Paul Brown and all their predecessors in Columbus, back to Doc Wilce and beyond.

Coaching in Columbus is not quite like coaching in New Haven. When Francis Schmidt had the Ohio State job, he drove his car into a filling station to have the oil changed and stayed behind the wheel, drawing plays in a notebook while the car was raised on a hoist.

Oblivious to the world around him, the coach pored over his X's and O's, devising an intricate double reverse, setting up a defense to stop it, trying something else. At length he came up with a play that looked unstoppable. With a small cry of triumph, he slapped the notebook shut, opened the door, stepped out and fell ten feet to the concrete.

PAPA BEAR

1979

The Chicago Bears, who have been more cuddly than grizzly most of the last 15 years, are in Philadelphia today, bucking for the half-championship of the National half of the National Football League, but Papa Bear is not with them. George Stanley Halas is the last survivor of that little group of willful men who sat on running boards in Ralph Hay's Hupmobile showroom in Canton, Ohio, on September 17, 1920, and laid the foundation of the N.F.L.

Six weeks short of his eighty-fifth birthday, George finds travel difficult, and this last week has been especially hard on him. Early last Sunday morning his fifty-four-year-old son Muggs, president of the Bears, died of a massive coronary. It took a lot out of George but, except when he was at the wake and the funeral, he has continued to keep regular hours in the club office in the Loop.

Papa Bear is a flaming wonder. As the team he founded winds up its 60th season, he still functions as owner, chairman of the board and chief executive officer. In forty of those seasons he was also the coach, and the Bears have not won a championship since he fired himself for the fourth and last time. In bad weather he has twinges in the hip he injured as an outfielder in the 1919 training camp of the New York Yankees (that was a year before they got Babe Ruth), but he is still tough as a boot.

"There was never any question that George was tough," Red Grange writes in the foreword to a handsome book, *The Chicago Bears—An Illustrated History* by Richard Whittingham (Rand McNally). "At times there were factions on the team . . . one time in 1934, before going out to practice, he said he wanted to talk to us. Instead he started to call certain players by name and told them to line up in two different groups. Then George said, 'Here are the guys who are breaking up the team into factions, and I'll fight you all, one by one or all together.' And that was the end of the factions."

George was seventy-three the last time he retired as coach. "I knew it was time to quit," he said, "when I was chewing out the referee and he walked off the penalty faster than I could keep up with him."

As with most athletes, it was the legs that went first, not the spirit, not the capacity for rage. In his foreword, Grange tells of George's clashes with his friend Jim Durfee, a referee in the 1920's:

> When Halas was riding him hard one day, Jim began marching off a five-yard penalty. Halas got really hot. "What's that for?" he hollered.
>
> "Coaching from the sideline," Jim yelled back. (You couldn't do that in those days.)
>
> "Well," said George, "that just proves how dumb you are. That's fifteen yards, not five."
>
> "Yeah," said Jim, "but the penalty for your kind of coaching is only five yards."
>
> Another day Jim was penalizing the Bears 15 yards, and Halas cupped his hands and yelled, "You stink!" Jim just marched off another fifteen yards, then turned and shouted, "How do I smell from here?"

George's eyes still flash when he remembers how a referee robbed the Bears in 1920, when they were the Decatur Staleys. They played 13 games that first season, and the only team that scored against them legitimately was the Hammond Pros, whom Decatur whipped, 28–7. In Chicago the Staleys were leading the Racine Cardinals, 6–0, late in the game when the Cardinals completed the sideline pass. The receiver ducked behind a knot of spectators who had crowded onto the field and with his civilian interference ran in for a touchdown. Not wishing to become suddenly dead, the referee allowed the score, and the Cardinals won, 7–6.

In 1975, W. B. Wolfan of Chicago forwarded a letter from George. And it began: "Yes, I did make an offer to now President Gerald Ford to join the Bears after the 1935 College All-Star game against our team. I might add that the Bears' bid exceeded the $50 per game offer from Curly Lambeau of Green Bay. However, Jerry Ford turned both of us down with the explanation that he intended to go on to Yale for his law degree and wasn't interested in pro football."

The Halas memory remains keen for details like those. Eleven teams were represented when the league was formed in that Canton auto agency, and after the meeting it was announced that the franchise fee was $100 each. Actually, George says, nobody paid anything. "I doubt if there was a hundred bucks in the whole room."

Whittingham's lively history borrows an anecdote from *My Life with the Redskins* by Corinne Griffith, the star of silent films who married George Preston Marshall, the late owner of the Washington club. She tells of a sidelines' shouting match between Marshall and Halas during the 1937 championship game after Marshall, infuriated because a Bear had taken a punch at Sammy Baugh, stormed down to the playing field:

> George [Marshall] stomped back to the box, snorted as he sat down and, of course, took it out on me.
> "What's the matter with you? You look white as a sheet!"
> "Oh, that was awful!"
> "What was awful?"
> "That horrible language. We heard every word."
> "Well, you shouldn't listen."
> "Oh, you. And right in front of the ladies . . . And as for that man Halas!" Every hair of George's raccoon coat bristled. "He's positively revolt—"
> "Don't you dare say anything against Halas." George was actually shaking his finger under my nose. "He's my best friend!"

THE MOST IMPORTANT THING

NEW HAVEN, 1947

"Gentlemen," the sainted Tad Jones is alleged to have said in the cathedral hush before a Yale-Harvard game, "you are about to play football for Yale. Never again in your lives will you do anything so important—"

America has been through two world wars, a world-wide depression, and had a couple of flings at inflation since then and yet, corny as it seems, the young Yales appeared actually to feel that T. Jones was right when today's 31–21 affair with the Harvards ended.

As the last whistle blew, a great passel of Yales swarmed onto the field to hug the combatants to their bosoms and even from the press box you could see grins as broad as Kate Smith upon the soiled faces of the belligerents. There was a brief, ecstatic huddle, and then Levi Jackson, the tall, dark, and handsome fullback of the Yales, broke away from his companions and raced across the field to pump any and all Harvard hands within reach. Meanwhile, a small boy snatched the cap of G. Frank Bergin, the umpire, and fled with the official in pursuit.

The cap-snatch was brought off on Harvard's twenty-yard line. The small miscreant fled to Yale's goal line on a long, clean, eighty-yard dash, circled to his right and raced back ten yards, then angled off into the crowd with the stolen haberdashery still in his possession. Mr. Bergin, puffing, gave up.

This was far and away the most spectacular play of the long, gray day. But such post-game shenanigans were no more than frosting on an extraordinarily fancy cake. The show itself was the thing, and it was the greatest thing since the invention of the wheel.

Here were two teams that had made a career of failure and had enjoyed staggering success at it. One had lost four games, the other three. Neither had beaten anyone of importance. And so, between them, they drew a crowd of 70,896, biggest gathering this holy of holies has attracted in seventeen years.

It was a hairy crowd, wrapped thickly in the skins of dead animals and festooned with derby hats, pennants and feathers of crimson and blue. It wore the pelts of mink and beaver and raccoons. Indeed, counting the coon coats in any section of the Bowl, you could be excused for assuming Coolidge was still President. Here and there a moth took wing as some fur-bearing customer flapped his arms in an effort to keep warm. It was concluded that although the science of offensive football was advanced by every play, the entertainment set the fur industry back thirty years. There were enough crew haircuts in evidence to supply the Fuller Brush Company for the next generation.

All the appurtenances of elegance were present. The bands paraded and postured between halves according to the strictest dictates of tradition. The Harvard tootlers wore crimson jackets and ice cream pants. From the waist up they looked like a road company chorus out of *Rose Marie*. From there down, they suggested Good Humor men on holiday.

The Yales came oompah-ing onto the scene after their guests were done. Yale costumes its bandsmen to impersonate bellhops in a good but unpretentious hotel. The somber ranks of blue shifted and twitched and maneuvered, deploying into fascinating but undecipherable formations. The only one which could be spelled out from the press loft seemed to be a salute to the Reliable Jersey House. It appeared to read: "Yale minus 7."

Critics agreed the Yale band was two steps faster than Harvard's. This was approximately the difference between the two teams. Harvard passed, but Yale ran. Rather, Yale marched, driving relentlessly in short, savage bursts, chewing out yardage with a persistence which Harvard couldn't resist. Thus Yale scored first, and was tied scarcely more than a minute later when Harold Moffie raced down from his flanker position on the right side, got behind Ferd Nadherny and made a casual catch of Jim Kenary's pass into the end zone.

Yale clawed down for another touchdown and Harvard responded with one of its own, fashioned chiefly on two plays. One was a forward pass to Chip Gannon, who faked two tacklers out of their underwear on a slick run. The other was a bolt through the middle by Paul Lazzaro on a fake pass-and-buck play which is called the bear trap because the Chicago Bears no longer use it.

So the score was tied again, but it stood to reason it wouldn't stay that way. You couldn't expect Harvard to keep on coming up with one-play touchdowns to match a team that could grind out gains as Yale was doing. Harvard finally gave Yale an unearned chance by roughing the New Haven kicker and drawing a penalty for same. This resulted in the winning touchdown. A little later, a low snapback from center loused up a Harvard punt, giving the ball to Yale for the score that made the game safe.

It was noted that the incredibly erudite Harvard coach, Dr. R. Harlow, made unique use of the free substitution rule. He would haul a guy out of the game, give him special instructions and run him back in again, all in one pause between plays. He did this with a couple of his key men just before the first half ended. The results were significant. On the next play, Yale intercepted a Harvard pass.

ART ROONEY

1970

Arthur J. Rooney is a man of such reckless daring that he once entrusted his Pittsburgh Steelers to Johnny Blood, an unfettered soul whose tenure as playing coach Rooney would sum up later in two sentences: "On most teams the coach worries about where the players are at night. Our players worried about the coach."

Evidently Art's five sons inherited their sire's boldness, for even as New York racing cries havoc, they are buying Yonkers Raceway for $47 million. When they take over the world's biggest harness track, the Rooneys' sports enterprises will compare in magnitude with the Roman Empire. They operate thoroughbred racing in Philadelphia, at Liberty Bell Park pending construction of a new track; professional football in Pittsburgh; and dog racing at the Palm Beach Kennel Club. Art still bets blithely on steeds carrying the silks of his Shamrock Farm. He always bet blithely.

"I didn't necessarily know more about horses than the next guy," he said the other day, "but I might have known a little more about playing. I never was afraid to bet."

He was retelling the tale of his big score at Saratoga in 1936, which has become a legend. According to most accounts, he slapped the bookmakers around for more than a quarter-million that day, but when Art tells the story he never mentions the amount.

"I went to Harrisburg," he said, "with Buck Crouse, the great middleweight fighter, and Harry Earl for a dinner the plumbers' union was giving our friend Charlie Anderson, their international vice president. From there we kept on driving to New York and got to Empire City just before the first race. I bet $20 with a bookmaker in the grandstand ring and won $700 or $800. We'd moved into the clubhouse by that time, so I went back to the grandstand to give the bookie a chance to get even. I had three or four winners and wound up knocking him out of the box.

"That was a Saturday and we went to Joe Madden's restaurant where the football crowd hung out. The next morning Buck and Madden and I were driving to Saratoga in Madden's old car. It broke down three or four times and the radiator kept boiling over going over the mountains.

"Monday, opening day at Saratoga, was a terrible day. If I remember right, a couple of horses were killed by lightning. I had Tim Mara's figures but sometimes I'd see something the charts didn't see, like a change of jockeys or post position, and I'd use my own judgment. I was betting with Peter Blong, who was working in the ring for Frank Erickson that day, and after I'd hit him for about three winners he said, 'That's enough.' Peter was right up there with the big books like Tom Shaw, and very sharp. If Erickson had been there I'm sure he would have kept on taking my action.

"Anyway, I came close to sweeping the card. In those days they ran only eight races, maybe only seven. I was sitting with Bill Corum, the sportswriter, who saw what I was doing and wrote a column about me breaking the books. He did it mostly to needle George Marshall down in Washington. By that time Marshall owned the Redskins and he was a reformed horseplayer. At least, he knew more about horses than any of us, and he was dead against anybody in the league betting.

"After Corum wrote the story it got bigger and bigger. One of the Hearst papers assigned a reporter to go to the track with me every day. On days when I'd lose he'd play it down and when I won he'd make it much bigger than it was. He told me he liked the assignment and had to make me seem like a live guy because his paper wouldn't be interested in a dead one."

The legend goes that Art sent most of his winnings to his brother Dan, a missionary priest in China.

"I sent Dan some money," he said, "but nowhere near the amount I've read about. In those days you could have bought most of China for that kind of money."

This was bread cast upon the waters, and it came back as soybeans. Some years after the Saratoga incident, Art and a Chicago friend, Jerry Nolan, were deep in the commodities market. They were selling soybeans short, gambling on a big crop and falling market.

"Riding home from New York one day," Art said, "I read a little item in the *Times* about floods in China. I called Father Dan, who was the superior in the Franciscan house in Boston. 'You got any Chinese priests in the house?' I asked him. Turned out there were a couple. They got in touch with the bishop in Hong Kong and sure enough, floods were playing hell with the soybean crop. I called Nolan and we switched our position and made a nice score."

Another time Art and a dozen others were trying to corner cocoa. Art confided in a friend who was connected with the Hershey, Pennsylvania, hockey team. The friend was aghast. "You've got more cocoa than we have in Hershey," he said. Art took it as a warning and sold out. His partners rejected the advice and got burned.

Then there was Westminster, who won the Double Event Handicap under Art's colors at Tropical Park. This was really two races, run twelve days apart. Westminster won both divisions and legend says Art cleaned up just under a million.

Maybe stories like these explain why his Steelers have never won a championship. Art has succeeded at so many things the law of compensation has to get in its licks somewhere. Son of a prosperous saloonkeeper, Art was a kid football player courted vainly by Knute Rockne of Notre Dame, a baseball player signed by the Chicago Cubs and Boston Red Sox, an amateur boxing champion in both the lightweight and welterweight divisions, a successful fight promoter.

"I could have gone to the Olympics," he said, "but I turned pro. I fought a kid named, I think it was Joe Azevedo on a Pinkey Mitchell–Tommy O'Brien card in Milwaukee and my manager, Dick Guy, talked about matching me with Benny Leonard. But I don't know, the style of fighter I was I might have wound up without all my buttons."

ARMY'S RED BLAIK

1959

When West Point's football team was wiped out in that carnival of brassbound stupidity, military buckpassing and bureaucratic bungling which was erroneously called a "cribbing scandal," Red Blaik wanted more than anything else in the world to chuck his job into the Hudson. He wasn't merely discouraged, as any coach might be, at the prospect of starting all over without the fine football material that his organization had assembled and that he had trained painstakingly.

He was passionately on the side of the kids. He did not try to conceal or condone the mistakes they had made but he defended them fiercely as boys of good character and he resented bitterly the slur upon their honor. They were, he felt, at least as much sinned against as sinning, and he knew of no other way to make his position clear than to leave the academy with them.

In his distress, he consulted the man he has respected above all others, his old boss, General Douglas MacArthur.

"Don't quit under fire," the general said, and the colonel said, "Very good, sir."

He stayed on the job and gave it his best, and there never was anything better than that. Now the job is done, and he has resigned. It is as simple as that. He gave all of himself that the job demanded, and it demanded a great deal, and he got it done, and now he is free.

Because he dedicated himself to football without reservations, Earl Blaik understands better than most what the pressures of big-time coaching are. When his younger son, Bob, went into coaching, Red didn't actively oppose him, but he would have preferred that the boy —an honor graduate in physics at Colorado—employ his talents otherwise.

"You can put the same amount of endeavor into something else," he said, not to Bob but to friends, "and, from a selfish standpoint, be infinitely better off. It's a rarity when an individual can take successive years of the pressure of this sort of thing."

He took more years of it than most. As far back as 1933 when he was an assistant at Army, he was keenly aware of the heartburn. Army played Illinois that year, and on the field before the game Blaik encountered Illinois' realistic little Bob Zuppke. Red mentioned the nervousness he felt.

"I'm burning up inside," Zup said. "If I weren't I'd have been out of this game long ago."

Blaik will miss football for a time, but there will be compensations. "Now," he said, "I won't have to expose myself to that cold November air." There'll be other things he won't have to be exposed to, as another coach named Clipper Smith noted some years ago.

Clipper was a lot like Red Blaik in the sense that he too was a perfectionist who drove himself without mercy. He coached for a long time, in college and among the pros, on the West Coast and the East, before retiring to a job in industry.

"How do you feel now on Saturday afternoons?" he was asked. "Do you miss it badly?"

"I did at first," he said, "but after a while—well, you can't imagine how it feels not to have to sit still and watch an eighteen-year-old kid run out on that field with your salary check fluttering between his fingers."

No doubt it's corny, but it is also entirely true that if Red Blaik misses football for a while, football will miss him a great deal longer. He is a great coach, he has been a symbol of decency especially to the young men he helped grow up, and there never was a man more faithful to his principles or his friends.

He is not an easy man to know. Those who do know him are utterly devoted to him.

N.F.L. IN AMERICAN HISTORY

1976

In a hot flush of patriotism, the National Football League has jumped aboard the Bicentennial bandwagon and is sponsoring an essay contest for high school students from fourteen to eighteen years of age. For the best paper on "The Role of the N.F.L. in American History," first prize is a $10,000 college scholarship and second is a $5,000 scholarship. There are ten scholarships worth $1,000 each. In addition, the winner gets an all-expense trip to Super Bowl X in Miami next January with his, her or its parents. The following is submitted in the hope of helping young minds to think along productive lines.

N.F.L. Bicentennial Essay Contest
Box 867
Winona, Minn.

I think pro football is boss and quite historic. I like to read books about pro football, like *Semi-Tough* and *North Dallas Forty*. My little sister likes them, too, and is learning most of the words.

The N.F.L. has made contributions to legal history, medical history and pharmaceutical history. In fact, the Houston Ridge Case was a milestone in all three areas. Houston Ridge was a defensive end with the San Diego Chargers who got hurt and sued the club, the team doctor and the league. He said they gave him pep pills to kill the pain so he could keep on playing after he was hurt. He said he did keep on playing and got hurt worse. He was on crutches a long time.

There was testimony that the Chargers' trainer made phys-ed history by leaving a package of "bennies" or "greenies" or "uppers" in each locker before each game. After the game if a player was afraid he wouldn't sleep that night, they gave him "downers" to settle his nerves.

A druggist testified that he sold 10,000 amphetamines to Irv Kaze, the business manager of the Chargers. "Did you expect Mr. Kaze to ingest 10,000 pills himself?" the druggist was asked. He didn't answer. This is a whole chapter in the history of pharmacology.

Houston Ridge was paid more than $300,000 to settle his suit. That was pretty historic. Later Pete Rozelle, commissioner of the N.F.L., put eight of the Chargers' players on probation for using drugs and fined them different amounts. He fined the club $20,000 and Harland Svare, the general manager, $5,000.

This year the Chargers have played eight games and lost them all. Historians think they ought to go back on greenies.

George Burman, who was a reserve center on the Washington Redskins, is one of the most historic Americans since George Washington. In his Farewell Address, President Washington said: "I hold the maxim no less applicable to public than to private affairs, that honesty is always the best policy."

So when somebody asked George Burman about taking dope he said sure, lots of Redskin players smoked grass and ate bennies. This made a lot of people in pro football sore, but today George Burman is a professor of economics at Carnegie-Mellon University, which used to be Carnegie Tech. He tells it like it is about laissez-faire and gross national product.

Our teacher says Samuel Gompers and Eugene V. Debs were great Americans because they did a lot for the labor movement in this country. She also says David Dubinsky, John L. Lewis and Walter Reuther made contributions.

So did Norm Van Brocklin of the National Football League. He was coach of the Atlanta Falcons and when the players went on strike in the summer of 1974 he called up the team representative, Ken Reaves.

"You and your picket sign are going to New Orleans," Norm Van Brocklin told Ken Reaves.

About the same time the Chicago Bears traded away three players including their player representative, Mac Percival. Their owner, George Halas, made a statement that has gone down in history. "This is the greatest thing that's happened to the Bears in five years," he said. "We got rid of those malcontents. It's a great day, a great day!" Since then the Bears have had no malcontents and very few football players.

On November 22, 1963, an opera was having its premiere in a brand-new opera house in Munich. After the first act, word came that President John F. Kennedy had been assassinated in Dallas 6,000 miles away. The theater closed and the people went home. In Rome, Italian taxi drivers draped a cab in black and parked it in front of the

United States Embassy. In Israel, every shop closed in every town and kibbutz. In the United States while mourners filed past a flag-draped coffin in the Capitol Rotunda, the National Football League played a full program of games.

That didn't prove the N.F.L. callous or insensitive to history, though. They always play "The Star-Spangled Banner" at N.F.L. games, and the pièce de résistance between halves at Super Bowl IV was a re-enactment of the Battle of New Orleans. The British won.

"I would rather be right than President," said Henry Clay, statesman.

"I don't care what others think, so long as I satisfy myself," says Al Davis, managing general partner of the Oakland Raiders.

4.

Baseball

SENT TO BED HUNGRY

1981

When Gene Michael was rehired as manager of the New York Yankees starting in 1983, George M. Steinbrenner III said: "It's like a
child doing something bad at the dinner table. You send him to bed
without dinner, but he's back down for breakfast in the morning."

The child George III had in mind was Eugene Richard Michael,
age forty-four. The bad thing Gene Michael had done at dinner was
stand up on his hind legs like a man and declare for publication that
he was sick to death of George's interminable nagging, carping and
fault-finding, and invite his employer to fire him here and now or
shut up about it.

After reading about sending the kid to bed without dinner, a friend
of Red Reeder said: "This makes it clear to me that those two guys
Steinbrenner beat up on the elevator must have been ten and
eleven."

Michael's ultimatum was a challenge, of course, and an immature,
half-formed mind cannot let a challenge pass. There have not been
many better examples than this of the way sports promoters think.

George III picked up the challenge and acted on it, firing Michael
as manager to satisfy his own macho appetite but keeping him in the
company for later use. George III knew there would be later use for
Gene; he admires Michael as a student of baseball, respects him as
a bachelor of science in education and esteems him as a contempla-
tive numismatist, but not even Steinbrenner has the crust to fire Bob
Lemon right now, considering Bob's record with the team. So when
Lemon said he'd like to be manager one more year, George III said,
"Goodie!" and put everything on the back burner.

Fortunately for the manager pro tem, Lemon, and the manager
presumptive, Michael, George III then struck a bargain with Ron
Guidry's lawyer, John Schneider. That was fortunate for Yankee
managers of the foreseeable future, because in the foreseeable future
the Yankees would not win a pennant without Guidry. He is the
franchise, and he can show the figures to prove it.

In no one of his five seasons since he became a member of the
starting rotation, including the amputated season of 1981, has Guidry
won fewer than 11 games. It goes without saying that the Yankees
have not had 11 games to spare in any recent year.

Guidry's big league record starting in 1977 is 79 games won, 27 lost,
for a winning percentage of .743. The Yankees in those seasons won
451 games and lost 303 for a percentage of .598. Ron is the stopper
who ends losing streaks, the fireball who wins the big ones, the bull

of the woods. Nobody else on the squad can assume that role. Also, he is going to be the only homegrown Yankee; all his playmates, save only Bobby Murcer, were nurtured in other gardens.

Now that Steinbrenner and Guidry have reached agreement—or what passes for agreement before George III has signed a paper—there may be time for inquiry into the future of Reggie Jackson. It must come as a new and perhaps disturbing experience for Reggie to discover another player's contract affairs commanding wider attention than his. It had to happen, though, just as Reggie will have to attain his thirty-sixth birthday next May.

A year ago the big baseball news concerned Dave Winfield and his obscene financial terms with George III. Perhaps that gave Jackson a taste of what it would be like when he was no longer playing the lead in the Bronx Follies. However, it was known then that his contract was valid for 1981; he could bide his time in a supporting part until the starring role was his again.

Now, though, he was a free agent and nobody was looking his way. All eyes were on Guidry. The situation may change this week. The teams bidding, or prepared to bid, against the Yankees for Jackson are supposed to be Baltimore, Atlanta and California.

One would be disposed to throw Baltimore out as a serious contender. As Earl Weaver, the Orioles' manager, says: "Must you have Jackson to win the championship? Yes? Then get him. Could you win without him? We'd have a pretty good chance. Then don't tap out for him."

The Braves' Ted Turner is a different breed of operator. If Turner wants something he'll let no obstacle get in his way, and if you don't like his team or his town or his mustache he'll talk your resistance away.

Angel management comes at a free agent just as rapaciously as the Braves, and Southern California offers compelling charms to some individuals. To suggest that Reggie Jackson may be such an individual is not necessarily absurd.

CONNIE MACK'S INEVITABLE DAY

1952

In the winter of 1883 a skinny young cobbler's assistant who hated cobbling shoved his catcher's glove into his pocket—it was a kid glove, skin-tight, with the fingers cut off—and went out through the snows of New England and got a job as a professional baseball player with Meriden, of the Connecticut State League. He knew then, of course, that the career he was starting would have to end some day.

Throughout his sixty-seven years in baseball, Connie Mack has been aware that the day of departure must inevitably arrive. So has everybody else. But those who have known him have known also that when the time did come, it would come as a shock. It came yesterday. It was a shock.

A shock, but not a surprise, for it is not exactly a secret that Connie will be eighty-eight years old on December 23. The only surprise regarding his retirement as manager of the Athletics stems from the appointment of Jimmy Dykes as his successor instead of Connie's son Earle. For years Connie insisted that Earle, and Earle alone, would succeed him, and certainly Earle fancied himself for the job over a good many years.

Only a week ago there was a story out of Philadelphia suggesting that Dykes was through with the Athletics, and it quoted Connie thus: "I hope Jimmy finds something good, real good."

So now Jimmy has found something, but how good it is remains to be seen. He is manager of a bad ball team with a barren farm system and a financial future that is a topic of wide speculation, because Earle Mack and his brother, Roy, went in hock to buy the club.

Seems as though there's always got to be a catch in it when Dykes takes a new job with the A's. Sold to the White Sox in 1932, he returned to the A's as coach in December 1948, and Connie welcomed him thus at the winter meetings in Chicago: "Jimmy, I'm afraid we can't pay you enough money."

"Keeeripes!" Jimmy wailed. "Do we have to start in where we left off sixteen years ago?"

But it isn't Jimmy Dykes whose name is uppermost in mind today. It is Connie Mack and the shocking, indigestible knowledge that from now on when the Athletics go out to play, the old man won't be sitting in the dugout erect on his little rubber cushion, his scorecard held stiffly over his bony knees, his Adam's apple jiggling above that high hard collar (he still buys them by the dozen from a firm in St. Louis).

For one who traveled with Connie Mack for ten seasons, it would require at least ten years to tell about this glorious old guy who has been baseball's high priest and patriarch, one of its keenest minds, its priceless ambassador, one of its sharpest businessmen, certainly its most indestructible myth.

The plaster saint that they made of him in his old age, the prissy figurehead whose strongest expletive was "Goodness gracious!"—that was pure myth. The man was a ballplayer in the days when baseball was a roughneck's game, and he did all right in the game. He was not a roughneck and not profane by habit, but on occasion he could cuss like any honest mule-skinner. Yes, and when he was younger he played the horses and drank liquor.

He could be as tough as rawhide and as gentle as a mother, reasonable and obstinate beyond reason, and courtly and benevolent and fierce. He was kindhearted and hardfisted, drove a close bargain, and was suckered in a hundred deals. He was generous and thoughtful and autocratic and shy and independent and altogether completely lovable.

There was a day when the Athletics, having broken training camp in Anaheim, California, and having left there Lena Blackburne, one of the coaches, with a leg infection, started out of San Francisco for an exhibition game. It was a nippy morning and somebody asked Connie if he wanted the auto window closed against the chill.

"Dammitohell!" Connie exploded. "I'm all right, don't worry about me! Everybody's always fussing about me. Mrs. Mack says: 'Con, wear your rubbers. Con, put on your overcoat.' So I put on my coat and rubbers and go out to buy medicine for her!

"And that Blackburne!" He was getting madder and madder. "It's 'Boss, are you warm enough? Boss, are you comfortable? Boss, you better come inside and rest.' And where is Blackburne? Lying down there in Anaheim on his tail, dammit!"

It may have been that same day that he nearly broke a rookie's heart by telling him he was going back to the minors and then, a couple of hours later, changed his mind and kept the kid, explaining apologetically: "At my age a man's got a right to do what he wants to do once, anyhow." (The rookie opened the season with the Athletics and was a bum and had to go back, after all.)

One day Wally Moses, who was a holdout, burst from the room where he'd been haggling with the boss and tore out of training camp on the run, his face as white as paper. Another day Connie confided that in all his years of baseball there'd been two unpleasant tasks he'd never got used to: sending a young fellow back to the minors, and arguing with a ballplayer over salary.

He meant it when he said that, and whatever he'd said that other time to Moses, he meant that, too. There never was another like Connie. There never will be.

HENRY AARON'S FINEST HOUR

1974

The only way it could have been better would have been for Henry to hit the very first pitch, the one thrown by Gerald Ford.

Of all the contributions Hank Aaron has made to baseball in twenty blameless years, of all his accomplishments as a player and his acts of graciousness, generosity and loyalty as a person, none was half so valuable as his achievement of yesterday. It isn't only that his 714th home run matched a record that for more than forty years was considered beyond human reach, and it isn't particularly important that this courteous, modest man has at last overtaken Babe Ruth's roistering ghost. What really counts is that when Henry laid the wood on Jack Billingham's fast ball, he struck a blow for the integrity of the game and for public faith in the game.

With one stroke he canceled schemes to cheapen his pursuit of the record by making it a carnival attraction staged for the box office alone, and he rendered moot two months of wrangling between the money-changers and the Protectors of the Faith.

Standard-bearer in the latter camp was Bowie Kuhn, whose rare exercise of authority as baseball commissioner brought about Aaron's presence in the lineup. When the game's upright scoutmaster notified the Atlanta Braves that he expected Aaron to play two of three of the team's early games, he brought back to memory an observation made some years ago by the late Tom Meany as toast-master at a sports dinner in Toots Shor's.

"Ford Frick just reached for the rye bottle," Tom announced between introductions. "It's his first positive move in four years."

This is the sixth season in office for Frick's successor-once-removed, and nothing he did in the first five years was anywhere near as important as his action in this matter. Bill Bartholomay, the Braves' president, meant to keep Aaron on the bench through the first three games in Cincinnati in the hope that crowds would fill the Atlanta park to see Henry go after Ruth's record in the 11-game home stand that opens Monday night.

Kuhn realized that in the view of most fans, leaving the team's clean-up hitter out of the batting order would be tantamount to dumping the games in Cincinnati. He explained to Bartholomay what self-interest should have told the Braves' owner, that it is imperative that every team present its strongest lineup every day in an honest effort to win, and that the customers must believe the strongest lineup is being used for that purpose.

When Bartholomay persisted in his determination to dragoon the living Aaron and the dead Ruth as shills to sell tickets in Atlanta, the commissioner laid down the law. With a man like Henry swinging for him, that's all he had to do.

Thanks to Mrs. Herbert Aaron's muscular son, 2:40 P.M., April 4, 1974, will stand until further notice as Bowie Kuhn's finest hour.

That was the time of day when Henry hit the ball, and although his 715th home run will mean more to him because it will advance him into a class all by himself, it was his finest hour, too.

To be sure, he didn't realize that beforehand. While the controversy that Bartholomay started was going on, Henry said some foolish things. He talked about protecting the Atlanta box office and about the rights of Atlanta's dwindling body of customers. He said it didn't matter whether he played or not because the Braves weren't going anywhere this year.

When they said, "Suppose the commissioner orders the Braves to play you," he said that in that event he guessed the commissioner would have to make out Cincinnati's batting order, too. This smart-aleck line must have been fed to him, for Henry isn't a smart aleck.

Had he given it any thought he would have realized that there was no need for Kuhn to worry about the Cincinnati batting order because nobody in the Reds' organization was playing tricks for box-office purposes. Kuhn knew he could rely on Sparky Anderson to start the team he considered most likely to win. If he could have placed the same reliance in the Braves' brass, he would never have set a precedent by pre-empting the manager's responsibility.

As it turned out, there was nothing contrived about the locale or the timing of the event. It happened in the first inning on Henry's first time at bat and the hit produced the first runs of the season.

It was witnessed by a standing-room-only crowd of 52,154 who weren't lured in by Aaron but rather by the local tradition that dictates that every ambulatory citizen of Cincinnati must attend the opening game even if he doesn't show up again all summer. It wasn't even postponed till tomorrow, when the box office could use a special attraction and the game will be on national television.

The way Henry did it removed all taint of commercialism. For this day, at least, the business of baseball made way for sport.

MIRACLE OF COOGAN'S BLUFF

1951

Now it is done. Now the story ends. And there is no way to tell it. The art of fiction is dead. Reality has strangled invention. Only the utterly impossible, the inexpressibly fantastic, can ever be plausible again.

Down on the green and white and earth-brown geometry of the playing field, a drunk tries to break through the ranks of ushers marshaled along the foul lines to keep profane feet off the diamond. The ushers thrust him back and he lunges at them, struggling in the clutch of two or three men. He breaks free, and four or five tackle him. He shakes them off, bursts through the line, runs head-on into a special park cop, who brings him down with a flying tackle.

Here comes a whole platoon of ushers. They lift the man and haul him, twisting and kicking, back across the first-base line. Again he shakes loose and crashes the line. He is through. He is away, weaving out toward center field, where cheering thousands are jammed beneath the windows of the Giants' clubhouse.

At heart, our man is a Giant, too. He never gave up.

From center field comes burst upon burst of cheering, Pennants are waving, uplifted fists are brandished, hats are flying. Again and again the dark clubhouse windows blaze with the light of photographers' flash bulbs. Here comes that same drunk out of the mob, back across the green turf to the infield. Coattails flying, he runs the bases, slides into third. Nobody bothers him now.

And the story remains to be told, the story of how the Giants won the 1951 pennant in the National League. The tale of their barreling run through August and September and into October. . . . Of the final day of the season, when they won the championship and started home with it from Boston, to hear on the train how the dead, defeated Dodgers had risen from the ashes in the Philadelphia twilight. . . . Of the three-game playoff in which they won, and lost, and were losing again with one out in the ninth inning yesterday when—Oh, why bother?

Maybe this is the way to tell it: Bobby Thomson, a young Scot from Staten Island, delivered a timely hit yesterday in the ninth inning of an enjoyable game of baseball before 34,320 witnesses in the Polo Grounds. . . . Or perhaps this is better:

"Well!" said Whitey Lockman, standing on second base in the second inning of yesterday's playoff game between the Giants and Dodgers.

"Ah, there," said Bobby Thomson, pulling into the same station after hitting a ball to left field. "How've you been?"

"Fancy," Lockman said, "meeting you here!"

"Ooops!" Thomson said. "Sorry."

And the Giants' first chance for a big inning against Don Newcombe disappeared as they tagged Thomson out. Up in the press section, the voice of Willie Goodrich came over the amplifiers announcing a macabre statistic: "Thomson has now hit safely in fifteen consecutive games." Just then the floodlights were turned on, enabling the Giants to see and count their runners on each base.

It wasn't funny, though, because it seemed for so long that the Giants weren't going to get another chance like the one Thomson squandered by trying to take second base with a playmate already there. They couldn't hit Newcombe, and the Dodgers couldn't do anything wrong. Sal Maglie's most splendrous pitching would avail nothing unless New York could match the run Brooklyn had scored in the first inning.

The story was winding up, and it wasn't the happy ending that such a tale demands. Poetic justice was a phrase without meaning.

Now it was the seventh inning and Thomson was up, with runners on first and third base, none out. Pitching a shutout in Philadelphia last Saturday night, pitching again in Philadelphia on Sunday, holding the Giants scoreless this far, Newcombe had now gone twenty-one innings without allowing a run.

He threw four strikes to Thomson. Two were fouled off out of play. Then he threw a fifth. Thomson's fly scored Monte Irvin. The score was tied. It was a new ball game.

Wait a moment, though. Here's Pee Wee Reese hitting safely in the eighth. Here's Duke Snider singling Reese to third. Here's Maglie wild-pitching a run home. Here's Andy Pafko slashing a hit through Thomson for another score. Here's Billy Cox batting still another home. Where does his hit go? Where else? Through Thomson at third.

So it was the Dodgers' ball game, 4 to 1, and the Dodgers' pennant. So all right. Better get started and beat the crowd home. That stuff in the ninth inning? That didn't mean anything.

A single by Al Dark. A single by Don Mueller. Irvin's pop-up, Lockman's one-run double. Now the corniest possible sort of Hollywood schmaltz—stretcher-bearers plodding away with an injured Mueller between them, symbolic of the Giants themselves.

There went Newcombe and here came Ralph Branca. Who's at bat? Thomson again? He beat Branca with a home run the other day. Would Charley Dressen order him walked, putting the winning run on base, to pitch to the dead-end kids at the bottom of the batting order? No, Branca's first pitch was a called strike.

The second pitch—well, when Thomson reached first base he turned and looked toward the left-field stands. Then he started jumping straight up in the air, again and again. Then he trotted around the bases, taking his time.

Ralph Branca turned and started for the clubhouse. The number on his uniform looked huge. Thirteen.

THE WINTER PASTIME

MONTREAL, 1981

When Bowie Kuhn surrendered authority to schedule postseason baseball games to his television masters eleven years ago, he sowed the seeds that ripened yesterday in this popular ski resort.

With the National League pennant race down to its last match, winter hit the summer game with an icy fist. Montreal awoke to sullen gray skies, bitter rain and a temperature of 37 degrees, 5 above freezing. The baseball commissioner was not responsible for the Sunday weather and only indirectly to blame for Montreal's presence in the pennant playoff. (If he hadn't dissected the season with a Bowie knife, these games would be in St. Louis, where Indian summer is often aglow at this time of year. The Cardinals and Cincinnati Reds had the best won-lost figures over the whole summer, but the Expos and Dodgers qualified for the playoffs by winning the second half.) Anyway, the playoffs are a league matter; only the World Series is the commissioner's baby.

However, this is the sort of thing Bowie has been warned about ever since he let TV switch World Series play from 1 P.M. to prime time.

This game was scheduled for 4 P.M. because NBC, which was doing the television, had contractual commitments to professional football, and baseball is afraid to compete with that game for Nielsen ratings. However, shortly after that hour with the pitchers and their playmates already warming up, the rain that had abated for half an hour started falling again, the infield was again covered with a tarpaulin, and customers in unroofed seats in Stade Olympique either fled or broke out umbrellas.

TV monitors announced "rain delay," but there was no official statement and rumors spread that Don Ohlmeyer of NBC had ordered an hour's postponement to get football off the tube.

A call was made to Freddie Aronson at the Montreal weather information office. He said showers would continue, possibly as late as 7:30 P.M., but the temperature had warmed to 50 degrees. A fierce wind blew in from the outfield with gusts of 20 to 25 miles an hour.

Today would be worse, Aronson said. Snow was forecast, but nothing that would stay on the ground. The wind would reach 33 miles an hour and temperatures would hang in the 30's.

At 4:52, the rain slowed, groundskeepers in long raincoats folded the infield tarp, spectators applauded and a few players emerged from the dugouts. Men with long-handled squeegees worked on a puddle around the shortstop's position, aided by the Zamboni machines that had been prowling unprotected areas.

Almost immediately, rain poured down and the tarp was replaced. At 5:20 the organ struck up and those customers still in the stands actually sang, chorusing their favorite, "The Happy Wanderer": "Fol-daree, fol-darah!"

At 6:35, after one more abortive attempt to uncover the field, it was announced that the game was "still on hold" and that Chub Feeney, the National League president, would have a further announcement at 7:15.

About the same time, television monitors carried an announcement that the game had been postponed until 1 P.M. today. Reporters scuttled for telephones but the announcement had been a phony. The network had been practicing. It was a dry run on a wet, wet day.

It had been an afternoon of unrelieved discomfort, not to say misery. Not even Bowie Kuhn, all-wise, all-merciful, all-powerful, could have controlled the weather, but the miserable conditions revived complaints about the way baseball is run.

"These people," a man was saying, "have no pride and no confidence in their sport. Wouldn't you think that just once one of them would say, 'This is the national game, and the playoffs and World Series are the jewels in our crown. Because it is great entertainment, television would want to buy it and we will be happy to sell the rights on our terms.'

"TV would buy it, baseball wouldn't have to fear football and wouldn't be subservient to the space cadets."

As seven o'clock drew near, shouts and whistles rose from the stands. Cowbells jangled. Rain came pelting down while Zambonis tried to mop up lakes just beyond the infield. Four of the Expos, who have come to regard this weather as normal, played pitch-catch briefly and retired. The clock passed 7:20 without the promised announcement.

Finally at 7:30 the public-address system spoke the unwelcome words: The game was postponed until 1:05 today.

There were scattered boos. Terry Francona, a spare outfielder with the Expos, did a swan dive in the pond behind first base. He was cheered.

JOE DiMAGGIO

1947

After the Yankees chewed up the Dodgers in the second game of the World Series, Joe DiMaggio relaxed in the home club's gleaming tile boudoir and deposed at length in defense of Pete Reiser, the Brooklyn center fielder, who had narrowly escaped being smitten upon the isthmus rhombencephali that day by sundry fly balls.

The moving, mottled background of faces and shirt collars and orchids, Joe said, made a fly almost invisible until it had cleared the top deck. The tricky, slanting shadows of an October afternoon created a problem involving calculus, metaphysics, and social hygiene when it came to judging a line drive. The roar of the crowd disguised the crack of bat against ball. And so on.

Our Mr. Robert Cooke, listening respectfully as one should to the greatest living authority on the subject, nevertheless stared curiously at DiMaggio. He was thinking that not only Reiser but also J. Di-Maggio had played that same center field on that same afternoon, and there were no knots on Joe's slick coiffure.

"How about you, Joe?" Bob asked. "Do those same factors handicap you out there?"

DiMaggio permitted himself one of his shy, toothy smiles.

"Don't start worrying about the old boy after all these years," he said.

He didn't say "the old master." That's a phrase for others to use. But it would be difficult to define more aptly than Joe did the difference between this unmitigated pro and all the others, good, bad, and ordinary, who also play in major-league outfields.

There is a line that has been quoted so often the name of its originator has been lost. But whoever said it first was merely reacting impulsively to a particular play and not trying to coin a mot when he ejaculated: "The sonofagun! Ten years I've been watching him, and he hasn't had a hard chance yet!"

It may be that Joe is not, ranked on his defensive skill alone, the finest center fielder of his time. Possibly Terry Moore was his equal playing the hitter, getting the jump on the ball, judging a fly, covering ground, and squeezing the ball once he touched it.

Joe himself has declared that his kid brother, Dominic, is a better fielder than he. Which always recalls the occasion when the Red Sox were playing the Yanks and Dom fled across the county line to grab a drive by Joe that no one but a DiMaggio could have reached. And the late Sid Mercer, shading his thoughtful eyes under a hard straw hat, remarked to the press box at large: "Joe should sue his old man on that one."

Joe hasn't been the greatest hitter that baseball has known, either. He'll not match Ty Cobb's lifetime average, he'll never threaten Babe Ruth's home-run record, nor will he ever grip the imagination of the crowds as the Babe did. Or even as Babe Herman did. That explains why the contract that he signed the other day calls for an estimated $65,000 instead of the $80,000 that Ruth got. If he were not such a matchless craftsman he might be a more spectacular player. And so, perhaps, more colorful. And so more highly rewarded.

But you don't rate a great ballplayer according to his separate, special talents. You must rank him off the sum total of his component parts, and on this basis there has not been, during Joe's big-league existence, a rival close to him. None other in his time has combined such savvy and fielding and hitting and throwing—Tom Laird, who was writing sports in San Francisco when Joe was growing up, always insisted that a sore arm "ruined" DiMaggio's throwing in his first season with the Yankees—and such temperament and such base running.

Because he does so many other things so well and makes no specialty of stealing, DiMaggio rarely has received full credit for his work on the bases. But travel with a second-division club in the league for a few seasons and count the times when DiMaggio, representing the tying or winning run, whips you by coming home on the unforeseen gamble and either beats the play or knocks the catcher into the dugout.

Ask American League catchers about him, or National Leaguers like Ernie Lombardi. Big Lom will remember who it was who ran home from first base in the last game of the 1939 World Series while Ernie lay threshing in the dust behind the plate and Bucky Walters stood bemused on the mound.

These are the reasons why DiMaggio, excelled by Ted Williams in all offensive statistics and reputedly Ted's inferior in crowd appeal and financial standing, still won the writers' accolade as the American League's most valuable in 1947.

It wasn't the first time Williams earned this award with his bat and lost it with his disposition. As a matter of fact, if all other factors were equal save only the question of character, Joe never would lose out to any player. The guy who came out of San Francisco as a shy lone wolf, suspicious of Easterners and of Eastern writers, today is the top guy in any sports gathering in any town. The real champ.

CURT FLOOD'S THIRTEENTH AMENDMENT

1969

Curt Flood was nineteen years old and had made one hit in the major leagues (a home run) when his telephone rang on December 5 of 1957. The call was from the Cincinnati Reds advising him that he had been traded to the St. Louis Cardinals.

"I knew ballplayers got traded like horses," he said years later, "but I can't tell you how I felt when it happened to me. I was only nineteen, but I made up my mind then it wouldn't ever happen again."

It happened again last October. The Cardinals traded Flood to Philadelphia. "Maybe I won't go," Curt said. Baseball men laughed. Curt makes something like $90,000 a year playing center field, and less than that painting portraits in his studio in Clayton, Missouri. "Unless he's better than Rembrandt," one baseball man said, "he'll play."

It was a beautiful comment, superlatively typical of the executive mind, a pluperfect example of baseball's reaction to unrest down in the slave cabins. "You mean," baseball demands incredulously, "that at these prices they want human rights, too?"

Curtis Charles Flood is a man of character and self-respect. Being black, he is more sensitive than most white players about the institution of slavery as it exists in professional baseball. After the trade he went abroad, and when he returned his mind was made up. He confided his decision to the twenty-four club representatives in the Major League Players Association at their convention in San Juan, Puerto Rico.

He told them it was high time somebody in baseball made a stand for human freedom. He said he was determined to make the stand and he asked their support. The players questioned him closely to make sure this was not merely a ploy to squeeze money out of the Phillies. Then, convinced, they voted unanimously to back him up.

Realizing that if Flood lost his case through poor handling they would all be losers, the players arranged—through their executive director, Marvin Miller—to retain Arthur J. Goldberg, former Secretary of Labor, former Justice of the Supreme Court, former United States ambassador to the United Nations, and the country's most distinguished authority on labor-management relations.

Baseball's so-called reserve clause, which binds the player to his employer through his professional life, had been under fire before. Never has it been attacked by a team like this.

The system is in deep trouble, and yesterday's action by the baseball commissioner, Bowie Kuhn, did nothing to help it out. Because the news was out that Flood was going to take baseball to court, Kuhn released to the press the following correspondence:

"Dear Mr. Kuhn," Flood wrote on December 24, 1969, "after twelve years in the major leagues I do not feel that I am a piece of property to be bought and sold irrespective of my wishes. I believe that any system that produces that result violates my basic rights as a citizen and is inconsistent with the laws of the United States and of the several states.

"It is my desire to play baseball in 1970, and I am capable of playing. I have received a contract offer from the Philadelphia club, but I believe that I have the right to consider offers from other clubs before making any decisions. I, therefore, request that you make known to all the major league clubs my feelings in this matter, and advise them of my availability for the 1970 season."

Kuhn replied:

Dear Curt: This will acknowledge your letter of December 24, 1969, which I found on returning to my office yesterday.

I certainly agree with you that you, as a human being, are not a piece of property to be bought and sold. That is fundamental in our society and I think obvious. However, I cannot see its application to the situation at hand.

You have entered into a current playing contract with the St. Louis club which has the same assignment provisions as those in your annual major league contracts since 1956. Your present playing contract has been assigned in accordance with its provisions by the St. Louis club to the Philadelphia club. The provisions of the playing contract have been negotiated over the years between the clubs and the players, most recently when the present basic agreement was negotiated two years ago between the clubs and the Players Association.

If you have any specific objections to the propriety of the assignment I would appreciate your specifying the objections. Under the circumstances, and pending any further information from you, I do not see what action I can take, and cannot comply with your request contained in the second paragraph of your letter.

I am pleased to see your statement that you desire to play baseball in 1970. I take it this puts to rest any thought, as reported earlier in the press, that you were considering retirement.

Thus the commissioner restates baseball's labor policy. "Run along, sonny, you bother me."

CHRISTMAS SPIRIT

1975

Obviously, the arbitration award making Andy Messersmith and Dave McNally free agents came as no surprise to the men who own baseball, for they already had a paper prepared and signed firing the arbitrator. As soon as Peter Seitz delivered his opinion, John Gaherin, the owners' representative in labor matters, handed him a letter dismissing him as umpire in grievance cases. The owners and the players' union had agreed on Seitz as successor to another professional arbitrator, Gabriel Alexander of Detroit, slightly more than a year ago under an agreement providing that his services could be terminated by either party. Remembering that it was Peter Seitz who shook Catfish Hunter off Charley Finley's hook—they couldn't possibly forget—the powers, archangels and angels of the baseball hierarchy had decided before yesterday that they wanted an impartial arbitrator who would be more impartial on their side.

Along with the dismissal notice went a demand that Seitz release no copies of his seventy-page opinion and refrain from discussing it, writing about it or making speeches about it.

He replied that he would not circulate the opinion because he felt it was the property of the parties involved. He added that he regarded the order to button his lip, coming from people who had just fired him, as the ultimate in arrogance.

If "arrogance" seems too mild a word, put it down to the fact that Peter Seitz is a man of judicial mind, temperate of speech, with a gift for understatement. Another man might have sent John Gaherin back to his bosses with a pointed suggestion for disposal of their pink slip.

In making the award, Marvin Miller, executive director of the Players' Association, concurred with Seitz, while the third member of the arbitration panel, Gaherin, voted the company way. The ruling will be appealed to the courts. Chances are baseball will attempt to carry it all the way to the Supreme Court. If it is confirmed, it will open another chink in the feudal edifice called the reserve system, but it will not put an end to the system.

All Seitz really decided was that when a contract says "for a period of one year" it does not mean two years or twenty or two hundred.

The standard one-year contract gives the employer an option on the player's services for a second year. Paragraph 10-A provides that if the player does not sign a new contract for the second year, the employer may unilaterally renew the old contract "for a period of one year on the same terms." The owners argue that "on the same terms" means "with another one-year option." That's how the reserve system works: it enables the employer to "reserve" the player for life, with or without a contract.

"No it doesn't," Peter Seitz ruled. His decision put baseball players in the same class as football players who play out their option and become free agents.

Messersmith and McNally, pitchers owned by the Los Angeles Dodgers and Montreal Expos, refused to sign 1975 contracts because they were not satisfied with the terms. Messersmith pitched all summer and won 19 games. With a record of 3–6 in June, McNally gave up and went home, spending the rest of the season on the disqualified list. Both went to arbitration, contending that now that the option season was over they were entitled to free agency.

First the owners went to court to argue that this was not a proper subject for arbitration. Federal Judge John W. Oliver in Kansas City refused to issue an injunction, but had the parties stipulate that either side could come back and ask for a review of the arbitrator's decision. That will be baseball's next step.

In making the award, Seitz pointed out that he was not making a judgment on the merits of the reserve system but was merely interpreting language that had been agreed upon. As he read it, that language said and meant "for a period of one year," so the players had discharged their obligations and were free.

Weeks ago he reminded both sides that they were engaged in negotiations for a new basic agreement on working conditions, which include the reserve system. He urged them to meet immediately and try to bargain out the issue instead of waiting for a quasi-judicial opinion. They did not meet.

"But," he said yesterday, "it still isn't too late. If this finding is destructive to the reserve system, if it is a blow to the national game, there is still time for them to sit down and ameliorate the blow. As I understand it, the Players' Association is not opposed to the reserve system, it is opposed to the reserve system with its present restrictions."

It is excellent advice. It will be acted upon exactly the way similar advice has been acted upon in the past: "These," the owners and their lawyers will say as they have said time and again, "are matters best left to collective bargaining." Then they refuse to bargain.

Yes, and Merry Christmas to you, too.

THE GAME THEY INVENTED FOR WILLIE

OAKLAND, 1973

When Willie got the hit, Ray Sadecki and Harry Parker were watching on television in the clubhouse of the New York Mets. For a moment there was silence. Then Sadecki, who had pitched an inning and one-third, turned to Parker, who had pitched one inning. "He had to get a hit," Sadecki said. "This game was invented for Willie Mays a hundred years ago."

It was the longest day in the long, long history of World Series competition, and for Willie Mays it was eternity. It was the second match in the struggle with the Oakland A's for the baseball championship of creation. It was the nineteenth such game for Willie in a span of twenty-two years. In the forty-third year of his life, this may have been the final bow for the most exciting player of his time. So he lost the game in the ninth inning, won it in the twelfth, came perilously close to losing it again—and walked away from disaster grinning.

Never another like him. Never in this world.

"Yesterday," a man told him, "you said you were going to let the kids win it the rest of the way. What do you say about the old folks now?"

Willie took a sip from a can of Coke. He lounged on a platform behind a microphone, one leg slung over a television receiving set. His jaw worked rhythmically on a cud of gum.

"What old folks you talkin' about?" he asked.

Strictly speaking, Willie never lost the game and never won it. It only seemed that way. When the Mets had the decision in hand, 6–4, in the last of the ninth, Mays fell down chasing a drive by Deron Johnson and the two-base hit that resulted started a rally that tied the score.

Willie had gone into the game as a pinch-runner and had fallen down rounding second, but that had been only an embarrassment without effect on the score. For the most spectacular outfielder of an era, though, that pratfall in center was catastrophic.

"I didn't see the ball," he said, and he wasn't the only one dazzled in the sun field of Oakland-Alameda County Stadium. "I tried to dive for it the last second. We had a two-run lead and I shoulda played it safe."

His chance for redemption came in the twelfth with the score still tied, two out and two Mets on the bases. The game had already gone on longer than any World Series match before, longer than the one between the Cubs and Tigers that consumed 3 hours 28 minutes in 1945.

Rollie Fingers, fifth of the six pitchers who worked for Oakland, threw a strike and Willie slashed at it, missing. Fingers threw another and Willie slapped it straight back, a bounder that hopped high over the pitcher's head and skipped on into center field, sending Bud Harrelson home with the run that put New York ahead.

"I think it was a fastball, up," Willie said. "I'd seen Fingers a lot on television and he likes to work inside and outside, up and down. Yesterday was the test. He threw me a fastball, then gave me a breaking pitch and came back with a fastball, so I knew he'd feed me 80 percent fastballs."

Waxed mustache twitching angrily, Fingers flipped his glove away in disgust. One play later the Oakland manager, Dick Williams, sent Fingers away, too, but more in sorrow than in anger. By that time Cleon Jones had singled to load the bases, and errors soon would let in three more runs.

With New York in front, 10–6, Reggie Jackson opened the rebuttal. He drove a mighty shot high and deep toward the wall in center.

Willie went back to the fence, set himself and saw the ball drop in front of him.

"I saw it," he said afterward, "and in a close game I might have had a chance on it, but we had a four-run lead then and I didn't want to kill myself because we got a lot more games to play."

"But Willie," a man said, "you fell down in center field. What happened out there?"

"Two balls come out there," he said. "That's most of it." His voice dropped, took on a comforting tone. "You've seen me play enough. I wasn't out there long today. You know when I play regular. . . . But I'm not a player that makes excuses."

Excuses? Some of those who heard him could remember the catch he made off Cleveland's Vic Wertz in the World Series of 1954, the time he ran down Carl Furillo's drive, spun completely around and threw out Billy Cox at the plate, the impossible chance he grabbed off Roberto Clemente of Pittsburgh. To be sure, this time Jackson scored and the A's went on to fill the bases. But excuses? Not for Willie, ever.

THE METS' MIDNIGHT MASSACRE

1977

In the emotional aftermath of M. Donald Grant's Midnight Massacre, one significant fact emerged yesterday: contrary to what the Mets' chairman of the board had been saying and his tame columnist had been writing, Tom Seaver was not demanding renegotiation of his contract. He was not welshing. He was prepared to fufill the commitments that extended through the 1978 season, provided the club would start negotiations now on a new agreement for the seasons of 1979–80–81. He would of course have sought a salary for those years comparable with the pay now drawn by lesser players who became free agents last fall. The best pitcher in baseball made this clear to the passel of reporters, photographers and broadcasters who flocked to Shea Stadium to watch him clear out his locker and depart for the Cincinnati Reds. He also set the record straight on national television.

Grant had been saying that Seaver had demanded to be traded. "It is with sincere regret," M. Donald's statement read, "that we have met Tom Seaver's request and traded him to Cincinnati."

"I never demanded to be traded," Tom Seaver said, "until Wednesday."

"They didn't want to renegotiate," he said of the Mets, "and I can understand that. But they did seem willing to talk about 1979–80–81."

They seemed that way Tuesday when Seaver, in Atlanta with team, talked by phone with Lorinda de Roulet, the Mets' president. She was "reasonable and lovely," said Tom's wife Nancy.

The next day Seaver read some garbage to the effect that his troubles with the brass stemmed from Nancy's resentment of the fact that Nolan Ryan, husband of her friend Ruth, got a bigger salary than Tom's for pitching for the California Angels. That tore it. "I want out," Seaver told the club. Even as he did, he sensed that the club's attitude had stiffened since his talk with Mrs. de Roulet. He suspected that Grant was infuriated because the pitcher had gone over his head.

For weeks Joe McDonald, the general manager, had been trying to get something of value for Seaver, without success because other clubs knew he was in a bind. Wednesday night he accepted the inevitable—a sophomore pitcher, two minor-league outfielders and a utility infielder. Pat Zachry, the pitcher, was a good rookie last year but hasn't been getting people out this season. To replace Doug Flynn, the infielder, Cincinnati got Rick Auerbach, whom the Texas Rangers had picked up after the Mets turned him loose.

Before bringing off that clinker, the Mets had telephoned San Diego to ask: "Would you accept Dave Kingman for Valentine and another player?"

Robert John Valentine is a part-time infielder-outfielder with a crooked leg and a batting average of .172. He was considered a bright prospect when he got out of Stanford University, but in 1973 he ran into the wall in Anaheim, California, and suffered a double fracture of the right leg. The next year he had a shoulder separation. The Padres hadn't thought of trading for Kingman, but " it was a deal we had to make," said Alvin Dark, their manager. As the "other player" the Mets had asked for, San Diego selected Paul Siebert, a pitcher fresh from the minors known primarily as the son of an old first baseman with the Philadelphia Athletics, Dick Siebert.

From the talent pool that had enabled them to reach last place in their division, the Mets had now subtracted the best pitcher in baseball and one of the best home-run hitters. They also subtracted Mike Phillips, a utility infielder who can hit for distance. To replace these three they received seven silhouettes but not one regular player.

Perhaps all seven will become useful players, maybe stars, though the laws of probability are against it. So is the record of the club's earlier adventures in the flesh market. While the Shea Stadium clientele surveyed the wreckage, some wondered what might have been. Suppose this team had its present personnel plus Seaver, Kingman, Nolan Ryan, Rusty Staub and Amos Otis, all former Mets. It would be in first place, or near it.

"How about Bowie Kuhn?" one fan asked. "He has vetoed other deals. Does he feel this one is in the best interests of baseball?"

Having Tom Seaver pitch for the Reds is not in the best interests of Walter O'Malley's Dodgers, whose fat lead over Cincinnati has been dwindling. When Walter discovers that Sparky Anderson has already calculated Seaver's place in the rotation so he will be fit and rested for a start against the Dodgers next weekend, Bowie's phone may start ringing.

CASEY STENGEL'S TESTIMONY

1981

A young woman asked, "What was Casey Stengel like?" I thought she was pulling my leg until I realized that she was nine years old when Casey, retiring as manager of the New York Mets, dropped out of public view. "Casey Stengel," I said, "was—well, just a minute." I dug up my copy of Casey's testimony before the Senate Subcommittee on Antitrust and Monopoly on July 9, 1958. It seems to me that those of us who covered Casey in his time owe it to history to reintroduce him to readers in this fashion at least once a decade.

Senator Estes Kefauver: Mr. Stengel, you are the manager of the New York Yankees. Will you give us very briefly your background and your views about this legislation?

Stengel: Well, I started in professional ball in 1910. I have been in professional ball, I would say, for forty-eight years. I have been employed by numerous ball clubs in the majors and in the minor leagues.

I entered in the minor leagues with Kansas City. I played as low as Class D ball, which was at Shelbyville, Kentucky, and also Class C ball and Class A ball, and I have advanced in baseball as a ballplayer.

I had many years that I was not so successful as a ballplayer, as it is a game of skill. And then I was no doubt discharged by baseball in which I had to go back to the minor leagues as a manager, and after being in the minor leagues as a manager, I became a major league manager in several cities and was discharged, we call it discharged because there is no question I had to leave.

And I returned to the minor leagues at Milwaukee, Kansas City and Oakland, California, and then returned to the major leagues. In the last ten years, naturally, with the New York Yankees, the New York Yankees have had tremendous success and while I am not a ballplayer who does the work I have no doubt worked for a ball club that is very capable in the office.

I have been up and down the ladder. I know there are some things in baseball thirty-five to fifty years ago that are better now than they were in those days. In those days, my goodness, you could not transfer a ball club in the minor leagues, Class D, Class C ball, Class A ball.

How could you transfer a ball club when you did not have a highway? How could you transfer a ball club when the railroads then would take you to a town you got off and then you had to wait and sit up five hours to go to another ball club?

How could you run baseball then without night ball? You had to have night ball to improve the proceeds, to pay larger salaries, and I went to work, the first year I received $135 a month. I thought that was amazing. I had to put away enough money to go to dental college. I found out it was not better in dentistry. I stayed in baseball.

Any other questions you would like to ask me?

Kefauver: Mr. Stengel, are you prepared to answer particularly why baseball wants this bill passed?

Stengel: Well, I would have to say at the present time, I think that baseball has advanced in this respect for the player help. That is an amazing statement for me to make, because you can retire with an annuity at fifty and what organization in America allows you to retire at fifty and receive money?

Now the second thing about baseball that I think is very interesting to the public or to all of us is that it is the owner's fault if he does not improve his club, along with the officials in the ball club and the players.

Now what causes that?

If I am going to go on the road and we are a traveling ball club and you know the cost of transportation now—we travel sometimes with three Pullman coaches, the New York Yankees, and I'm just a salaried man and do not own stock in the New York Yankees. I found out that in traveling with the New York Yankees on the road and all, that it is the best, and we have broken records in Washington this year, we have broken them in every city but New York and we have lost two clubs that have gone out of the city of New York.

Of course, we have had some bad weather. I would say that they are mad at us in Chicago, we fill the parks. They have come out to see good material. I will say they are mad at us in Kansas City, but we broke their attendance records.

Now on the road we only get possibly 27 cents. I am not positive of these figures, as I am not an official. If you go back fifteen years or if I owned stock in the club, I would give them to you.

Kefauver: Mr. Stengel, I am not sure that I made my question clear.

Stengel: Yes, sir. Well, that is all right. I am not sure I'm going to answer yours perfectly, either.

Senator Joseph C. O'Mahoney: How many minor leagues were there in baseball when you began?

Stengel: Well, there were not so many at that time because of this fact: anybody to go into baseball at that time with the educational schools that we had were small, while you were probably thoroughly educated at school, you had to be—we had only small cities that you could put a team in and they would go defunct.

Why, I remember the first year I was at Kankakee, Illinois, and a bank offered me $550 if I would let them have a little notice. I left there and took a uniform because they owed me two weeks' pay. But I either had to quit but I did not have enough money to go to dental college so I had to go with the manager down to Kentucky.

What happened there was if you got by July, that was the big date. You did not play night ball and you did not play Sundays in half of the cities because of a Sunday observance, so in those days when things were tough, and all of it was, I mean to say, why they just closed up July 4 and there you were sitting there in the depot. You could go to work someplace else, but that was it.

So I got out of Kankakee, Illinois, and I just go there for the visit now.

Senator John A. Carroll: The question Senator Kefauver asked you was what, in your honest opinion, with your forty-eight years of experience, is the need for this legislation in view of the fact that baseball has not been subject to antitrust laws

Stengel: No.

Carroll: I had a conference with one of the attorneys representing not only baseball but all of the sports, and I listened to your explanation to Senator Kefauver. It seemed to me it had some clarity. I asked the attorney this question: What was the need for this legislation? I wonder if you would accept his definition. He said they didn't want to be subjected to the *ipse dixit* of the federal government because they would throw a lot of damage suits on the *ad damnum* clause. He said, in the first place, the Toolson case was *sui generis,* it was *de minimus non curat lex.*

Stengel: Well, you are going to get me there for about two hours.

Kefauver: Thank you, very much, Mr. Stengel. We appreciate your presence here.

Mr. Mickey Mantle, will you come around?

Mr. Mantle, do you have any observations with reference to the applicability of the antitrust laws to baseball?

Mantle: My views are just about the same as Casey's.

DIZZY DEAN'S DAY

ST. LOUIS, 1934

Through the murk of cigarette smoke and liniment fumes in the Cardinals' clubhouse a radio announcer babbled into a microphone.

"And now," he read with fine spontaneity from a typewritten sheet prepared hours in advance, "and now let's have a word from the Man of the Hour, Manager Frank Frisch."

The Man of the Hour shuffled forward. He had started changing clothes. His shirttail hung limply over bare thighs. The Man of the Hour's pants had slipped down and they dragged about his ankles. You could have planted petunias in the loam on his face. The Man of the Hour looked as though he had spent his hour in somebody's coal mine.

Beside him, already scrubbed and combed and natty in civilian clothes, awaiting his turn to confide to a nationwide audience that "the Cardinals are the greatest team I ever played with and I sure am glad we won the champeenship today and I sure hope we can win the World Series from Detroit," stood Dizzy Dean, destiny's child.

There was a conscious air of grandeur about the man. He seemed perfectly aware of and not at all surprised at the fact that just outside the clubhouse five thousand persons were pressing against police lines, waiting to catch a glimpse of him, perhaps even to touch the hem of his garment.

He couldn't have known that in that crowd one woman was weeping into the silver fox fur collar of her black cloth coat, sobbing, "I'm so happy! I can't stand it!" She was Mrs. Dizzy Dean.

All afternoon Dizzy Dean had seemed surrounded by an aura of greatness. A crowd of 37,402 persons jammed Sportsman's Park to see the game that would decide the National League pennant race. To this reporter it did not appear that they had come to see the Cardinals win the championship. Rather, they were there to see Dizzy come to glory.

It was Dean's ball game. He, more than anyone else, had kept the Cardinals in the pennant race throughout the summer. He had won two games in the last five days to help bring the Red Birds to the top of the league. Here, with the championship apparently hinging upon the outcome of this game, was his chance to add the brightest jewel to his crown, and at the same time to achieve the personal triumph of becoming the first National League pitcher since 1917 to win 30 games in a season.

And it was Dizzy's crowd. Although the game was a box office "natural," it is doubtful that, had it not been announced that Dean would pitch, fans would have been thronged before the Dodier street gate when the doors were opened at 9:30 A.M. They were, and from then until game time they came in increasing numbers. Eventually, some had to be turned away from lack of space.

Packed in the aisles, standing on the ramps and clinging to the grandstand girders, the fans followed Dizzy with their eyes, cheered his every move.

They whooped when he rubbed resin on his hands. They yowled when he fired a strike past a batter. They stood and yelled when he lounged to the plate, trailing his bat in the dust. And when, in the seventh inning, with the game already won by eight runs, he hit a meaningless single, the roar that thundered from the stands was as though he had accomplished the twelve labors of Hercules.

The fact was, the fans were hungry for drama, and that was the one ingredient lacking. With such a stage setting as that crowd provided, with such a buildup as the National League race, with such a hero as Dizzy, Mr. Cecil B. DeMille would have ordered things better.

He would have had the New York Giants beat Brooklyn and thus make a victory essential to the Cards' pennant prospects. He would have had Cincinnati leading St. Louis until the eighth inning, when a rally would have put the Red Birds one run ahead. Then Mr. DeMille would have sent ex-St. Louis Hero Jim Bottomley, now one of the enemy, to bat against Hero Dean, with Cincinnati runners on every base. And he would have had Dizzy pour across three blinding strikes to win the ball game.

In the real game there was no suspense. Cincinnati tried, but the Cards couldn't be stopped. They just up and won the game, 9–0, and the pennant, and to blazes with drama.

Still, drama is where you find it. The crowd seemed to find it in the gawky frame of Mr. Dean, and in the figures on the scoreboard which showed Brooklyn slowly overhauling the Giants in their game in the east.

Dean was warming up in front of the Cardinal dugout when the first-inning score of the New York–Brooklyn game was posted, showing four runs for the Giants and none for the Dodgers. As an apprehensive "Oooooh!" from the fans greeted the score, Dizzy glanced toward the scoreboard. Watching through field glasses, this reporter saw his eyes narrow slightly. That was all. A moment later he strolled to the plate, entirely at ease, to accept a diamond ring donated by his admirers.

Then the game started, and for a few minutes the customers' attention was diverted from their hero by the exploits of some of his mates.

In the first inning Ernie Orsatti, chasing a low drive to right center by Mark Koenig, raced far to his left, dived forward, somersaulted, and came up with the ball. To everyone except the fans in the right field seats it seemed a miraculous catch. The spectators closest to the play were sure they saw Orsatti drop the ball and recover it while his back was toward the plate. But everyone screamed approbation.

Magnificent plays, one after another, whipped the stands into a turmoil of pleasure. In Cincinnati's second inning, after Bottomley had singled, Leo Durocher scooted far to his right to nail a grounder by Pool and, in one astonishingly swift motion, he pivoted and whipped the ball to Frisch for a forceout of Bottomley.

Again in the fourth inning, there was a play that brought the fans whooping to their feet. This time Frisch scooped up a bounder from Pool's bat and beat Koenig to second base, Durocher hurdling Frisch's prostrate body in order to avoid ruining the play. A few minutes earlier Frisch had brought gasps and cheers from the stands by stretching an ordinary single into a two-base hit, reaching second only by the grace of a breakneck headfirst slide.

Play by play, inning by inning, the crowd was growing noisier, more jubilant. Cheer followed exultant cheer on almost every play.

Meanwhile the Cards were piling up a lead. Meanwhile, too, Brooklyn was chiseling runs off New York's lead, and the scoreboard became a magnet for all eyes. When Brooklyn scored two runs in the eighth inning to tie the Giants, Announcer Kelly didn't wait for the scoreboard to flash the news. He shouted it through his megaphone, and as fans in each succeeding section of seats heard his words, waves of applause echoed through the stands.

Shadows were stretching across the field when Cincinnati came to bat in the ninth inning. The National League season was within minutes of its end. The scoreboard long since had registered the final tallies for all other games. Only the tied battle in New York and the contest on this field remained unfinished.

Dean lounged to the pitching mound. The man was completing his third game in six days. He was within three putouts of his second shutout in those six days. He didn't seem tired. He hardly seemed interested. He was magnificently in his element, completely at ease in the knowledge that every eye was on him.

The first two Cincinnati batters made hits. Dizzy was pitching to Adam Comorosky when a wild yell from the stands caused him to glance at the scoreboard. The Dodgers had scored three runs in the tenth. New York's score for the inning had not been posted.

Seen through field glasses, Dean's face was expressionless. He walked Comorosky. The bases were filled with no one out. Was Dizzy tiring, or was he deliberately setting the stage for the perfect melodramatic finish?

The scoreboard boy hung up a zero for the Giants. The pennant belonged to the Cardinals. Most pitchers would have said, "the hell with it," and taken the course of least resistance, leaving it to the fielders to make the putouts.

But this was Dean's ball game. Seen through a haze of fluttering paper, cushions and torn scorecards, he seemed to grow taller. He fanned Clyde Manion. A low roar rumbled through the stands. The fans saw what was coming. Dizzy was going to handle the last three batters himself.

Methodically, unhurriedly, he rifled three blinding strikes past Pinch-Hitter Petoskey. Was that a faint grin on Dizzy's face? The roar from the stands had become rolling thunder. The outfielders foresaw what was coming. They started in from their positions as Dizzy began pitching to Sparky Adams.

They were almost on the field when Adams, in hopeless desperation, swung at a pitch too fast for him to judge. His bat just tipped the ball, sending it straight upward in a wobbly, puny foul fly to DeLancey.

Dean didn't laugh. He didn't shout or caper. The man who has been at times a gross clown was in this greatest moment a figure of quiet dignity. Surrounded by his players he walked slowly to the dugout, a mad, exultant thunder drumming in his ears.

LOATHSOME PLOY: THE D.H.

1980

The outlook wasn't brilliant for the Mudville ten that day;
The score stood four to two with but one inning more to play . . .

Chances are Ernest L. Thayer, who created the mighty Casey, and DeWolf Hopper, whose recitations immortalized him, have got beyond the stage of whirling in their graves. The game they knew as baseball, the nine-man game, is played only in the National League and Japan's Central League today, and it came perilously close to eradication from the National League the other day. By the narrowest of margins, the league voted against adopting the loathsome designated hitter rule in slavish imitation of the American League.

As Bill Lee, the thinking man's pitcher, pointed out several years ago, the designated hitter serves one useful purpose. It relieves the manager of all responsibility except to post the lineup card on the dugout wall and make sure everybody gets to the airport on time.

Once there was a theory that devising strategy, dictating and altering tactics, matching wits with the licensed genius across the way were part of the manager's job and that his degree of success in these areas accounted for his ranking in his profession. In the ten-man game, most decisions are made for the manager automatically. If he wants to phone his bookmaker in the third inning, there is seldom anything else demanding his attention.

The only excuse anybody gives for adopting the d.h. rule is that baseball is in a rut and cries aloud for some change, any change. The fact is, baseball has had longer to test and polish its rules than any other team game in the country, and this process of evolution has produced a code that seldom demands change because it is beautiful in its fairness and balance. If you don't know a rule governing a certain situation, give it some thought; when you have arrived at a decision that is fair to both sides, you will have the rule as it is written.

Tested, altered and adjusted over a century, the rules for nine-man baseball became a triumph of checks and balances. There are moves the manager can make in the interest of offense, but he must pay for them. When to remove the pitcher used to be, and in the National League still is, one of the major decisions up to a manager. Suppose the pitcher allowed a run in the first inning and none since. It is now the eighth inning, it is his turn to bat, and the team is still trailing, 1–0. The pitcher is strong enough to work at least a couple more innings but he can't win without a run and he isn't likely to contribute much to the offense.

If you take him out for a pinch-batter, you lose his services and must rely on the bull pen, and that's the way it should be. This charming balance is a major factor in the attraction of the game.

With the corruption called designated hitter, the balance is destroyed, the challenge to the manager eliminated. He pinch-hits for the pitcher every time around, and it costs him nothing. National League managers have to think; American Leaguers don't, and maybe that helps explain the result of the annual All-Star Game.

A designated hitter has added a few points to the team batting average and presumably added a few runs to the season's score. The men who own baseball have long had the notion that more hitting and scoring produces more business, but there is no proof of that. The d.h. rule is in its eighth year now, and as yet nobody has been overheard saying, "Let's go out and watch the designated hitter."

By the winter of 1972 the governing intellects in the American League were in a panic. For more than a decade A.L. attendance had run substantially behind business in the National League. One year the N.L. had drawn 17,324,857, a tidy 5,456,297 more than the American.

"So what can we do about it?" the Americans asked one another.

"My cook says the public wants more hitting and scoring," one replied.

"Well," said another, "suppose we pinch-hit for the pitcher every time up but let the pitcher stay in the game. Think that might add some pizzazz?"

"Can't hurt to try," said still another. "Sure, it changes the whole game but who cares? Alexander Cartwright is dead."

So it came about, and the changes were immediately reflected at the box office. That is, the American League and its ten-man game continued to run behind the National League every year, millions behind, until 1977, when it added franchises in Seattle and Toronto, expanding to fourteen clubs while the Nationals remained at twelve.

Then A.L. figures inched up, edging past the other league for the first time in many years. In the American League press guide, the 1979 attendance of 22,371,979 is marked with two asterisks denoting "major league and professional sports league record." Broken down on a team-by-team basis, the American League average was 1,597,-999 and the Nationals? 1,764,468. And still those chumps almost went for the d.h.

TED WILLIAMS SPITS

1958

By now some modern Dickens, probably in Boston, must surely have brought out a best seller entitled *Great Expectorations*. It was a $4,998 mistake when Ted Williams chose puritanical and antiseptic New England for his celebrated exhibition of spitting for height and distance. In easygoing New York's insanitary subway the price is only $2.

It was bush, of course. There is no other way to characterize Williams' moist expression of contempt for fans and press, even though one may strive earnestly to understand and be patient with this painfully introverted, oddly immature thirty-eight-year-old veteran of two wars.

In his gay moods, Williams has the most winning disposition and manner imaginable. He can be charming, accommodating and generous. If Johnny Orlando, the Red Sox maître de clubhouse and Ted's great friend, wished to violate a confidence he could cite a hundred instances of charities that the fellow has done, always in deep secrecy.

This impulsive generosity is a key. Ted is ruled by impulse and emotions. When he is pleased, he laughs; in a tantrum, he spits. In Joe Cronin's book, this falls $5,000 short of conduct becoming a gentleman, officer and left fielder.

The price the Boston general manager set upon a minute quantity of genuine Williams saliva, making it the most expensive spittle in Massachusetts, suggests that the stuff is rarer than rubies. However, this is one case where the law of supply and demand does not apply.

Actually the $5,000 figure is a measure of Cronin's disapproval of his employee's behavior and an indication of Ted's economic condition. Rather than let the punishment fit the crime, Cronin tailored it to the outfielder's $100,000 salary. As it is, considering Williams' tax bracket, chances are the federal government will pay about $3,500 of the fine, though it may cause some commotion around the Internal Revenue Bureau when a return comes in with a $5,000 deduction for spit.

Baseball has indeed put on company manners since the days when pitchers like Burleigh Grimes, Clarence Mitchell and Spittin' Bill Doak employed saliva as a tool of the trade and applied it to the ball with the ceremonious formality of a minuet.

Incidentally, the penalty was applied after Williams drew a base on balls which forced home the winning run for Boston against the Yankees. He must have realized that a few more victories at those prices would leave him broke, yet the next night he won another game with a home run. With Ted, money is no object.

Nobody has ever been able to lay down a rule determining how much abuse a paid performer must take from the public without reciprocation. It was either Duffy or Sweeney, of the great old vaudeville team, who addressed an audience that had sat in cold silence through the act:

"Ladies and gentlemen, I want to thank you for giving us such a warm and encouraging reception. And now, if you will kindly remain seated, my partner will pass among you with a baseball bat and beat the bejabbers out of you."

Baseball fans consider that the price they pay for admission entitles them to spit invective at a player, harass him at his work and even bounce a beer bottle off his skull. It is not recalled that Williams' hair was ever parted by flying glassware, but verbal barbs from Fenway Park's left-field seats have been perforating his sensitive psyche for years.

There are those of a sympathetic turn who feel it was high time Williams be permitted to spit back. Miss Gussie Moran, trained in the gentle game of tennis, remarked on the radio that she approved, "as long as he didn't spray anybody." As in tennis, Gussie believes, marksmanship and trajectory count.

All the same it is a mark of class in a performer to accept cheers and jeers in stride. One of the soldier citizens of the Boston press— it could have been Johnny Drohan—pointed this out to Williams years ago. Ted was a kid then, a buff for Western movies.

Hoots and jeers were a part of the game, the man said, and everybody in the public eye had to learn to accept them.

"Take actors, for instance, Ted. You see one in a good show and you applaud and go around talking about how great he is. Then you see him in a bad vehicle and you say, 'He stinks. Whatever gave me the idea he could act?' "

"Oh, no, Johnny," Ted protested, "not that Hoot Gibson. He's *always* great!"

PLAYED ON A TIN WHISTLE

1947

The other day in Newark, Larry MacPhail gave an interview in which he (a) vowed there wasn't enough evidence adduced at the Sarasota–St. Petersburg "trials" to justify suspending Leo Durocher for five minutes, and (b) conceded that in granting the interview he was violating Happy Chandler's gag rule, but (c) swore redundantly that nobody could shut him up, and (d) denied that he had ever been Chandler's sponsor, before or after that jocund critter's election as baseball commissioner.

Incidentally, as this is written, word comes from Cincinnati that Chandler has rejected an appeal by the Brooklyn club to reopen the Durocher case and has declared it is closed. Which it isn't. Which it cannot be. Which the jocular commissioner is going to have to learn, apparently the hard way. More on that shortly.

Now, as to MacPhail's interview, there is more here than a mere statement by the complainant against Durocher that Durocher got a bum rap. MacPhail, it must be remembered, was the man who blew the whistle on Durocher, and what has happened to Leo must be on MacPhail's conscience. If he feels Durocher got a bum rap, the only one he can blame is himself.

In popping off about the case, however, the president of the Yankees has openly and flagrantly defied the authority of the commissioner. The day after the decision was announced, he called a press conference and therein violated Happy's edict of silence. Since then Charley Dressen, the Yankee coach who was also suspended by Chandler, has appeared in uniform each day at the ball park in open defiance of the spirit of Chandler's order.

And now MacPhail, having entered an official plea on Durocher's behalf, pops off again in a reckless challenge of the royal edict. The fact that one is in ardent agreement with MacPhail on this point doesn't alter the fact that he has publicly tossed down the gage to Chandler, who cannot ignore the challenge without making himself more ridiculous than ever.

It is now clearly up to the commissioner. He can either throw the book at MacPhail for an offense infinitely more aggravated than any crime Durocher committed, or he can back down, admit he is licked, and get out.

Chandler has said repeatedly that if the test ever came and the baseball people refused to accept his authority, he would resign. "And," he always adds, "I've never been out of a job."

Well, here's the test and here's his chance. He must whip MacPhail or run. And whichever course he takes, it is difficult to see how the result can fail to establish Durocher as the greatest benefactor of baseball since Doubleday.

It is noteworthy that Ford Frick, president of the National League, concurred with the Brooklyn club in seeking reconsideration of the Durocher case. Since MacPhail's formal request for similar action was made through Will Harridge, the president of the American League is also drawn into line on Durocher's side.

These men, Ford Frick and Will Harridge, are men who have the best interests of baseball at heart. If Chandler stubbornly holds out against them, where will the public conclude that his interest lies? On the side of baseball and justice, or on the side of a fifty-thousand-dollar job?

Broaching a small cask of bile in Cleveland the other day in response to published criticism of his administration, Chandler spoke enviously of sportswriters, who, he thought, must be in communion with the spirit of Judge Landis, since they can guess what action Laughing Boy's predecessor would have taken on any given problem. The commissioner said he had no such contact with the other world and, consequently, had to depend on his own judgment, an unfortunate substitute.

Actually, it demands no gift of second sight to know what Landis would have done in a given situation. Any commissioner who would take the trouble to study up on his job would know what Landis did do in similar circumstances.

For example, it is difficult to believe that Landis ever would have permitted the Brooklyn-Yankee quarrel to reach the malodorous state it achieved during the spring. But when an unpleasant situation did become publicly unpleasant, he saw to it that the solution was publicly arrived at.

Thus in the case of Bill Cox, president of the Phillies, who took to the radio microphone to enlist fan support for himself when he had been unfrocked for betting on ball games. It had become a publicized, if not public, issue, and so Landis conducted a public hearing on Cox's fruitless appeal for vindication.

The judge never tried to snatch an issue out of the headlines and settle it in a dark room. On the contrary, when Cox's attorney hinted that he could, but would prefer not to, introduce evidence that "might not be so good for baseball," the judge rared up and snapped: "If it is bad for baseball, by all means produce it!"

Read the record on the judge, Mr. Chandler, and you won't have to envy anyone who can guess what he would have done. You'll know what he would have done, because you'll know what he did do. His form was clearly established.

Recently Dan Parker quoted Mr. Chandler to the effect that an unholy alliance existed among Mr. Parker, Tom Meany, Dave Egan, of Boston, this bureau, and others who have not always seen eye-to-eye with the commissioner. "And I wouldn't be surprised," Mr. Parker said Mr. Chandler said, "if there's a lot of money behind it."

I wish to state, using the first person, that if I can get paid for thinking Happy Chandler has performed like a clown and a mountebank, then I want all of that kind of money I can get. Ordinarily I have to work for mine.

O'MALLEY'S HOUSE OF HORRORS

1956

Walter O'Malley, president of the world champion Dodgers of Jersey City, shares with other persuasive men a gift for supporting an argument with figures that can't easily be checked. James Thurber, when he wishes to smash an adversary in debate, employs a similar tactic. "As you know, of course," he says, "the Prestwick Report settles all doubts on that score," etc. The other fellow has not read the Prestwick Report, partly because there is no such thing, and backs off in mortified surrender ashamed of his ignorance.

John McNulty, passing without credentials through a gate at the racetrack attended by a Pinkerton who does not know him, merely jerks a thumb toward the man behind him in line and says, "He's all right, he's with me." If you are vouching for another, it stands to reason that you're all you pretend to be and probably more.

Back to O'Malley. He has said more than once that physical maintenance of Ebbets Field cost $100,000 a year. When he first proposed moving some of Brooklyn's home games to Jersey City, a question was raised about the expense of restoring a ball park that had been abandoned for years to mosquitoes and automobile races. O'Malley said pooh, it could be done for $25,000.

While amateur mathematicians were pondering these figures—$25,000 to convert a racing plant into a ball park and $100,000 to maintain a ball park as a ball park—Jersey authorities came up with an estimate of $129,000 for the refurbishing job. Is it still Mr. O'Malley's plan, as he said in the beginning, to pay for the reconditioning plus $10,000 rental? That seems to add up to an investment of $139,000 for seven games in a park that holds 10,000 fewer customers than Ebbets Field.

After attending the Abbey Theater in Dublin, Roger Bannister, the foot-racer, wrote: "I asked myself why every Irish phrase has a link with the heavens. Why did even their pennies bear harps?" No other Irishman excels Walter O'Malley at musical keening, at crying with a loaf of bread under each arm.

Almost every season, it is the gate for the last game that enables the Dodgers to break even. They'd have finished in the red if the World Series hadn't gone seven games. Yet over the last ten years, the Dodgers have done more business at home and on the road than any other club in the National League. How do the others manage to get by?

In the last three seasons, of course, Milwaukee attendance has offered a phenomenon unmatched in baseball. The Boston-Milwaukee total over a decade, however, doesn't touch Brooklyn's figures for the same period.

Moreover, the Dodgers own their park. For one lacking the president's acknowledged financial acumen, it is difficult to understand how he expects to increase his net by paying rent in a smaller playground, while maintenance costs continue at home.

In his campaign to persuade Brooklyn fans that Ebbets Field is a house of horrors which they should not visit, O'Malley has declared repeatedly that the Dodgers can't play there after 1957. Why not? They own the joint. Nobody's foreclosing.

If an ideal site were available in Brooklyn, could the Dodgers assume the huge expense of building a new stadium? Authorities have not encouraged a belief that the city would build them a new store. What's with O'Malley, then? Does he have his eye on some distant city?

If he were to propose moving now to Minneapolis or Los Angeles, the other owners would surely say: "Abandon the second-best corner in the league? Look, up to now we've moved only the dead horses. Act your age, Walter."

A couple of years hence, however, after constant reiteration of Dodger woes dramatized by such devices as the Jersey City caper, the owners might come to accept the theory that Brooklyn is a ghost borough, and a change of venue might be approved.

There is no pretense here of ability to read a mind as deep as Mr. O'Malley's. Bannister had an encounter with the Irish grasp of finance when he sought to tip a Dublin porter for carrying his bag.

"Sure," the man scoffed, "and what would I be doing charging a handsome fellow like yourself, and you with all the Olympic glory of Zeus, and the gods of Ancient Greece, on your jacket? If I were to charge you, and heaven forbid that I should, 'twould be only three-pence. Why don't you make it a shilling?"

NO CRUSADES FOR CAMPANELLA

1958

It was after dinner on a March evening in Dodgertown, the Brooklyn baseball team's tropical concentration camp at Vero Beach, Florida. A jukebox was going full-blast in the big lounge where the players took their ease, talking, reading, playing cards, checkers, or pool.

"Come here," said Frank Graham, Jr., who was the Dodgers' publicity director then. "Get a load of this."

He pushed open a screen door and nodded toward the rear of the administration building where the kitchen is.

"This club," he said with justifiable pride, "has the highest-paid orange-juice squeezer in the world."

Sitting on a bench beneath the stars, helping the kitchen help and gabbing away thirteen to the dozen, was Roy Campanella, the most valuable player in the National League and one of the greatest catchers ever to pick a runner off second base.

The dishwasher and cooks and waiters were his pals. So were the players and coaches and newspaper men, the Pullman porters and dining-car staff and cab drivers. That's the way it always has been with the ample and amiable, cheerful and disarming gentleman who was carried, critically injured, into Community Hospital, Glen Cove, Long Island, before dawn yesterday.

In the great social contribution which baseball has made to America since 1946, Jackie Robinson was the trail blazer, the standard-bearer, the man who broke the color line, assumed the burden for his people and made good. Roy Campanella is the one who made friends.

No crusades for Campy. All he ever wanted was to live right and play ball. If he can never play again—and reports of the terrible damage suffered in an auto crash suggest that he never can—it will be a deep sorrow. He will be grateful, nevertheless, to be alive.

Campy has an uncomplicated appreciation of the good things that have happened to him, and a capacity for honest, unquestioning gratitude. If he were asked why he should be grateful for his chance in baseball—why he or any other decent person in a democracy should feel it necessary to thank anybody for letting him do what he could do superlatively—Roy would frown thoughtfully and answer something like this:

"Maybe I don't have to, but just the same I'm grateful it happened to me. I can remember when it couldn't happen."

If he comes successfully through the present crisis, everybody will be grateful.

"The thing about Campy," a fellow said one day, "he never knew he was a Negro until he went out to play ball."

That isn't quite so, of course, but it has elements of truth. Son of a white father, he grew up in a Philadelphia neighborhood that was as much white as black and the streets and schools and playgrounds where he spent his boyhood made no question of color.

When he was fifteen and good enough to become a professional, no scouts from organized baseball knocked at his door. A bid from the Bacharach Giants was more than he expected. After that, it was the Baltimore Elite Giants and winter ball in Latin America, and it was a good life. Roy never asked for more until Branch Rickey offered more.

Even then, he only half believed the chance was real. Probably full realization of the changes he was seeing didn't come until the night in Nashua, New Hampshire, when his manager, Walter Alston, was chased out of a game and asked Campy to take charge. Alston isn't much for making speeches. Giving the nod to Campy in front of the other players, he was saying without words: "You are more than the best and smartest ballplayer on this club. You are a leader. These fellows respect you. They're white and you're not and it's never going to make any difference again."

For ten years, Campy has brought pleasure to millions. Fans watching him work were looking over the shoulder of an artist. It was even better at the squad games in Vero Beach, where one could get close enough to hear as well as see him. Joking with the hitters, encouraging the pitcher, he always had charge of those games.

"All right," he would tell a young pitcher in the last inning, "you're leading by five runs. Just throw hard down the middle, because even with good hitters the percentage is three to one against 'em."

"Only trouble with Newk," he said on one occasion when Don

Newcombe was having indifferent success, "he don't push hisself."

Campy never hesitated to push hisself. Right now he's got millions pulling.

REGGIE JACKSON'S THREE HOMERS

1977

It had to happen this way. It had been predestined since November 29, 1976, when Reginald Martinez Jackson sat down on a gilded chair in New York's Americana Hotel and wrote his name on a Yankee contract. That day he became an instant millionaire, the big honcho on the best team money could buy, the richest, least inhibited, most glamorous exhibit in Billy Martin's pin-striped zoo. That day the plot was written for last night—the bizarre scenario Reggie Jackson played out by hitting three home runs, clubbing the Los Angeles Dodgers into submission and carrying his supporting players with him to the baseball championship of North America. His was the most lurid performance in 74 World Series, for although Babe Ruth hit three home runs in a game in 1926 and again in 1928, not even that demigod smashed three in a row.

Reggie's first broke a tie and put the Yankees in front, 4–3. His second fattened the advantage to 7–3. His third completed arrange ments for a final score of 8–4, wrapping up the championship in six games.

Yet that was merely the final act of an implausible one-man show. Jackson had made a home run last Saturday in Los Angeles and another on his last time at bat in that earthly paradise on Sunday. On his first appearance at the plate last night he walked, getting no official time at bat, so in his last four official turns he hit four home runs.

In his last nine times at bat, this Hamlet in double-knits scored seven runs, made six hits and five home runs and batted in six runs for a batting average of .667 compiled by day and by night on two seacoasts three thousand miles and three time zones apart. Shakespeare wouldn't attempt a curtain scene like that if he was plastered.

This was a drama that consumed seven months, for ever since the Yankees went to training camp last March, Jackson had lived in the eye of the hurricane. All summer long as the spike-shod capitalists bickered and quarreled, contending with their manager, defying their owner, Reggie was the most controversial, the most articulate, the most flamboyant.

Part philosopher, part preacher and part outfielder, he carried this

rancorous company with his bat in the season's last fifty games, leading them to the East championship in the American League and into
the World Series. He knocked in the winning run in the twelve-
inning first game, drove in a run and scored two in the third, furnished the winning margin in the fourth and delivered the final run
in the fifth.

Thus the stage was set when he went to the plate in last night's
second inning with the Dodgers leading, 2–0. Sedately, he led off
with a walk. Serenely, he circled the bases on a home run by Chris
Chambliss. The score was tied.

Los Angeles had moved out front, 3–2, when the man reappeared
in the fourth inning with Thurman Munson on base. He hit the first
pitch on a line into the seats beyond right field. Circling the bases for
the second time, he went into his home-run glide—head high, chest
out. The Yankees led, 4–3. In the dugout, Yankees fell upon him. Billy
Martin, the manager, who tried to slug him last June, patted his
cheek lovingly. The dugout phone rang and Reggie accepted the call
graciously.

His first home run knocked the Dodgers' starting pitcher, Burt
Hooton, out of the game. His second disposed of Elias Sosa, Hooton's
successor. Before Sosa's first pitch in the fifth inning, Reggie had
strolled the length of the dugout to pluck a bat from the rack, even
though three men would precede him to the plate. He was confident
he would get his turn. When he did, there was a runner on base again,
and again he hit the first pitch. Again it reached the seats in
right.

When the last jubilant playmate had been peeled off his neck,
Reggie took a seat near the first-base end of the bench. The crowd
was still bawling for him and comrades urged him to take a curtain
call but he replied with a gesture that said, "Aw, fellows, cut it out!"
He did unbend enough to hold up two fingers for photographers in
a V-for-victory sign.

Jackson was the leadoff batter in the eighth. By that time, Martin
would have replaced him in an ordinary game, sending Paul Blair to
right field to help protect the Yankees' lead. But did they ever bench
Edwin Booth in the last act?

For the third time, Reggie hit the first pitch but this one didn't take
the shortest distance between two points. Straight out from the plate
the ball streaked, not toward the neighborly stands in right but on
a soaring arc toward the unoccupied bleachers in dead center, where
the seats are blacked out to give batters a background. Up the white
speck climbed, dwindling, diminishing, until it settled at last halfway
up those empty stands, probably 450 feet away.

This time he could not disappoint his public. He stepped out of the dugout and faced the multitude, two fists and one cap uplifted. Not only the customers applauded.

"I must admit," said Steve Garvey, the Dodgers' first baseman, "when Reggie Jackson hit his third home run and I was sure nobody was listening, I applauded into my glove."

TWO MAVERICKS DEPART

1980

The two liveliest minds in baseball left the game high and dry last week, and it's going to take more than snap judgment to decide whether this left the game richer or poorer. Did the welcome departure of Charlie Finley compensate for the loss of Bill Veeck?

"I called Lee MacPhail after the deal," Veeck said yesterday from his hospital bed in Chicago, "and asked 'How lucky can a guy get? This must be your biggest single week in twenty decades.' "

As owner of the Oakland A's, Finley picked a fight with the American League president every hour on the hour, and between skirmishes MacPhail had to deal with some of Veeck's more outlandish promotions.

"What did Lee say?" Bill was asked.

"You know what a gentleman he is," Veeck said.

Finley sold the A's for about $12.5 million. Veeck and his partners got $20 million for the Chicago White Sox. When you consider that the New York Mets, who had lost money for three years in a row, finished last three times and last season had their smallest home attendance ever—788,905—went for $21.1 million last winter, and that the Baltimore Orioles, American League champions whose home business touched a record 1,681,009, changed hands for $12 million, you have to wonder about baseball economics. Oakland, if possible, cares less about baseball than Baltimore; attendance last season was 306,763.

"There's one big difference," Veeck said. "We had a very valuable piece of property the other clubs didn't have—the real estate. We spent from $3.25 million to $3.5 million on it just in the few years since we've had the club. This is thirty-odd acres, the biggest contiguous piece of land in South Chicago.

"Count that as worth $7 million and it brings the price of the ball club down to $13 million, in the same area as Oakland and Baltimore. The Mets, of course, are something else."

There is no reason to think that Finley would ever want to return to baseball and less than none to believe that he would not be blackballed if he tried. He ran the cheapest and loudest operation in the big leagues and his contributions would be a pleasure to forget—green and gold play suits; Herb Washington, the Olympic sprinter, as designated runner; night World Series games; a mule in the outfield.

Brassy vulgarity was his style.

Veeck, on the other hand, was born into baseball and belongs there. He is an independent thinker, imaginative, uninhibited, innovative. He is a promoter at heart but a baseball man at bottom and he always realized that his merriest promotional stunts would not enable a bad team to do good business.

"I still think our theories are sound," he said, "but we were a little short of scratch to make the operation go. I have been advising for a couple of years that we would be wise to sell the club because we were a stock company and so couldn't depreciate our players for tax purposes. We had to operate with 100-cent dollars while other clubs, limited partnerships or something, operated with 50-cent dollars because the government picked up the other half."

Bill had pledged everything he owned to buy the club, and the free agent era found him unable to spend enough to keep players like Richie Zisk, Oscar Gamble, Rich Gossage, Terry Forster, and Bobby Bonds.

"I don't earn as much as a utility infielder," he said a few years ago, "but baseball is my game and I can't let one or two high-priced players drive me out of it."

"I do think," he said yesterday, "that we have again put together a good bunch of youngsters, especially pitchers. We'd like them to be able to develop together as White Sox instead of drifting away one by one like the others."

As for Bill Veeck, the sixty-six-year-old entrepreneur, he'll be back. Baseball can't afford to let a mind like his go to waste.

"Once I catch my breath," he said. "Oops, Kingman just hit one out of sight." (He was obviously watching the Cubs' game on television.) "After I learn to breathe again, I'll start thinking about what to do." He is in the hospital for a respiratory ailment, his room is full of free oxygen so he can't smoke, but he hopes to be out next week.

Presumably he'll get enough from the club's sale to furnish a modicum of operating capital, maybe set him up again on the property in Easton, Maryland, which he left when he went to Chicago.

"I know you pledged everything you had to buy the club," it was remarked.

"Yes," he said, "and that place in Maryland was right in center field."

WINNING BY STRIKING OUT

BROOKLYN, 1941

It could happen only in Brooklyn. Nowhere else in this broad, untidy universe, not in Bedlam nor in Babel nor in the remotest psychopathic ward nor the sleaziest padded cell could The Thing be.

Only in the ancestral home of the Dodgers which knew the goofy glories of Babe Herman could a man win a World Series game by striking out.

Only on the banks of the chuckling Gowanus, where the dizzy-days of Uncle Wilbert Robinson still are fresh and dear in memory, could a team fling away its chance for the championship of the world by making four outs in the last inning.

It shouldn't happen to a MacPhail!

As Robert W. Service certainly did not say it:

> Oh, them Brooklyn Wights have seen strange sights.
> But the strangest they ever did see,
> Today was revealed in Ebbets Field
> When Owen fumbled strike three!

Among all the Yankee fans in the gathering of 33,813 who watched the fourth game of the World Series, only one was smiling when Tommy Henrich faced Hugh Casey in the ninth inning with two out, nobody on base, the Dodgers in front by one run, and a count of three balls and two strikes on the hitter.

That one gay New Yorker was Jim Farley, whose pink bald head gleamed in a box behind the Dodger dugout. He sat there just laughing and laughing—because he hadn't bought the Yankees, after all.

Then The Thing happened.

Henrich swung at a waist-high pitch over the inside corner. He missed. So did Catcher Mickey Owen. Henrich ran to first. Owen ran after the ball but stopped at the grandstand screen.

That was Mickey's biggest mistake. He should have kept right on running all the way back home to Springfield, Missouri.

That way he wouldn't have been around to see and suffer when Joe DiMaggio singled, Charley Keller doubled, Bill Dickey walked, Joe Gordon doubled, and the Dodgers went down in horrendous defeat, 7 to 4.

Out of the rooftop press box in that awful instant came one long, agonized groan. It was the death cry of hundreds of thousands of unwritten words, the expiring moan of countless stories which were to have been composed in tribute to Casey.

For just as Owen has taken his place among the Merkles and Snodgrasses and Zimmermans and all the other famous goats of baseball, so now Casey belongs with the immortal suckers of all time.

The all-American fall guy of this series—round, earnest Casey—was only one pitch short of complete redemption for his sins of yesterday.

Remember that it was he whom the Yankees battered for the winning hits in the third game of the series. It was he whom Larry MacPhail castigated for failing, in MacPhail's judgment, to warm up properly before relieving Fred Fitzsimmons yesterday.

Now he was making all his critics eat their words. He was making a holy show of the experts who snorted last night that he was a chump and a fathead to dream that he could throw his fast stuff past the Yankees.

He was throwing it past them, one pitch after another, making a hollow mockery of the vaunted Yankee power as each superb inning telescoped into the one before.

No one ever stepped more cheerfully onto a hotter spot than did Casey when he walked in to relieve Johnny Allen in the fifth inning.

The Yankees were leading, 3 to 2, had the bases filled with two out, and the hitting star of the series, Joe Gordon, was at bat.

Casey made Gordon fly to Jim Wasdell for the final putout, and from there on he fought down the Yankees at every turn.

He made Red Rolfe pop up after Johnny Sturm singled with two out in the sixth. He breezed through the seventh despite a disheartening break when DiMaggio got a single on a puny ground ball that the Dodgers swore was foul.

Leo Durocher said enough short, indelicate words to Umpire Lary Goetz on that decision to unnerve completely anyone within earshot. But Casey, determined to hear no evil and pitch no evil, shut his ears and shut out the Yanks.

In the clutch, the great Keller popped up. The ever-dangerous Dickey could get nothing better than a puerile tap to the mound.

So it went, and as Casey drew ever closer to victory the curious creatures that are indigenous to Flatbush came crawling out of the woodwork. They did weird little dances in the aisles and shouted and stamped and rattled cowbells aloft and quacked derisively on little reedy horns.

Their mouths were open, their breath was indrawn for the last, exultant yell—and then The Thing happened.

Far into this night of horror, historians pored over the records, coming up at last with a World Series precedent for "The Thing."

It happened in the first game of the 1907 series between the Cubs and Detroit, when the Tigers went into the ninth inning leading, 3 to 1. With two out and two strikes against pinch-hitter Del Howard, Detroit's Wild Bill Donovan called catcher Charley Schmidt to the mound for a conference.

"Hold your glove over the corner," Donovan said, "and I'll curve a strike into it."

He did, but Schmidt dropped the strike, Howard reached base, and the Cubs went on to tie the score. The game ended in darkness, still tied after twelve innings, and the Cubs took the next four contests in a row.

That's about all, except that it should be said the experts certainly knew their onions when they raved about the Yankee power. It was the most powerful strikeout of all time.

NEXT TO GODLINESS

BROOKLYN, 1947

The game has been over for half an hour now, and still a knot of worshippers stands clustered, as around a shrine, out in right field adoring the spot on the wall which Cookie Lavagetto's line drive smote. It was enough to get a new contract for Happy Chandler. Things were never like this when Judge Landis was in.

Happy has just left his box. For twenty minutes crowds clamored around him, pushing, elbowing, shouting hoarsely for the autograph they snooted after the first three World Series games. Unable to get to Lavagetto, they were unwilling to depart altogether empty-handed. Being second choice to Cookie, Happy now occupies the loftiest position he has yet enjoyed in baseball. In Brooklyn, next to Lavagetto is next to godliness.

At the risk of shattering this gazette's reputation for probity, readers are asked to believe these things happened in Ebbets Field:

After 136 pitches, Floyd Bevens, of the Yankees, had the only no-hit ball game ever played in a World Series. But he threw 137 and lost, 3 to 2.

With two out in the ninth inning, a preposterously untidy box score showed one run for the Dodgers, no hits, ten bases on balls, seven men left on base, and two more aboard waiting to be left. There still are two out in the ninth.

Hugh Casey, who lost two World Series games on successive days in 1941, now is the only pitcher in the world who has won two on successive days. One pitch beat him in 1941, a third strike on Tommy Henrich, which Mickey Owen didn't catch. This time he threw only one pitch, a strike to Tommy Henrich, and this time he caught the ball himself for a double play.

Harry Taylor, who has had a sore arm half the summer, threw eleven pitches in the first inning, allowed two hits and a run, and fled with the bases filled and none out. Hal Gregg, who has had nothing at all this summer—not even so much as a sore arm—came in to throw five pitches and retired the side. Thereafter Gregg was a four-hit pitcher until nudged aside for a pinch hitter in the seventh.

In the first inning George Stirnweiss rushed behind second base and stole a hit from Pee Wee Reese. In the third Johnny Lindell caught Jackie Robinson's foul fly like Doc Blanchard hitting the Notre Dame line and came to his feet unbruised. In the fourth Joe DiMaggio caught Gene Hermanski's monstrous drive like a well-fed banquet guest picking his teeth and broke down as he did so. Seems he merely twisted an ankle, though, and wasn't damaged.

Immediately after that play—and this must be the least credible of the day's wonders—the Dodger Sym-phoney band serenaded Happy Chandler. The man who threw out the first manager for Brooklyn this year did not applaud.

In the seventh inning two Sym-phoney bandsmen dressed in motley did a tap dance on the roof of the Yankees' dugout. This amused the commissioner, who has never openly opposed clowning.

In the eighth Hermanski smashed a drive to the scoreboard. Henrich backed against the board and leaped either four or fourteen feet into the air. He stayed aloft so long he looked like an empty uniform hanging in its locker. When he came down he had the ball.

In the ninth Lindell pressed his stern against the left-field fence and caught a smash by Bruce Edwards. Jake Pitler, coaching for the Dodgers at first base, flung his hands aloft and his cap to the ground.

And finally Bucky Harris, who has managed major-league teams in Washington, Detroit, Boston, Philadelphia, and New York, violated all ten commandments of the dugout by ordering Bevens to walk Peter Reiser and put the winning run on base.

Lavagetto, who is slightly less experienced than Harris, then demonstrated why this maneuver is forbidden in the managers' guild.

Cookie hit the fence. A character named Al Gionfriddo ran home. Running, he turned and beckoned frantically to a character named Eddie Miksis. Eddie Miksis ran home.

Dodgers pummeled Lavagetto. Gionfriddo and Miksis pummeled each other. Cops pummeled Lavagetto. Ushers pummeled Lavagetto. Ushers pummeled one another. Three soda butchers in white ran onto the field and threw forward passes with their white caps. In the tangle Bevens could not be seen.

The unhappiest man in Brooklyn is sitting up here now in the far end of the press box. The *v* on his typewriter is broken. He can't write either Lavagetto or Bevens.

HUTCH AND THE MAN

1958

France and Algeria heaved in ferment, South Americans chucked rocks at the goodwill ambassador from the United States, Sputnik III thrust its nose into the pathless realms of space—and the attention of some millions of baseball fans was concentrated on a grown man in flannel rompers swinging a stick on a Chicago playground called Wrigley Field.

Warren Giles, president of the National League, had come down from Milwaukee to sit in the stands and watch Stan Musial make his 3,000th hit against major-league pitching. When the event came to pass, the game would be halted. Giles would walk out on the field to congratulate Musial with full benefit of Kodak and formally present to him the ball he had struck—if it could be found. Then the Cubs and Cardinals would return to their play.

On his first time at bat, Musial made his 2,999th hit. He got no more that day. There were still only seven men in history who had made 3,000. To be sure, there were only eight who had made 2,999, but nobody thought of that. Giles left town.

"I'll do it tomorrow," Stan said, but just before dinner the Cardinals' manager, Fred Hutchinson, phoned Jim Toomey, the club publicity man, and asked him to notify the press that Musial wouldn't start the next day's game. Unless he were needed as a pinch-batter, Hutch would let him wait until the following evening to try for the big one before a home crowd in St. Louis.

At dinner, Toomey and the newspaper men and the club secretary, Leo Ward, talked about it. Musial hadn't asked to be held out the next day. Nobody in the St. Louis office had suggested it. It was Hutchinson's own idea, prompted by his respect and affection for Musial and his realization that Stan would derive a special satisfaction out of attaining his goal in the park where he had grown to greatness.

"Maybe I'm speaking out of turn," said Bill Heinz, who was there on a magazine assignment, "but it seems to me Hutch is sticking his neck out. His team got off to a horrible start and now it's on a winning streak and he's got a championship game to play tomorrow, without his best man because of personal considerations.

"Not that the guy hasn't earned special consideration, but from a competitive point of view I think it's wrong. If the Cardinals lose tomorrow, Hutch will be blasted. He'll be accused of giving less than his best to win and it will be said the club rigged this deliberately for the box office, gambling a game away to build up a big home crowd."

"You're absolutely right," another said. "I've been thinking the same thing and I'm glad somebody agrees."

They talked it over but didn't mention it to Hutchinson. He's the manager. He must have known what he was doing.

Now it was the next day and Musial was sunning himself in the bullpen and the Cubs were leading, 3 to 1. Gene Green, a rookie outfielder, was on second base. It was a spot for a pinch-batter. Hutch beckoned.

Musial hit the sixth pitch to left field for two bases, scoring Green. The game stopped, Hutchinson walked out to second and shook hands. Frank Dascoli, umpiring at third base, got the ball when it was returned from the outfield and gave it to Musial. Eight cameras fired away.

You don't see that often. They don't stop games in the major leagues and let photographers invade the playing field to celebrate individual accomplishment. Baseball is as ceremonious as a Graustarkian court, but they butter the Golden Bantam before the game, not during play. Maybe this sort of thing has been done before, but not in thirty years of firsthand observation.

When the last picture was taken, Hutchinson called for a runner and Musial left the game. The manager was sticking his neck out again. The score was still 3 to 2 against the Cardinals and Musial's bat might still be needed to win, but Hutchinson took him out. It could be that Hutch lost sight of the score in the theatrics of the moment. It is no discredit to him if, just for that little while, the personal triumph of one great man meant more to the manager than team success.

As it turned out, the Cardinals kept the rally going and won the game. The next night Musial got his twenty-one guns from the fans in St. Louis, and on his first time at bat acknowledged the salute by flogging one over the pavilion in right.

So everything worked out happily. The way it happened was theatrical but it wasn't staged. There was nothing planned, nothing tawdry, no prearranged billing to disfigure the simple reality. Stan got his hit in honest competition, and it helped his team win.

Like anybody else, Musial relishes personal success and takes pleasure in the honors he wears so gracefully. Above all, though, he's a ballplayer in a team game, and the object is to win. Circumstances saved his greatest moment from the carnival vulgarity that would have debased it. That was good for baseball, good for the Cardinals, good for Hutchinson, and good for The Man.

BABE RUTH: ONE OF A KIND

1973

Grantland Rice, the prince of sportswriters, used to do a weekly radio interview with some sporting figure. Frequently, in the interest of spontaneity, he would type out questions and answers in advance. One night his guest was Babe Ruth.

"Well, you know, Granny," the Babe read in response to a question, "Duke Ellington said the Battle of Waterloo was won on the playing fields of Elkton."

"Babe," Granny said after the show, "Duke Ellington for the Duke of Wellington I can understand. But how did you ever read Eton as Elkton? That's in Maryland, isn't it?"

"I married my first wife there," Babe said, "and I always hated the goddamn place." He was cheerily unruffled. In the uncomplicated world of George Herman Ruth, errors were part of the game.

Babe Ruth died twenty-five years ago but his ample ghost has been with us all summer and he seems to grow more insistently alive every time Henry Aaron hits a baseball over a fence. What, people under fifty keep asking, what was this creature of myth and legend like in real life? If he were around today, how would he react when Aaron at last broke his hallowed record of 714 home runs? The first question may be impossible to answer fully; the second is easy.

"Well, what d'you know!" he would have said when the record got away. "Baby loses another! Come on, have another beer."

To paraphrase Abraham Lincoln's remark about another deity, Ruth must have admired records because he created so many of them. Yet he was sublimely aware that he transcended records and his place in the American scene was no mere matter of statistics. It wasn't just that he hit more home runs than anybody else, he hit them better, higher, farther, with more theatrical timing and a more flamboyant flourish. Nobody could strike out like Babe Ruth. Nobody circled the bases with the same pigeon-toed, mincing majesty.

"He was one of a kind," says Waite Hoyt, a Yankee pitcher in the years of Ruthian splendor. "If he had never played ball, if you had never heard of him and passed him on Broadway, you'd turn around and look."

Looking, you would have seen a barrel swaddled in a wrap-around camel-hair topcoat with a flat camel-hair cap on the round head. Thus arrayed he was instantly recognizable not only on Broadway in New York but also on the Ginza in Tokyo. "Baby Roos! Baby Roos!" cried excited crowds, following through the streets when he visited Japan with an all-star team in the early 1930's.

The camel-hair coat and cap are part of my last memory of the man. It must have been in the spring training season of 1948 when the Babe and everybody else knew he was dying of throat cancer. "This is the last time around," he had told Frank Stevens that winter when the head of the H. M. Stevens catering firm visited him in the French Hospital on West 30th Street, "but before I go I'm gonna get out of here and have some fun."

He did get out, but touring the Florida training camps surrounded by a gaggle of admen, hustlers and promoters, he didn't look like a man having fun. It was a hot day when he arrived in St. Petersburg, but the camel-hair collar was turned up about the wounded throat. By this time, Al Lang Stadium had replaced old Waterfront Park where he had drawn crowds when the Yankees trained in St. Pete.

"What do you remember best about this place?" asked Francis Stann of the *Washington Star.*

Babe gestured toward the West Coast Inn, an old frame building a city block beyond the right-field fence. "The day I hit the adjectival ball against that adjectival hotel." The voice was a hoarse stage whisper; the adjective was one often printed these days, but not here.

"Wow!" Francis Stann said. "Pretty good belt."

"But don't forget," Babe said, "the adjectival park was a block back this way then."

Ruth was not noted for a good memory. In fact, the inability to remember names is part of his legend. Yet he needed no record books to remind him of his own special feats. There was, for example, the time he visited Philadelphia as a "coach" with the Brooklyn Dodgers. (His coachly duties consisted of hitting home runs in batting practice.) This was in the late 1930's when National League games in Philadelphia were played in Shibe Park, the American League grounds where Babe had performed. I asked him what memories stirred on his return.

"The time I hit one into Opal Street," he said.

Now, a baseball hit over Shibe Park's right-field fence landed in 20th Street. Opal is the next street east, just a wide alley one block long. There may not be five hundred Philadelphians who know it by name, but Babe Ruth knew it.

Another time, during a chat in Hollywood, where he was an actor in the film *Pride of the Yankees,* one of us mentioned Rube Walberg, a good lefthanded pitcher with the Philadelphia Athletics through the Ruth era. To some lefthanded batters there is no dirtier word than the name of a good lefthanded pitcher, but the Babe spoke fondly:

"Rube Walberg! What a pigeon! I hit twenty-three home runs off him." Or whatever the figure was. It isn't in the record book but it was in Ruth's memory.

Obviously it is not true that he couldn't even remember the names of his teammates. It was only that the names he remembered were not always those bestowed at the baptismal font. To him Urban Shocker, a Yankee pitcher, was Rubber Belly. Pat Collins, the catcher, was Horse Nose. All redcaps at railroad stations were Stinkweed, and everybody else was Kid. One day Jim Kahn, covering the Yankees for the *New York Sun,* watched two players board a train with a porter toting the luggage.

"There go Rubber Belly, Horse Nose and Stinkweed," Jim said.

Don Heffner joined the Yankees in 1934, Ruth's last year with the team. Playing second base through spring training, Heffner was stationed directly in the line of vision of Ruth, the right fielder. Breaking camp, the Yankees stopped in Jacksonville on a night when the Baltimore Orioles of the International League were also in town. A young reporter on the *Baltimore Sun* seized the opportunity to interview Ruth.

"How is Heffner looking?" he asked, because the second baseman had been a star with the Orioles in 1933.

"Who the hell is Heffner?" the Babe demanded. The reporter should, of course, have asked about the kid at second.

Jacksonville was the first stop that year on the barnstorming trip that would last two or three weeks and take the team to Yankee Stadium by a meandering route through the American bush. There, as everywhere, Ruth moved among crowds. Whether the Yankees played in Memphis or New Orleans or Selma, Alabama, the park was almost always filled, the hotel overrun if the team used a hotel, the railroad depot thronged. In a town of 5,000, perhaps 7,500 would see the game. Crowds were to Ruth as water to a fish. Probably the only time on record when he sought to avert a mob scene was the day of his second marriage. The ceremony was scheduled for 6 A.M. on the theory that people wouldn't be abroad then, but when he arrived at St. Gregory's on West 90th Street, the church was filled and hundreds were waiting outside.

A reception followed in Babe's apartment on Riverside Drive, where the 18th Amendment did not apply. It was opening day of the baseball season but the weather intervened on behalf of the happy couple. The party went on and on, with entertainment by Peter de Rose, composer-pianist, and May Singhi Breen, who played the ukulele and sang.

Rain abated in time for a game next day. For the first time, Claire Ruth watched from a box near the Yankees' dugout, as she still does on ceremonial occasions. Naturally, the bridegroom hit a home run.

Rounding the bases, he halted at second and swept off his cap in a courtly bow to his bride. This was typical of him. There are a hundred stories illustrating his sense of theater—how he opened Yankee Stadium (The House That Ruth Built) with a home run against the Red Sox, how at the age of forty he closed out his career as a player by hitting three mighty shots out of spacious Forbes Field in Pittsburgh, stories about the times he promised to hit a home run for some kid in a hospital and made good, and of course the one about calling his shot in a World Series.

That either did or did not happen in Chicago's Wrigley Field on October 1, 1932. I was there but I have never been dead sure of what I saw.

The Yankees had won the first two games and the score of the third was 4–4 when Ruth went to bat in the fifth inning with the bases empty and Charley Root pitching for the Cubs. Ruth had staked the Yankees to a three-run lead in the first inning by hitting Root for a home run with two on base. Now Root threw a strike. Ruth stepped back and lifted a finger. "One." A second strike, a second upraised finger. "Two." Then Ruth made some sort of sign with his bat. Some said, and their version has become gospel, that he aimed it like a rifle at the bleachers in right center field. That's where he hit the next pitch. That made the score 5–4. Lou Gehrig followed with a home run and the Yankees won, 7–5, ending the Series the next day.

All the Yankees, and Ruth in particular, had been riding the Cubs unmercifully through every game, deriding them as cheapskates because in cutting up their World Series money the Chicago players had voted only one-fourth of a share to Mark Koenig, the former New York shortstop who had joined them in August and batted .353 in the last month of the pennant race. With all the dialogue and pantomine that went on, there was no telling what Ruth was saying to Root. When the papers reported that he had called his shot, he did not deny it.

A person familiar with Ruth only through photographs and records could hardly be blamed for assuming that he was a blubbery freak whose ability to hit balls across county lines was all that kept him in the big leagues. The truth is that he was the complete ballplayer, certainly one of the greatest and maybe the one best of all time.

As a lefthanded pitcher with the Boston Red Sox, he won 18 games in his rookie season, 23 the next year and 24 the next before Ed Barrow assigned him to the outfield to keep him in the batting order every day. His record of pitching 29 2/3 consecutive scoreless innings in World Series stood 43 years before Whitey Ford broke it.

He was an accomplished outfielder with astonishing range for his bulk, a powerful arm and keen baseball sense. It was said that he never made a mental error like throwing to the wrong base.

He recognized his role as public entertainer and understood it. In the 1946 World Series the Cardinals made a radical shift in their defense against Ted Williams, packing the right side of the field and leaving the left virtually unprotected. "They did that to me in the American League one year," Ruth told the columnist, Frank Graham. "I coulda hit .600 that year slicing singles to left."

"Why didn't you?" Frank asked.

"That wasn't what the fans came out to see."

He changed the rules, the equipment and the strategy of baseball. Reasoning that if one Babe Ruth could fill a park, sixteen would fill all the parks, the owners instructed the manufacturers to produce a livelier ball that would make every man a home-run king. As a further aid to batters, trick pitching deliveries like the spitball, the emery ball, the shine ball and the mud ball were forbidden.

The home run, an occasional phenomenon when a team hit a total of twenty in a season, came to be regarded as the ultimate offensive weapon. Shortstops inclined to swoon at the sight of blood had their bats made with all the wood up in the big end, gripped the slender handle at the very hilt and swung from the heels.

None of these devices produced another Ruth, of course, because Ruth was one of a kind. He recognized this as the simple truth and conducted himself accordingly. Even before they were married and Claire began to accompany him on the road, he always occupied the drawing room on the team's Pullman; he seldom shared his revels after dark with other players, although one year he did take a fancy to a worshipful rookie named Jimmy Reese and made him a companion until management intervened; if friends were not on hand with transportation, he usually took a taxi by himself to hotel or ball park or railroad station.

Unlike other players, Ruth was never seen in the hotel dining room or sitting in the lobby waiting for some passerby to discard a newspaper.

Roistering was a way of life, yet Ruth was no boozer. Three drinks of hard liquor left him fuzzy. He could consume great quantities of beer, he was a prodigious eater and his prowess with women was legendary. Sleep was something he got when other appetites were sated. He arose when he chose and almost invariably was the last to arrive in the clubhouse, where Doc Woods, the Yankees' trainer, always had bicarbonate of soda ready. Before changing clothes, the Babe would measure out a mound of bicarb smaller than the Pyramid of Cheops, mix and gulp it down.

"Then," Jim Kahn says, "he would belch. And all the loose water in the showers would fall down."

The man was a boy, simple, artless, genuine and unabashed. This explains his rapport with children, whom he met as intellectual equals. Probably his natural liking for people communicated itself to the public to help make him an idol.

He was buried on a sweltering day in August 1948. In the pallbearers' pew, Waite Hoyt sat beside Joe Dugan, the third baseman. "I'd give a hundred dollars for a cold beer," Dugan whispered.

"So would the Babe," Hoyt said.

5.

Politics

RED TROTSKY TALKS TO RED SMITH

The red fire of revolution which forged the reputation of Leon Trotsky and was to become a worldwide conflagration is flickering out in the oldest, sleepiest village of the Western Hemisphere.

Today the arch-plotter of modern time sits in the study of a borrowed home in Mexico City's suburban Coyoacan, a mild and amiable and aimless old man pottering with old ideas.

The Great Revolutionist is somewhat bigger than a growler of beer and somewhat less fiery. Fumbling with the writings by which he earns a living, he exhibits all the wild-eyed revolutionary fervor, all the sinister aspect, all the mastery of men, all the compelling powers of oratory, all the irresistible ardor and magnetism of an elderly and not very successful delicatessen keeper in the Bronx, inking his fingertips over the month-end statements.

Leon Trotsky does not admit he is through any more than he says in so many words that he will return to the Soviet Union some day to lead Russia and the workers of the world.

But the latter obviously is what he means when he says:

"Stalin's biggest mistake was in exiling me. He thought if he sent me out of the country, he could ruin me by reviling and libeling me in the press, in all the agencies of propaganda which he controls.

"But outside of Russia I have gathered a new group around myself. I still do harm. My writings, my books, what I say, they penetrate into Russia. I do harm."

Harm. He says it like a small boy insisting "I'm tough. I carry matches."

It was mid-afternoon when word came to the Athletics training camp that Trotsky would see the Philadelphia newspapermen. Probably he had not been told these newspapermen worked only in the children's department, the sports staff.

Probably, too, it was the first time in his life any group of interviewers met him on a completely equal footing of understanding; they knew precisely as much about Communism as he did about baseball.

The suburb in which the exiled war minister of Lenin is holed up became the first permanent white settlement on the continent when Hernando Cortez made it his headquarters for the assault upon the Aztec capital of Mexico City. Today it is the quiet, characterless sort of middle class residential district you might notice as your train pulls out of Des Moines.

Its placidity emphasizes the incongruity of the squad of armed Mexican police lounging in the dusty, half-paved street that leads to a house owned by Señora Frieda Rivera, wife of the revolutionary artist Diego Rivera, who collects so many capitalist dollars for painting murals lampooning the capitalist system.

Behind the tall gate of heavy oak, kept closed and barred, live Rivera's guests—Trotsky and his wife; an American secretary, Bernard Wolfe, former instructor of political science at Yale and Bryn Mawr; a French-Dutch secretary; a Czech secretary. The Riveras live elsewhere.

Wolfe admitted the newspapermen. A pistol butt protruded from his waistband. An ornament, he said, as Trotsky had no fear of violence.

Wolfe ushered the visitors through a tiny patio, knobby with stone Aztec gargoyles, across the narrow brick veranda which makes a promenade along the bright azure wall of the house, and into the study.

No stage setting in this room, a rather bare rectangular chamber containing a half-dozen leather-backed chairs, a long table cluttered with papers, a few shelves of books, three crystal balls suspended from the ceiling.

Trotsky entered briskly, almost, but not quite, dapper in dark gray pin-striped suit without a vest, soft striped shirt with attached collar, dark tie. His mustache and goatee are gray, his pompadour white. He seems older than his fifty-seven years, possibly because, like the very young and very old, he talks only of himself.

"Any Hearst papers?" he inquired as introductions were made. None. He seated himself at the desk, exchanged shell-rimmed glasses for pince-nez, showed flashing white teeth in a smile.

"That is a great advantage."

Hearst papers are to him the "fascist press." How could he keep them from getting his statements? Possibly they got them through the Mexican papers.

"When the next trials start I shall not give statements to the Mexican papers," he continued. "Not through unfriendliness, but because the reactionary interests and the Soviet try to use them to make it appear I am meddling in politics here.

"It was so in Norway. Although I kept aloof from politics, the Stalin Government kept trying to entangle me, and succeeded, until the Norwegian elections revolved about my personality."

He spread his hands in a deprecatory gesture that said "Innocent little me in Norwegian politics!"

His English is fairly fluent, heavily accented. Now and then he gropes for an Americanism, turns quickly to Wolfe for prompting or assurance that he has used the right word.

Mention of the next trials sent him off pell-mell into his favorite subject, the conspiracy trials in Russia, which he contends are pure fake, trumped up for propagandist purposes.

How long does he expect such trials to follow one another?

"Until world opinion has become finally convinced either of the truth or falsity of the Gaypayoo's charges and the alleged 'confessions.'

"You see, each trial has left doubts. In the recent Radek trial it was mentioned that I had a meeting, a friendly conversation in Berlin, with Rudolf Hess, the Vice Führer. Many people wondered how I could be on friendly terms with Hess.

"I predict the next trial, of the Germans accused of sabotage, will purport to give details of that meeting."

Does he believe Kamenev and Zinoviev and other convicted "plotters" have been shot?

"Yes. Keeping such men in prison would be too dangerous, like storing up bombs. There were, for example, two political adversaries of mine who were arrested and 'confessed' to conspiracies. When I read the confessions, it did not seem possible they could be false, for I knew the honesty of these men.

"Later I heard their story. They had been promised freedom for confessing, but were not given their freedom. So they began to stir up trouble in prison. Then they were shot."

Why do men continue to "confess" if they are shot anyway?

"Common sense would tell them to refuse, to say, 'No, it is not true. I will not compromise my memory, the memory of my children so.'

"But a man is in a row of cells. Now and then one is taken out and shot. The Gaypayoo comes and says, 'You see what happened to your friend. Confess and you will live.'

" 'Those who confessed are dead, too,' the man says, but the Gaypayoo says, 'No. Radek, he is not dead. Others are not dead. You have a chance.'

"So for a hope, for a straw to grasp, this man confesses to what he did not plot. And the infernal conveyor, the endless belt of trials by which the Stalin bureaucracy justifies itself before the world, moves on."

What of Stalin, the man?

"He is the complete bureaucrat. He could exist only in a bureaucracy. He did not build the machine; he is a product of the machine. Separate him from the machine and he is nothing."

Why does the Soviet feel the need of making Trotsky the archvillain, the man behind the plots in all these trials?

A shrug. "Because I am their adversary."

Then do they still fear him so much?

This pleased him. He smiled broadly. "I, too, am astounded, but so it is."

He closed the interview on that note, his blue eyes sparkling with what seemed a juvenile exultation over being considered a very tough party.

Departing, the newspapermen surveyed the premises briefly, found the single-story house slightly cramped, inquired as to how the Great Revolutionist spends his day.

Seems he arises about 7:30 A.M., walks in the patio, eats, writes some, dictates some. Mostly, it seems, he just putters.

HARRY TRUMAN RETURNS

CHICAGO, 1956

The old champ came striding down the aisle with outriders in front of him and cops behind, and memory recaptured the classic lines which once described Jack Dempsey's entrance in a ring:

> Hail! The conquering hero comes,
> Surrounded by a bunch of bums.

This was Harry ("Give 'em hell") Truman, last Democrat to hold the heavyweight title, coming out of retirement now to slug it out with the clever young contender, Ad Stevenson. The arena was a hotel ballroom, the ring a curving battery of microphones, the crowd made up of working stiffs assigned to a press conference. Stevenson wasn't there in the flesh but you could sense his presence, a stick-and-move guy, tough for even a young adversary to hit solidly.

The old champ looked fit, square of shoulder and springy of tread, his skin clear, his eyes bright behind the glittering glasses. No roll of middle-aged flesh showed under the gray double-breasted; his blue polka-dotted bow tie spread wings for bold flight.

But how about the old legs?

At the bell, the left flicked out in a practiced jab. "I am deeply touched by the anxiety of the press and so many of our illustrious columnists about my political judgment." It was a light jab but he felt it get home.

He glanced about the room with a cocky, crooked grin. McGurk used to give that same grin to the fighter he drew to illustrate H. C. Witwer's *Leather Pusher* stories. Jim Braddock's ruddy kisser wears it today.

Inwardly, a ringsider applauded. "Attaboy, Harry! Tell 'em what you did to Pawling Tom Dewey."

A moment more of light sparring, then Harry moved to the attack. His voice was cold and level. Stevenson's counsel of moderation "was, in fact, a surrender of the basic principles of the Democratic party." "I am shocked that any liberal Democrat would advocate or encourage the abandonment of the New Deal and the Fair Deal as out of date." Stevenson is not "a dynamic and fighting candidate." "He cannot win the election by himself."

"There is nothing personal about my attitude toward Governor Stevenson." In the room there was undeceived laughter, but the old champ kept his face straight, going through with the feint. "In fact, I like him personally.

"That's all." He stepped back, as though to let his adversary fall forward.

Stevenson didn't go down. The attack had been meant to shatter him, explode his title pretensions and leave the field to Ave Harriman, but Ad was still on his feet and coming in. Questions hit Harry from all directions.

"Mr. President, you just said that recent events showed that Adlai Stevenson lacks a fighting spirit. What recent events are you referring to?"

"I didn't say that, I said his recent actions show that he lacks the fighting spirit to win an election."

"Which recent events would you refer to, sir?"

"His moderation, his tie-up with the conservatives of the Democratic party."

"Any specific actions?"

"Your judgment is as good as mine."

He was backing and circling, grabbing and parrying, doing a Missouri waltz, and the legs were going. He came up on his toes. "I think he [Stevenson] would need the help of an old man from Missouri," and he laughed with the crowd.

Ken Overlin was like this in his last days as middleweight champion, still sure he could lick any bum they threw in with him. The young ones came along, though, and licked Ken. They always do.

Once Harry slipped but recovered swiftly. He said he had told Stuart Symington by telephone: "Get yourself out here if you expect to—uh"—win the nomination?—"do anything about the Missouri delegation," he finished, laughing over the slip with the others.

Toward the end he seemed impatient for the final bell. "Gentlemen," he said, "I think that is enough," and he lifted his hands. Somehow, one was reminded of Abe Attell as an old man fighting a kid in St. Louis. A few fast rounds, and then Abe turned to the crowd.

"Gentlemen," he said. "I am Abe Attell, featherweight champion of the world. I have always given you a good show. This is as far as I can go."

The old champ had come in briskly. Now he went out slowly. They never come back.

YOU PAY FOR THIS

1951

Ever since Senator Estes Kefauver and His Rascals burst upon the television scene as the biggest act in show business since Little Egypt, this nation has been undergoing government-by-flashbulb. It is an underprivileged lawmaker indeed who does not sit on a committee investigating something, with full benefit of camera. If the inquiry concerns sports, so much the better, because sports are widely read and the politician is thus forced to submit to the distasteful experience of seeing his name in headlines. This mortifies the flesh and chastens the timorous statesman, making him a better public servant.

Congressman Emanuel Celler of Brooklyn is chairman of a judiciary subcommittee examining baseball for traces of acute monopoly. In an effort to avoid publicity, the group started by interviewing that celebrated authority on constitutional law, Mr. Ty Cobb. Since then the caliber of witnesses has diminished and lately the congressmen have been calling in sportswriters.

When instructions to appear and give testimony were received here, a tiny worm of suspicion reared its impertinent head. Considering the scarcity of lawyers, baseball players, managers and club owners in the ordinary press box, one wondered whether the statesmen were primarily interested in first-hand information or in straightening out columnists who had viewed the subcommittee's project without enthusiasm.

Mr. Celler was advised by telegraph, prepaid: "Have nothing to contribute and could serve no useful purpose. If you insist on wasting my time and the taxpayers' money, will arrange to appear."

The chairman replied by letter: "I am disappointed you feel assisting the subcommittee would waste your valuable time. Your wire will be read into the record."

On the chance that this was not done, the message is quoted here, for the record. On that comradely note, arrangements were made to use up two working days, not enormously valuable, going to Washington. Other witnesses have traveled farther at greater expense.

Not all eleven members of the subcommittee and its six-member staff attend every hearing. Of those present at this particular session, the most articulate were Mr. Celler, who likes witnesses to mention Brooklyn; Patrick J. Hillings, a pleasant young man whose voters live in California and who keeps asking how about a third major league on the West Coast; Kenneth B. Keating, a pretty good needler from Rochester; and William M. McCulloch of Ohio, who remarked at one point, "Now let's see if I know where we are."

They heard Thomas J. Halligan, president of the Central League, tell stories about what he once said to Judge Kenesaw Mountain Landis and what Happy Chandler once said to him.

Then Bill Werber, a former third baseman who now sells insurance, said baseball was dandy.

Then Russ Lynch, sports editor of the *Milwaukee Journal,* said the owners of major league clubs operating farm teams were selfish dastards. He said they'd go and grab players like Willie Mays and Hank Thompson out of the minors and pay them major league salaries just because the owners were greedy for pennants.

As noon approached, Mr. Keating got up to depart. Mr. Lynch halted him. "You're from Rochester," Mr. Lynch said. Mr. Keating smiled.

"I think I can predict," Mr. Lynch said, "that you've got a pennant coming up soon in Rochester."

Mr. Keating beamed all over. He said he had heard the Red Wings were acquiring half a dozen new players. Were they pretty good?

"Some of them," Mr. Lynch said.

Mr. Keating said he was delighted.

Mr. Celler declared a recess, explaining that some bills were coming up in Congress. Seems there was something to do with appropriating money for a centennial celebration at West Point, or something, and unexpected argument developed in the House, so the hearing resumed after lunch with Joseph R. Bryson of South Carolina, presiding, and E. Ernest Goldstein and John Paul Stevens, of counsel for the subcommittee, asking questions in the absence of others.

Mr. Bryson is one of the group's two Southerners. The other, Edwin E. Willis of Louisiana, had spoken up once. He had asked Mr. Lynch how "your fraternity" felt about the farm system, and what the press reaction would be "if I signed a recommendation" to abolish farms.

In the afternoon, Franklin Wetherill Shepard Yeutter of the *Philadelphia Bulletin* said he liked baseball the way it is.

The last witness was just about finished when Mr. Celler returned. The witness had been asked whether a team in a big city was likely to draw more customers than one in a smaller city. The answer, after some thought, was probably.

Mr. Celler said issues before the subcommittee were complex. He said several bills applying to baseball were pending and it was up to the committee to study them, wasn't it?

"You will forgive my conviction," the witness said, "that in these times, there are graver matters to consider."

ONE DRUNK, UNARMED

1963

Between halves of the Army-Navy football game last year, cadets and midshipmen formed a double row across the field and John F. Kennedy walked between the ranks from a flag-draped box in the west stands to another in the east.

Hatless and without an overcoat in the November cold, he went jauntily—one football fan among 100,00. He was a Navy veteran but he was also Commander in Chief of the Army. In the first half he had seen Navy take a lead of 15–6.

Halfway across, a drunk broke through the line and was almost within arm's reach of the President when Secret Service men grabbed him. Laughter started in the crowd but choked off.

Suppose the drunk hadn't been drunk? Suppose he had a gun? It could have happened there in Philadelphia, before 100,000 witnesses.

No doubt the 64th Army-Navy game will come off as scheduled next Saturday, if anybody cares. It is difficult to conceive of anybody caring but life has to go on, and work, and probably play, too.

John Kennedy enjoyed games as a participant and spectator, and sports had his hearty official support as President.

There is no disposition here to condemn the few college authorities who did not call off their games yesterday or the men in the National Football League who decided to go through with today's schedule. A while back some promotion man on the *Herald Tribune* lumped the paper's book reviewers and drama and television critics and a few others into a group he called the Tastemakers but this peanut stand wasn't included.

What seems bad taste to one man is plain common sense to another. What one considers decent respect is mawkish in other eyes.

Maybe it's important to determine whether the St. Louis Cardinals can upset the Giants in Yankee Stadium today, whether the Bears can push on against the Steelers in Pittsburgh. There's a race to be finished and there's money invested. Money.

Maybe a lot of people will feel it perfectly proper to attend. Like it or not, we newspaper stiffs will have to be there because that's our job as much as it's Y. A. Tittle's job.

If Yale and Harvard had played yesterday, we'd have had to be there, too. Thank heaven they didn't. Work must go on, but there'll be other days to shiver in that crepe-gray heap called Yale Bowl being lighthearted about a game for children.

KENT STATE

1970

It is time for some of our professional sports leaders to declare that the games must go on because that is how those kids at Kent State would have wanted it.

This was the theme when John Kennedy was murdered and when Robert Kennedy was murdered and when Martin Luther King Jr. was murdered. Indeed, Spec Richardson, the psychic general manager who minds store in Houston, knew so well what Robert Kennedy would have wanted that he slapped fines on Rusty Staub and Bob Aspromonte for refusing to play on the day of mourning for the senator.

Joe L. Brown of Pittsburgh either did or did not fine Maury Wills for the same offense—he didn't have the guts to say—and Milt Pappas, the pitcher who led a protest by Cincinnati players, was swiftly traded to Atlanta.

Ken Fairman, athletic director at Princeton, isn't sure how the kids at Kent State would have wanted it, and isn't putting pressure on athletes who have suddenly lost interest in the playground.

"They feel very deeply about this," Fairman says. "They're dropping out because they feel they can't go out and have fun in sports. . . . They always have a veto. They are not hired by us to play athletics."

Princeton's unbeaten tennis team has quit for the year, eight lacrosse players have left the squad, three basketball players have packed it in, and so have three oarsmen on the heavyweight crew.

The Princeton track team is down to eighteen athletes and Herman Stevenson, the captain, is trying to organize a boycott of the Heptagonal Games this weekend at Yale. Steve Tourek, the crew captain at Dartmouth, wants all oarsmen to wear black headbands in the Eastern sprint championships Saturday.

The Columbia baseball team canceled last Tuesday's game with

Manhattan College. At least one football player at Stanford stayed away from spring practice.

"These kids are for the most part very conservative kids," Ken Fairman says. "One kid says to our lacrosse coach, you told us not to play unless we have a 100 percent commitment, and I can't."

They're bums. They just don't feel like playing games. I don't feel like writing about games. I'm a bum. An old bum. I try to think about sports and I just keep hearing a too-familiar voice repeating on radio and television: "I have a plan to end the war. I promise you I can achieve a just peace."

Richard Milhous Nixon says what happened at Kent State was an "unfortunate incident" and implies that the kids who were slaughtered had nobody but themselves to blame because "when dissent turns to violence it invites tragedy."

Spiro T. Agnew says that what happened was "predictable and avoidable." That's the polysyllabic way to say, "I told you so."

To Mr. Nixon, young people who detest the war in Vietnam and oppose his invasion of Cambodia are "bums." To Mr. Agnew they are "tomentose exhibitionists."

In most colleges, athletes are regarded as conservatives, often correctly. Some are just muscular jocks with limited interests beyond the playing field, and most of them are kept too busy to have much time for campus movements. More and more of them, however, are speaking out against the notion that they are part of the President's "Silent Majority."

In fact, unless his hearing has failed badly, Mr. Nixon must be aware of voices of dissent in many quarters that have been quiet until recently, in his own party and even in his own Cabinet. That was a remarkable letter he got from his Secretary of the Interior protesting the President's insensitivity and the Vice President's blackguarding of youth.

Walter J. Hickel is the Alaskan who said conservation was overrated, whereupon Nixon handed him the Interior Department, making him the National Conservation Commissioner. Now Walter has concluded that the President was overrated.

OUTPOINTING THE SUPREME COURT

1971

In the morning Cassius Muhammad Ali Clay stopped into a store on 79th Street on Chicago's South Side and bought an orange. He was getting back into his car when the storekeeper came running and hugged him. "I'm so happy for you!" the man cried.

"You're free! You're free! The Supreme Court says so!"

It was a mismatch. As eight members of the court saw it—Justice Thurgood Marshall abstained—the government never laid a glove on the former heavyweight champion of the world, whom the Department of Justice was trying to send to prison as a draft dodger.

"He lost a unanimous decision last time out," said Angelo Dundee, who was in Muhammad's corner when Joe Frazier administered the whipping that cleared the title in March. "I'm glad he won a unanimous decision this time."

Those who love justice are glad, too, with one tiny reservation. The decision leaves Ali free to fight Jimmy Ellis, his sparring partner, in Houston July 26. Is this what the framers of the Constitution sought to accomplish when they created the United States Supreme Court?

Because it was never possible to believe that Muhammad Ali received fair and impartial treatment from his draft board, it was felt here that the Supreme Court would surely rule in his favor. Now that this has come to pass, a chronological review of developments might help us all to see the facts straight.

When he reached draft age, Cassius flunked his mental test and was rejected for military service. Later, standards were dropped to a level below the grade he had scored, and without a second test he was called up. He claimed exemption on the ground that his membership in the Nation of Islam, called the Black Muslims, forbade him to fight in any war except a holy war declared by Allah.

(Nations at war always say God is on their side, but there are in existence few formal declarations of war signed by the Almighty. Still, that was Ali's position.)

His case was referred to an examiner who recommended that he be classified a conscientious objector, but the draft board rejected the recommendation. This was unusual enough to raise questions about the draft board's impartiality. The questions were underlined by reports that the board's files were fat with newspaper clippings, and it wasn't hard to guess at the nature of this material. A professional fighter refusing to fight had not inspired much editorial applause.

When Ali delivered a sermon, it didn't sound much like the sermons heard in most churches. Doubts were expressed about the Muslim faith qualifying as a religion. This is pretty impertinent, like a Catholic saying Jews, Moslems, and Unitarians don't have a religion because they don't accept the divinity of Christ.

At any rate, Ali was classified 1-A, and on April 28, 1967, he refused to accept induction. This was a clear violation of the Selective Service Act, for which he was convicted, drawing a five-year sentence and $10,000 fine. Four years of appeals and arguments followed.

Even before his conviction, boxing commissioners moved with obscene haste to lift his license and declare his championship vacant.

New York State and a few others named Frazier as Ali's successor to the title. The World Boxing Association recognized Ellis. Frazier settled that dispute by stopping Ellis in five rounds.

At long last, a court held that the New York State Athletic Commission had been unreasonable and arbitrary in unfrocking the champion. After three and a half years, Ali was allowed back in the ring. Frazier whipped him and they split a $5 million purse.

In all this time, there couldn't possibly be any doubt about Ali's sincerity. He knew in the first place that he could have accepted induction and served his hitch boxing exhibitions at troop entertainments without ever hearing a shot fired. He chose instead to sacrifice years of his youth and millions in possible earnings, and take his chances on a stretch in the freezer.

Even the government prosecutors conceded that he was both religious and sincere. But because he has called Vietnam a white man's war and said he didn't have no quarrel with them Viet Congs, they argued his objections were political and racist.

Now the Supreme Court says his position was "surely no less religiously based" than the positions of other conscientious objectors. Because it was unanimous, the opinion was not signed, but Justices John M. Harlan and William O. Douglas wrote concurring opinions of their own. A couple of frustrated sportswriters who had to get in theirs.

APARTHEID IN REVERSE

PRETORIA, SOUTH AFRICA, 1979

Sydney Maree, one of the two or three best mile runners in the world, is a victim of apartheid in reverse. The Villanova junior is a South African, and because the world sports community has ostracized South Africa in hope of persuading the government to abandon its policy of separate and unequal status for blacks, he is barred from international competition. Maree, who can do a mile in 3:53, may represent his university in intercollegiate meets like the National Collegiate Athletic Association championships, but may not run in the Olympics or the national Amateur Athletic Union championships, which might include a Polish pole-vaulter. The irony is that he is black.

"We are deeply disappointed," said Mrs. Christine Susan Marina Maree.

Then her face lit up. She said Sydney had just telephoned. He had said he was fine but suburban Philadelphia was getting cold. He had asked how she and her husband, Philip, would feel if he applied for American citizenship so he would be eligible for international meets.

She said slowly that they would have no objection, provided this would not prevent Sydney from coming home again. She said that running was Sydney's whole life and that she understood his frustration but she did not want to lose her son.

Sydney's mother is a slender women of quiet dignity. Entirely composed, she sat in the tiny front room of the house at 3 Letswalo Street in Atteridgeville, the black township outside this capital, where Sydney grew up and where she and Philip are bringing up Sydney's three younger brothers and sister—Patrick, Matthew, Stanley and Maria.

The house is like almost all others in Atteridgeville, a brick box with galvanized iron roof and a front door of sheet metal, sitting cheek by jowl with identical twins on an unpaved street of flinty red dust. There is a tiny plot of lawn in front, with one green shrub and a miniature triangle of flowers in bloom.

Joe Gemude, director of the Khazamula Sporting Club, had not known the Marees' address when he and a driver took a reporter over from Johannesburg. They had gone first to a house opposite the township's barren playing field, where a schoolteacher Joe knew gave directions to the right neighborhood. There Joe spoke in Sutu dialect to small boys, who grinned with delight when they heard the name Maree. Three of them jumped aboard for the ride to 3 Letswalo.

It was 4 P.M. Patrick Maree, a tall sixteen-year-old, thin as a stick, was home with an aunt. They said Mr. and Mrs. Maree would be home at six from their jobs in Pretoria. Mrs. Maree works in a coffee-roasting plant, Mr. Maree in the mint.

The visitors drove to the local hotel for a beer, then the driver took them to the home of a friend of his, a taxi driver. He went inside, and in a moment a smiling woman came out and invited the others in for tea. Her house was no bigger than its neighbors, but there was new leatherette furniture in the front room and a television set was playing. The visitors drank tea, made their manners and went back to Letswalo Street, where Mrs. Maree made them welcome.

She wore a white beret and a two-piece dress with a dark jersey. The front room was immaculate. There was no ceiling, just the galvanized roof. A kitchen table with a small tablecloth on top of the oilcloth took up most of the space. Against one wall, a glass-front china cabinet held many of Sydney's trophies—cups, statuettes, a silver track shoe. Mrs. Maree brought them all out on the table, left the room and returned with handfuls of smaller awards, medals and ribbons.

A color photograph of Sydney laughed down from the wall. Beside it was a wedding picture of his parents. Other family pictures hung on the walls. Mrs. Maree served tea and cookies.

She understands English but speaks Afrikaans. Joe Gemude interpreted. She said that when Sydney was a boy in Phatogeng School down the street, his game was soccer. At fifteen or sixteen he entered a technical school in Pretoria where kids were mustered for intramural sports on teams called Lions, Kudus, Elephants and such. Sydney was an Elephant.

"He doesn't look like one," it was suggested. Mrs. Maree laughed. He didn't run like one, either, though Elephants can get there rather soon. Sydney beat everybody in the Vleikfontein School and everybody in other schools and at length came the great day when he caught the attention of James Mokoka, the coach who made him.

They never looked back. At Villanova the track coach is Jumbo Elliott, whose eye is on every sparrow that runs, even sparrows 13,000 miles from Philadelphia's Main Line. So Sydney crossed the sea.

Would he be home for the Christmas holidays? Mrs. Maree didn't think so. He had some indoor meets ahead. In June, then? Maybe. But if he became eligible for a European tour or something, she would understand. By this time Philip Maree had come home, a little man composed mostly of smiles. Together they said they grieved when Sydney's ambitions were frustrated, but if anti-apartheid pressure could bring changes in this country, then his sacrifice might be worthwhile.

Mrs. Maree said something in Afrikaans. Joe Gemude translated. "He is such a pride to them," he said.

6.

Some Other Sports

A HUNDRED AND FOUR YEARS OLD

For a couple of guys who are going to be a hundred and four years old in August (fifty-two each, that is), Ben Hogan and Sam Snead looked remarkably youthful striding into the locker room after a two-day pitched battle on the fairways of the Houston Country Club.

Sam scowled blackly, disgusted with himself and furious at his long irons. Ben was imperturbable. Between them they have played sixty-seven years of professional golf and this was the first time the tight-lipped Hawk had whipped Snead in head-to-head combat.

It was Hogan's first television match, and if any distractions could weaken his frightening self-discipline they were all present here—frustrating delays, whirring cameras, violently erratic weather. A cloudburst had halted play on the third hole, leaving the greens drenched and heavy and the fairways deep in casual water; then came scorching sunshine and the standard Texas wind.

Impervious to everything, he had played eighteen perfect holes to beat par and Snead by three strokes with a 69.

The Houston Country Club has gold dust instead of sand in the traps and the greens are irrigated with oil. It is home base for those hackneyed caricatures, the Texas zillionaire and his lady hung with ice cubes.

"Beautiful round, Ben," said one old goat in the clubhouse. "But I was watching you putt back there on the thirteenth. Your stance was too open."

The four-time Open champion kept a straight face, realizing that although golf is an 'umbling game in Scotland, in Texas Humble means an oil company.

Incidentally, the Humble Company has a new office building in Houston whose forty-odd floors are staffed by employees from New York and New Jersey. The skyscraper is known as Yankee Stadium.

Snead was disconsolate because his long irons got him in trouble four times, but he scrambled sensationally. The seventh hole, for example, is a dogleg to the left around a thicket of tall trees. Along the left side behind the woods five traps yawn, one behind the other from turn to green.

Hogan hit an iron to the knee of the dogleg and had an open shot to the green. Sam tried to clear the trees with a wood, hit a pine, and his ball bounced back toward the tee. It wasn't humanly possible to get home from there, but somehow he whistled his second shot through the trees to the edge of the green beyond the last trap.

"You dodged a bullet there," said Fred Corcoran after Sam got down in two and halved the hole with a four.

"If I'da cleared the trees and drove the green," Sam said, "it woulda been a great tee shot."

"But I was lousy," he said at the end.

"No, you weren't," a man told him. "I'm so glad I was able to see this match. I'll remember it along with the War Admiral–Seabiscuit match race, Graziano-Zale, and Don Larsen's perfect game."

Somebody told Corcoran, who arranged the show for Shell's *Wonderful World of Golf*, that he ought to make it a series, five out of nine. Somebody else suggested teaming Snead and Hogan against Arnold Palmer and Jack Nicklaus.

If the round just filmed was the golfing equivalent of a Dempsey-Firpo rematch, the other would be like getting Dempsy and Joe Louis together. Only in golf is it possible to match the best of two eras.

Hogan would be interested. He can't resist a challenge. Waiting at the seventeenth tee, a man had said to him: "What a round you're having, Ben! Sixteen holes and you haven't missed a fairway, you haven't missed a green, you haven't missed a shot."

"Can't afford to miss," he said, "or you get beat."

"And that's something that's not to be tolerated, eh?"

"That's right," Ben said, unsmiling.

GENERAL OF THE ARMY

MAMARONECK, NEW YORK, 1974

On the seventeenth green Arnold Palmer ran down a 25-foot putt for a birdie, and a blind man within earshot might have thought he was back in 1960 on the Cherry Hills course at Denver. It was there fourteen years ago that Palmer started the last round seven strokes back and charged through the field to the United States Open golf championship, and that rabble called Arnie's Army came into being. The army has dwindled since those days, from thousands to hundreds, but at forty-four its leader still has that special personal quality that can move his idolators to rapture. Chances are there were no more than 500 spectators at the seventeenth—including two girls wearing buttons that read "Miller's Killers," identifying them as followers of the defending champion—but when the putt went down their cries could be heard clear across the Winged Foot Club's West Course.

"He did it and I didn't see it!" wailed a member of the ladies' auxiliary on the fringe of the crowd.

Minutes later one platoon broke away from the main body of

troops and gathered around a ball in the eleventh fairway of the East Course. Standing over his ball, Arnold could see a tiny patch of green and a wide stretch of sand between the spreading branches of a tree and a wooden scoreboard.

Taking his time, he hit over the scoreboard to the green about twenty feet from the flag. Two putts gave him his par and a score of 73 for the first round of the 74th National Open. For a man who has an average score of 70.82 for 1,892 rounds over twenty years, a 73 isn't exactly the stuff that dreams are made on. Yet such are the demands that Winged Foot makes this week, with its narrow fairways, tangled rough, slick greens and cruel pin placements, that Palmer's score put him among the leaders.

"I played the eighteenth perfectly," he said later. "Duck-hooked my drive, hit a six-iron to the green and took two putts."

"This whole week is going to be a week of disappointments," said Gary Player after taking the early lead with a 70. Among the deeply disappointed when he spoke were the 1961 champion, Gene Littler, with an 80; the 1963 winner, Julius Boros, 78; Ken Venturi, the last to win with a 36-hole final round, 84; and shooters like Tom Weiskopf, Dave Eichelberger, Bobby Nichols and Frank Beard, with 76 or 77.

Obviously, the biggest thing in this tournament is the course. Nobody is going to desecrate it with a 63 as Johnny Miller did in his final winning round at Pittsburgh's Oakmont course last year.

"There will be some good scores before the week is out," Palmer said, "and a lot of bad ones. The course is very good, but fair. The fairways are cut short and the greens are cut short, and it's better that way. I think it is the best course we've played in a long time. I'd like to see every course we play like this.

"It is very difficult, no question about it. You have to think on every shot and play for what you can get. You can't get reckless. They talk about shooting for the pin. There are some pins you can shoot for, but many where you don't dare.

"Who does this course favor? It favors the guy who is really playing well and thinking well. Sometimes on this course you'll have to play for bogeys. You just have to take them, and the guy who makes ten or twelve bogeys or less will have a pretty good chance."

The deity of the 1960's hasn't won since the Bob Hope Desert Classic of last year, hasn't taken a major championship since the Masters of 1964. He has earned a shade under $2 million in competition, though, and has the appearance of well-being to go with such figures. Now he sat at ease in the press tent, amiable as always in the so-familiar postmortem routine. The short sleeves of his sports shirt were tight on his biceps.

"I didn't play anything well," he said. "As a matter of fact, I played rather poor, but I thought well. For the first time in a long while I played golf. I made use of every shot I played."

"If your thinking was better than it has been," someone asked, "can you explain why?"

"I didn't want to shoot 85," Arnold said. "What will it take to win? I know what I'd like to have. I'd like to have 282 and just stay here all week and talk with you fellows. If the wind gets going and the greens stay slick the way they are, it could add up to anything. It's conceivable that 290 would win; on the other hand, it is conceivable that it would take 280.

"I think I can play aggressively and still play the way the course demands. I think I had to just shoot 73. Going for the pin when it's five feet from sand, that's not being aggressive. That's being stupid."

He strolled out to the practice tee and started hitting irons. Even there, he drew a pretty good gallery. Between shots he unzipped a pocket of his golf bag, fished out a little plastic bottle and, tilting his head back, squirted saline solution into his eyes while the hand that wore a golf glove held the eyelid up. That's why he looks different, a man thought. No glasses. He has switched to contact lenses.

THE ROUND JACK NICKLAUS FORGOT

1978

Jack Nicklaus's golf is better than his memory. When he came charging home in the Inverrary Classic last weekend, picking up four strokes on Grier Jones, three on Jerry Pate and Andy Bean, and two on Hale Irwin with five birdies on the last five holes, he was asked whether he had ever put on such a finish before. "I can't imagine any other time," he said. "It was the most remarkable thing I've ever seen in my life," said Lee Trevino, comparing it with Reggie Jackson's three home runs in the last World Series game and Leon Spinks' victory over Muhammad Ali. Well, it was remarkable but it wasn't unprecedented.

Fifteen years ago, Nicklaus and Arnold Palmer represented the United States in the World Cup competition at Saint-Nom-la-Bretèche near Versailles in France. If Jack has forgotten his performance there, perhaps he wanted to forget it. Maybe he deliberately put it out of his mind as too outrageously theatrical to bear remembering.

The things he did on the very first hole were downright scandalous. The hole was a legitimate par 5 for club members but a trifle short for a pro with Jack's power, measuring somewhere between 450 and 500 yards. In his four rounds, Jack played it eagle, eagle, eagle, birdie, and that was just for openers.

Bretèche may have been a trifle shorter than Inverrary's 7,127 yards, but this was no exhibition on a pitch-and-putt course, and the opposition was at least as distinguished as the field Nicklaus encountered last week. The World Cup, now twenty-five years old, is a movable feast that leaps from continent to continent, usually playing national capitals, matching two-man teams from virtually every land where the game is known. Though it hasn't the prestige of the United States or British Open, it is probably the closest thing there is to a world championship.

In 1963, Saint-Nom-la-Bretèche was a comparatively new course built on land that had been the royal farm when Louis XIV was top banana. The clubhouse, once the royal cow barn, was a splendid building of ivy-covered stone set in a terraced stableyard ablaze with roses, snapdragon, chrysanthemum and pansies.

The galleries had a touch of quality seldom associated with, say, Maple Moor in Westchester County. Among those who followed the play were two former kings and one former Vice President—Leopold of Belgium, the Duke of Windsor and Richard M. Nixon.

Before play started, Prince Michel de Bourbon-Parme, the club president, dispatched ten dozen fresh eggs to a nearby convent. This, he explained, was an ancient custom in the Ile de France. Anyone planning an outdoor binge like a wedding or garden party sent eggs to the poor and this assured him of good weather. The standard fee was one dozen eggs, but the Prince had laid it on to guarantee a week of sunshine.

Morning of the opening round found the Prince glowering through a clammy fog. "So," he said, "I am sending to the sisters to get back my eggs."

Soggy turf made the course play long for little guys, but not for Nicklaus. His second shot on the opening hole was twenty feet from the pin, and he ran down the putt for his first eagle 3. After that he had five birdies and three bogeys for a 67. Palmer's 69 gave the pair a tie for first place with Al Balding and Stan Leonard of Canada.

Prince Michel changed his mind about reclaiming the eggs, but the weather didn't relent. Day by day the fog thickened, until the green hills and yellow bunkers were all but blotted out. Realizing that if a hitter like Nicklaus tried to fire a tee shot into that soup the ball would never be seen again, officials postponed the final round for twenty-four hours.

It didn't help much. Next day a gray soufflé garnished the fairways. The climate dripped sullenly from the trees. Windsor and Leopold showed up as they had for each earlier round, but the weather reduced the gallery to a minimum. Reluctantly, the committee decided to cut the final round to nine holes. At this point Nicklaus and Palmer were tied with Spain's Ramon Sota and Sebastian Miguel for the team trophy, with Nicklaus and Gary Player all square in individual competition.

Automobiles were driven out past the first green, where they made a U-turn and parked with headlights on. From the tee, lights were blurred but visible, giving the players a target. For the first time in four rounds, Nicklaus needed four shots to get down. Then he got serious.

With that birdie for a start, he played the next five holes as follows: 3-3-3-3-3. When he walked toward the seventh tee, a spectator asked: "What are you going to do for an encore?"

"Try to finish," Jack said.

On the first six holes he had taken 19 shots. On the last three he took 13 for a 32. It won.

TO REACH THE UNREACHABLE STAR

1971

Bob Beamon, who reached an unreachable star three years ago, is about to attain another goal that sometimes seemed hopelessly remote. He will get a degree in sociology and anthropology next month from Adelphi University. After that, there must be a decision: to sell his height and speed and agility to the Harlem Globetrotters as a professional basketball player, to concentrate exclusively on some other job that would support his family, or to devote time and effort toward winning a place on the 1972 Olympic team and assaulting his own implausible world record in the long jump.

"There's good and bad in each," he said the other day. "To go professional and make money, that's good. Right now, I'm aiming for a good indoor season jumping off my left leg. If I went for the Olympics, would I be aiming to break my record or to win another gold medal? I think the fans would want to see me go for the record but I think I'd be most interested in the gold medal."

Perhaps there is no such thing as an unbeatable performance but for a reasonable facsimile thereof, Beamon's leap of 29 feet 2½ inches at the Mexico City Olympics October 18, 1968, does nicely.

In all of track and field, no other record has withstood attack like that in the long jump. In 1935 Jesse Owens leaped 26 feet 8¼ inches for a record that stood 25 years, far outlasting every other mark then in the books. Nobody touched it until 1960, when Ralph Boston squeaked past by three inches, and in the next eight years the world's best, including Boston, couldn't add six inches. Ralph still shared the recognized mark of 27-4¾ when Beamon took flight. When Beamon got back to earth, the record was smashed by almost two feet.

When Roger Bannister broke the four-minute barrier in the mile run it was like breaching a dike. Others rushed through like stampeding cattle. For a long time Cornelius Warmerdam was the only pole-vaulter in existence who could clear 15 feet. Once somebody caught him, the world record spurted off like a self-service elevator on a toot. Not so in the long jump. Since Beamon did 29 feet, nobody has done 28. In 1971, Ron Coleman and Norm Tate were the only men in the world to clear 27 feet, and each did it just once.

In Mexico, Beamon took off from his right foot, as he always had. In the winter, he pulled a hamstring muscle in that leg. He won the national championship in 1969, jumping 26-11 off his left foot, but he says he was plagued by injury after that.

"In one meet in Madison Square Garden," he said, "I started down the runway and just stopped. I think the directors of indoor meets decided I'd just make a token appearance to collect expense money, so instead of doing something about me personally they dropped the long jump and substituted the triple jump. I've met long jumpers who told me, 'You're the one who killed our event.'"

Bob played basketball one semester at Adelphi but didn't represent the school in track and field. Before the Olympics, he attended the University of Texas at El Paso, where his athletic scholarship was lifted because he boycotted a meet with Brigham Young in protest against the racial attitudes of the Mormon church, which runs Brigham Young.

"I had a lot on my mind in Mexico," he said. "I didn't know where I was going to school, things weren't smooth in my family. I stood to lose my home in El Paso. You know I fouled out on two qualifying jumps and only made it on my last. I don't think I could have done it except for Ralph Boston.

"To me, Ralph is the father of the field events—and the runners, too, for that matter. I'd been having trouble with the runway in Mexico, too fast. 'You're tight,' Ralph told me. 'Just take a little extra time, walk around, loosen up. Then take it nice and easy down the runway. If you have to take off before you reach the board, don't worry. Just be sure you don't foul.'

"They hadn't measured the two jumps where I fouled, but I could tell from where I landed they must have been around 28 feet. So I did what Ralph said, and qualified.

"The night before the finals, my wife was trying to phone me, I owed a great big telephone bill, everything was wrong. So I went into town and got me a shot of, uh, cognac. Cognac?"

He pronounced it hesitantly: "Kahn-yak?"

"Man, did I feel loose! I got a good sleep. I had the feeling my first jump was a good 27 feet. Maybe 27-4, something like that. They raised the white flag, meaning no foul, and then that thing, that drum that shows the distance, was turning around. I said, 'Ralph, did I do 27 feet?'

"Ralph was watching that thing. He's used to reading in meters. 'You did 29 feet,' he told me. I could hear the crowd roaring, but I couldn't get it through my head. Then I said, 'Well, when you win just remember that I held the world record a few minutes.'

"Ralph said, 'I've got news for you. I can't jump that far.' And just then it started to rain. Can you imagine?"

Moral: Brandy is a boy's best friend.

THE HIGH JUMPER'S SIN

1979

Greater love hath no organization than the Amateur Athletic Union, which will sacrifice its virtue for a high jumper. The jumper is Dwight Stones, former holder of the world record, whom the A.A.U. cast into outer darkness a year or so ago for soiling his hands with money won on a television show. Branded a professional and forced to stand in the pillory with a scarlet P embroidered on his shirtfront, Stones no longer was eligible for under-the-table payments from promoters of track meets.

This amounted to cruel and unusual punishment, violating the Eighth Amendment to the Constitution, so last week the A.A.U. recanted. "Give that dirty TV loot to us," the guardians of amateur purity told Stones. "We'll be smirched but you'll be scoured clean, and you can jump for a living instead of pumping gas or whatever you've been doing."

Stones had pulled down $33,663 on the TV show called *Superstars* and he wasn't eager to give all that bread away. Still, we're about to enter an Olympic year, when track and field interest and the expense accounts of star attractions traditionally skyrocket.

He said well, all right, he would buy back his amateur standing but he didn't want to debauch the A.A.U. with the whole bundle. He would give one-third of the TV swag to the national body, one-third to the Southern Pacific Association and one-third to the newly formed Athletics Congress.

That way all three groups would be sullied a little bit, but $11,221 wouldn't pollute any of them the way $33,663 would. As for Stones, he can look upon the payments as an investment.

In the dream world of amateur athletics, lucre is filthy if received openly. It is unselfish of the A.A.U. to begrime its own fingers in order that Stones' may be cleansed. Unselfish and understanding, for along with the reinstatement goes a tacit promise that when and if the young man talks business with promoters, the A.A.U. will not be listening.

As a matter of practical fact, Stones doesn't have to talk to promoters. There is at least one prominent foot-racer in the United States who never does. His wife handles that end of the business for him. Wage scales have risen so dramatically that a top box-office attraction, lacking a spouse with business sense, could afford to hire an agent.

"We're all professionals, rules don't mean anything," Frank Shorter, the marathon runner, told the President's Commission on Olympic Sports.

"There are no longer true amateurs in track," says Adriaan Paulen, president of the International Amateur Athletic Federation.

It is encouraging when somebody in Paulen's position talks that way, because it suggests that perhaps some in authority are beginning to face facts. This has not been so in the past. Though professionalism was probably as widespread in Jim Thorpe's time as it is today, the waxworks always looked the other way until an infraction was forced to attention.

Taking money didn't cost Stones his amateur standing. His sin was taking visible money, taking it openly. He didn't even jump for it, because participants in that TV show aren't allowed to compete in their specialty. The format is designed to prove that someone who excels in one area can be a dub in another; for instance, Joe Frazier, the boxer, nearly drowned in a swimming race on the show.

Stones didn't win the money as a high jumper. Today, amateurs are permitted to endorse sports apparel and serve as "consultants" to manufacturers of equipment, capitalizing on their athletic reputation more directly than Stones did. Trouble was, whenever Dwight won a dollar he did it on a coast-to-coast hookup.

It would appear that track and field authorities are creeping along the route tennis followed a decade ago when the amateur myth was discarded in favor of open competition. In a recent rule "clarification," the I.A.A.F. announced that in certain cases amateurs may now associate with professionals whereas in the past it was believed that an amateur couldn't say hello to a pro without catching a loathsome disease.

Under the new ruling, athletes like John Smith, the quarter-miler, and Brian Oldfield, the shotputter, who turned pro to tour with the defunct International Track Association, will be eligible for domestic meets but not international competitions. That is, they can compete against Americans but not if there is a Polish pole-vaulter in the meet. Seems like dipping a toe into the real world.

It has been a long time coming. After the 1972 Olympics in Munich, the International Olympic Committee appointed a subcommittee to recommend changes in the amateur rules. The subcommittee didn't exactly go off the deep end. Bob Giegengack of Yale, who was one of the group, summed up its proposals in one sentence: "Let's all be a little bit pregnant."

It is high time the babies were delivered.

THE MILE IS A MOCKERY

1981

One opinion that has been held here too long to be lightly dismissed is that if God had intended man to run He would have given him four legs, or at least made him late for a bus. To be sure, speed afoot might have been useful to some of the young ladies pursued by Jack the Ripper, but unnecessary running is a crime against nature. This goes for the joggers who clutter our country roads and infest our parks, and young men like Sebastian Coe and Steve Ovett who perform publicly in their underwear.

By breaking the world record every few days, those two Limeys are making a mockery of the mile race, which has been traditionally the core and kernel of any track meet. Mention the Millrose Games, and the discussion automatically turns to the Wanamaker Mile.

Today a world record endures for a week or less and the guy who breaks it can call his shot in advance, as Ovett did the other day in Koblenz, West Germany.

Still, slapping the event around with consummate disrespect hasn't made it unpopular with the masses. More than 22,000 buffs, considerably more than Oberwerth Stadium can handle, saw Ovett chip a piece off Coe's shiny new standard. Nearly 50,000 saw Coe on Friday.

It doesn't seem possible that twenty-seven years have passed since Roger Bannister broke what has been nicknamed the "four-minute barrier," yet it was May 6, 1954, when he did the deed.

Since man dropped out of a tree and took off with a saber-toothed tiger on his heels, no pedestrian had traveled 5,280 feet in four minutes. In 1864 one Charles Lawes of Great Britain had gone the distance in 4 minutes 56 seconds, and 90 years later Sweden's Gunder Hagg had lowered the record to 4:01.4.

May 6, 1954, five days after Determine won the Kentucky Derby, was gray and drizzly at Oxford but Bannister knew that if he waited for ideal weather in that blessed plot, that earth, that realm, that England, hardening of the arteries could set in first. So he ran, and the stopwatches read 3:59.4.

A month later John Landy did 3:58 flat and took the record to Australia, but in the Empire Games that August Bannister beat Landy in 3:58.8 with the Aussie also under four minutes. John's time was 3:59.6. The floodgates were open. Britain's Derek Ibbotson was the next to break the record, then came Herb Elliott of Australia, Peter Snell of New Zealand, France's Michel Jazy, Jim Ryun of the United States who lowered the mark twice, Filbert Bayi of Tanzania and John Walker, New Zealand.

Walker made 3:49.4 in 1975. That stood for five years, and then along came Coe and Ovett to exchange the record five times, three times in the last two weeks. Coe broke Walker's record and Ovett broke Coe's. On August 19 this year Coe took it back with a mile in 3:48.53 in Zurich, and exactly seven days later Ovett did 3:48.40.

Ovett held the record for two days. On Friday in Brussels, Coe snatched it back with a mile in 3:47.30.

Ovett's record was 13 one-hundredths under Coe's best previous effort. Coe's latest clocking, though, was more than a second below Ovett's.

Until recently, human timers worked events like this, hoping that each of them would hit his watch at the starting gun and hit it again at the exact moment the winner reached the tape. They measured time in tenths of a second and when they were lucky several timers got the same time down to a fraction.

Now an electric timer does the work, depending on the starting gun to activate the gismo and the winner to break a beam at the finish. This presumably accurate device splits times down to hundredths instead of tenths and can spot a winner that no human eye could detect.

No doubt this is a step forward, if anybody cares. When it comes to the difference between 3:48.53 and 3:48.40, the attention span here is measured in thousandths of a second.

Much more interesting than the numbers is the mental attitude involved. It doesn't make sense that scores of milers since 1954 have been faster than all the milers who preceded them in human history. It is obvious now that the barrier was psychological rather than physical.

For a millennium or two, nobody ran a mile in four minutes for the excellent reason that it was impossible. (To be sure, Glenn Cunning-ham says now that he broke four minutes in practice in high school and he and his coach kept it a secret, but that's no part of recorded history.) Then Roger Bannister showed that it was not impossible, and it was like divine revelation. Suddenly it got to be like this:

Jesse Abramson, covering a Boston track meet for the *New York Herald Tribune,* was in a taxi with a colleague and they were discuss-ing runners and their times. The cabbie spoke up:

"Anything that starts with four," he said, "is slow."

ROUNDBALL SCHOLAR

1964

Cecil John Rhodes, diamond king, empire builder and founder of the Rhodes Scholarships, was a ruthless tyrant who thought well of ath-letics, though he was no good at games himself. Since it was only eleven years before his death that James A. Naismith tacked up those peach baskets in the Springfield (Massachusetts) Y, there's no telling how Rhodes would have felt about roundball if he had lived into Bob Cousy's time.

There is, however, no need to speculate how Ned Irish, sometimes called Mr. Bounceball and sometimes Father Knickerbocker, feels about Cecil John Rhodes these days.

Ever since William Warren Bradley of Crystal City, Missouri, en-tered Princeton four years ago, Ned Irish has been waiting to snatch him for the New York Knicks. Indeed, when the National Basketball Association decided to abandon the territorial draft, it was extended through this season specifically to give the Knicks the rights to Brad-ley.

So now this studious history major has won a Rhodes Scholarship to Oxford. For the next two years, instead of practicing lay-ups in Madison Square Garden, he'll be reading for honors on the banks of the Cherwell where roundballs are for soccer players.

When Princeton plays Syracuse Monday afternoon in the Eastern Collegiate Athletic Conference's Holiday Festival, it will be the first Garden appearance of the young man who is considered the finest college player in the world.

The better he plays and the more applause he hears, the harder his playmates will ride him. He likes that. If his companions didn't give him the treatment he would be acutely uncomfortable.

"I don't care for all this attention on one player in a team game," says Bill van Breda Kolff, the coach, "and neither does he. To me he's one of twelve, which is the way he wants it. Fortunately he can handle it all. It doesn't change him, and we can't hide him."

Reluctantly, the coach went on. "The words are all so trite," he said. "Unassuming, level-headed, mature beyond his years—they're trite and true. He's just another guy, except that he shoots better than most, passes better, does almost everything better."

Crystal City (population 3,678) is about 50 miles down the Mississippi from St. Louis. Before Bill Bradley was born it had a girls' basketball team playing in a St. Louis league with Dee Beckman, now a member of the U.S. Olympic Committee, as the star. When Bill was in high school, and making all-America twice, he worked out regularly with the professional St. Louis Hawks.

"Above all," van Breda Kolff said, "it was the way he worked that made him. There are plenty of boys with his physical attributes (6 feet 5 inches, a shade over 200 pounds). There are some with his agility, his moves, his quick reactions.

"But kids who combine those talents with his capacity for work, his dedication—here are those trite words again—well, it's the combination that makes him.

"Mind you, he has weaknesses. He's been called a great defensive player, but he wasn't all that good taking rebounds because he isn't a natural jumper. The Olympics improved him in that respect. (Bradley was the only undergraduate on the team that won in Tokyo.) He played against bigger, stronger guys than he'd been used to and had to jump a little higher, block a little harder, grab the ball a little tighter.

"There's a story, it's awful corny but it's true. When Bill was a sophomore we played off with Yale for the Ivy League championship. Bill fouled out with a minute or so to go, but we were twelve or thirteen points ahead and it was safe. He sat beside me on the bench, the happiest, most excited kid.

" 'Can we get the net?' he asked. Sometimes kids go for those souvenirs.

" 'Come on, Bill,' I said. 'You're too old for that sort of stuff.'

" 'But I've never been on a championship team before,' he said, and he hadn't. Twice all-America in high school but never a championship. Well, you have to humor your stars a little. 'Okay,' I told him, 'get a scissors and when it's over we'll get you the net.'

" 'Oh,' he said, 'you don't understand. I want it for Artie.' Art Hyland, the captain.

"Pretty corny, eh? Still, I know if I asked him never to take a shot, he'd do it cheerfully. And if I told him it was best for the team if he shot every time he touched the ball, he'd be very unhappy but I think he'd do it. And I'd never be able to holler at him again."

A CASE OF MALNUTRITION

1947

A few more nights like the opening round of the National Invitation Basketball Tournament and the memory of Dr. Naismith, who perpetrated basketball, will cease to be a hissing and a byword around here. Indeed, get a few more guys like Rhode Island State's Ernie Calverly playing the game and some movie company is a cinch to do the life of Dr. Naismith, picturing him as a benefactor of the human race like Mme. Curie, Alexander Graham Bell and Al Capone.

This is written by one who would rather drink a Bronx cocktail than speak well of basketball. Yet it must be confessed that there hasn't been another sports show in years which lifted the hackles and stirred the pulse quite so thoroughly as the performance of young Calverly leading his team to an 82–79 overtime conquest of Bowling Green.

Calverly is a gaunt, pale young case of malnutrition who'd probably measure up as a fairly sizable gent in your living room, but looks like a waif among the goons who clutter up the courts. He may be, as alleged, the most detached defensive player on a team whose members seem to feel there is something sordid and unclean about defensive basketball. But when he lays hand on that ball and starts moving, he is a whole troop of Calverly, including the pretty white horses. The guy is terrific, colossal, and also very good.

Throughout the fevered match with Bowling Green, he was the man who set up Rhode Island's plays, taking the ball down the court, hiding it, passing it, shooting, dribbling, feinting, weaving, running the show with almost unbelievable dexterity and poise. He played without relief through a breakneck game that had others gasping inside the first quarter-hour and once he was knocked cold as an obsolete mackerel.

Making a pass, he tripped and hit the deck with his bony shoulder blades. As he lay there supine, the ball came back to him out of a scramble and he reached up and caught it and passed it off, and then passed out.

But despite his elegance, Bowling Green was winning the game as long as Don Otten remained in circulation. Otten is the Bowling Green center. He measures one-half inch less than seven feet from end to end and he looks and moves more like an institution than a man, with agonizing deliberation and great grinding of gears.

Joe DiMaggio would be hard pressed to throw a baseball over the top of Otten and there aren't any DiMaggios playing for Rhode Island. He loped gawkily around the joint with his mouth open and plucked rebounds off the backboard like currants off a bush, while waves of adversaries surged around him and bounced off in a sort of spray. When a teammate missed a shot he simply reached up and palmed the ball and pushed it down through the hoop.

With three minutes, twenty seconds to go he committed his fifth personal foul and was flung out. The crowd cheered and it wasn't applause; it was the rejoicing of Rhode Island fans, who figured they now had a chance.

There would have been no chance, however, without Calverly. A minute and ten seconds before the last horn, he took aim from a point near the center stripe and fired a long shot that went through the hoop as though it had eyes, squaring the match at 72–all. A moment later he was fouled and missed the throw that might have won. With ten seconds to play, Vern Dunham scored for Bowling Green, and that looked like the business. But somehow, in the scant time remaining, a Bowling Green player contrived to squeeze in another foul, giving Rhode Island the ball out of bounds at midfloor with two seconds remaining.

The ball came in to Calverly in the back court. There was no time for a pass or a play and from where he stood a field goal was impossible. So, with appalling calm, he shot a field goal. Time was up.

Over in front of the Rhode Island bench, substitutes were leaping around in a crazed sort of war dance, flinging arms aloft and shouting, and out on the floor Calverly's playmates were shouting and pummeling him and the kid had his head flung back and was laughing at the ceiling.

Well, Rhode Island scored eight fast points in the extra period and Bowling Green scored five, and with a minute and a half left Calvery set out to freeze the ball. He did a magical job, dribbling in and out and around and back, keeping an appraising eye on the enemy, passing when necessary and then squirming loose for a return pass.

Then the game was over and there was a threshing swirl of players and spectators in a knot on the floor and Calverly was shoved up out of the pack and rode off on the others' shoulders. Which was fair enough, since the others had ridden to victory on his. They rushed him out and he broke loose barely in time to get down and avoid being skulled where the exit ramp goes under the stands. They like to bashed his brains out.

BASKETBALL IN A CAGE

1951

If a man has any decent instincts at all, he's got to feel regret—not sympathy, but a sort of pain—over the crooked basketball players who are going to jail. He's got to feel bad because they are young guys whose lives are ruined. But he's got to applaud the decision of Judge Saul S. Streit to put the crooks in a cage.

There must be some deterrent to the spread of dishonesty in sports. Chances are it never occurred to the fakers that they could be put in jail for throwing in with sure-thing punks and dumping games for pay. Even the most stupid ones, who were dragged into college by the heels when they should have been working as longshoremen or grease monkeys, must have known that what they were doing was a dirty thing. They must have known that if the word ever got out, they would be put away as crumbs by the undergraduates and the neighbors and all decent associates.

Yet it is unlikely they realized they could be caught and tossed into the pokey. It is time that realization was brought home to everybody. There has been far too much breast-beating about unfortunate, immature lads who were led astray by hoodlums. Everybody has been too ready to forget that the most doltish of students in ballroom dancing and finger painting knew enough to count the money at payoff time. It is high time for the courts to teach what the colleges have neglected—that when you get caught stealing, there's a penalty for it. Maybe if that knowledge got around, it would make easy money look a little harder in young eyes.

It is unfortunate, of course, that these young men have to be put away. It is even more unfortunate that when they go behind the wall they will not be accompanied by their accomplices—the college presidents, the coaches, the registrars, the alumni, who compounded the felony. Regrettably, there is no law that can reach the educators who shut their eyes to everything except the financial ledgers of the athletic department, the authorities who enroll unqualified students with faked credentials, the professors who foul their academic nests by easing athletes through their courses, the diploma-mill operators who set up classes for cretins in Rope-Skipping IV and History of Tattooing VII, the alumni who insist on winning teams and back their demands with cash, the coaches who'd put a uniform on Lucky Luciano if he could work the pivot play. They're the bums who ought to go to jail with the fixers whom they encouraged. But they won't, and apparently they regret nothing except the fact that some crooks have been caught.

The most shocking feature of this whole sordid business is the attitude expressed by mature men entrusted with the guidance of the young.

"It isn't any of the judge's business in the first place," says Matty Bell, athletic director of Southern Methodist, about Judge Streit's comments on recruiting and subsidization in the Southwest.

"The public doesn't understand," says Clair Bee of Long Island University, "that the players were not throwing games. They were throwing points. They were not selling out to the extent that the public believed, and somehow the players did not feel that what they did was wrong."

Admittedly, the public's understanding of many things is faulty. Yet one can't help believing it surpasses the understanding of some men who are supposed to set an example for boys.

Recently a successful football coach was complaining about the bad press that college sports have received this year. He thinks the newspapers play up scandals and ignore news that puts athletics in a favorable light. "The sporting press," he said, "has let football down badly this year."

Foolishly, an effort was made to explain that the press wasn't letting football down. It was argued that many observers of the sports scene with a genuine respect for the good things in sports have been genuinely concerned about abuses and excesses which, they fear, threaten the very existence of amateur sports. It was foolish to attempt this explanation because the coach, a thoroughly honest, straight guy, doesn't want to see any imperfections in the game that makes him a good living. He should have tuned in the radio last Friday night when two newspapermen, probably the best friends football ever had in their field, laid some truths on the line.

These two men, Grantland Rice and Stanley Woodward, said all the things Judge Streit said later when he sentenced the basketball bagmen. They talked about the trapping and care and feeding of athletes, about slipping them through phony courses so they could make headlines and profits for the college with no danger of intellectual pursuits distracting them from the main job. They said that unless the colleges scrubbed up fast, there was sure to be a scandal that would invite the reformers to abolish intercollegiate sports altogether.

They are dead right, because if a college kid can dump a basketball game he can also dump a football game. As a matter of fact, who honestly believes it hasn't happened already?

ALLIGATOR MAN

PARIS, 1963

On a hill overlooking the fifth and fifteenth greens of Saint-Nom-la-Bretèche stands a house which visitors are told, cost a tidy $600,000 to build. Nearby is a more modest one, if you consider the Palace of Versailles modest compared to the Taj Mahal. It has a big alligator for a weather vane.

"Pretty nice digs for an amateur tennis player," a guy said to the owner, René LaCoste. Then the significance of the weather vane filtered through. "Oh, sure. I forgot you made those sports shirts with the alligator on the breast. You know, at Miami Beach they have armed guards at the city limits and no tourist is allowed in if he isn't wearing one."

"It is not the shirts," M'sieu LaCoste said. "More aviation and finance." Diffidently he explained that when he quit international tennis in 1928 he had gone to work for his father, an automotive tycoon, then invested in Bendix Aircraft, and things had gone swimmingly.

This was good to hear, for it is always good to know of an amateur tennis player making a buck without benefit of Jack Kramer. This amateur in particular, for he is one of the all-time greats: Back in the 1920's, in the golden age of Jack Dempsey and Bobby Jones, Man O'War and Bill Tilden, Red Grange and Babe Ruth, the whole world knew about the Three Musketeers of France—Henri Cochet, Jean Borotra and René LaCoste.

René had been watching Arnold Palmer, Jack Nicklaus and Gary Player lead a big gallery through the fifth hole on a practice round for the Canada Cup golf matches which begin today. As chairman of the greens committee at Saint-Nom, René has been worried about the fifth and the fifteenth because, he said, after a rain worms come up and do nasty things to the turf.

Apparently satisfied that the worms were under control, he led the way up to a tremendous lawn framed by the L-shaped house. Still in its first season, the lawn looks like a huge putting green, which is what it will be unless René decides to make it the first private grass court in the Ile-de-France. He hasn't made up his mind.

At the door visitors were greeted by Mme. LaCoste, and right away they understood why René, born to play tennis, is married to golf. In 1927 when he was Wimbledon champion, Mme. LaCoste was Mlle. Thien de la Chaune, the first foreigner ever to win the British Women's Amateur golf championship.

"I saw him play tennis," Mme. LaCoste said, "and he saw me play golf. In America, where I played very badly in your National Amateur because I loved America and was having too good a time. My cousin was a cousin of Jacques Brugnon, the fourth Musketeer, and we met through Jacques."

Mme. LaCoste wore a sports shirt complete with alligator. M'sieu LaCoste had a sports shirt with a scarf at the throat but a sweater concealed the insigne, if any. He is lean and keen, with straight hair turned gray. They have three golfing sons and a golfing daughter, which suggests that golfing genes are dominant, tennis recessive.

René plays to a handicap of six, still bats a tennis ball against the wall three or four hours a week in a small room in Paris. When he was practicing tennis four hours a day he would relax at golf, sometimes playing fifty-four holes nonstop.

"Then I had to take it seriously to beat her," he said.

"All our matches are decided on the last green," Mme. LaCoste said.

There's an old story about a pitching machine René built to fire tennis balls at him at 110 miles an hour. The story goes that after Bill Tilden's power beat him in 1925 he worked a year with the machine, came back and polished off Big Bill. It isn't exactly true.

"I built the machine," he said, "and it was very good because it would shoot the ball exactly the same way all the time. To do this hitting against a wall, you must be very good. Also you could aim it up and practice smashing a lob.

"But I had studied Tilden. He was tall and I reasoned that if you could keep the ball low and make him run, cross-court and short and long, you could beat him. In 1926 I beat Tilden and Bill Johnston in the Davis Cup and Borotra beat Johnston and we won the cup.

"That year in the U.S. singles Cochet, I think, beat Tilden, then Borotra beat Cochet and I beat Borotra in the final. It was 1927 when I beat Tilden in the final."

Like all who follow the game, LaCoste believes open pro-amateur play is the only hope for tournament tennis. Then he said a surprising thing. Greatest player of all time, in his book, is Ken Rosewall—"He controls the ball. The girls? First Suzanne Lenglen, then Maureen Connolly."

Frank Frisch will have him perpetually barred from the Elderly and Fraternal Affiliation of These Kids Today Couldn't Carry Our Shoes.

CHRISSIE

BOSTON, 1973

Chris Evert, who regards grass with less enthusiasm than some other eighteen-year-olds, is practicing on the clipped lawns of the Longwood Cricket Club here for the United States Open tennis championships in Forest Hills. Revisiting Forest Hills is a little like recapturing love's young dream, for it was on the turf of the West Side Tennis Club that her romance with the galleries burst into flower. Playing in her first National Open two years ago as a pigtailed pixie of sixteen with her neat features set in an expression of sweetly childish intensity, Chrissie captivated the fans completely as she won, and won, and won again before Billie Jean King defeated her in the semifinals.

What emotions are uppermost now as she returns to the scene of that popular triumph as an internationalist and professional with a chance to lift her prize money for the year over $100,000? Eagerness? Apprehension? Confidence? Anxiety? "Eagerness, I think," she said. "I'm grateful that I had a good Wimbledon. It convinced me I could play well on grass, after all."

Lissome and trig and fastidiously turned out in a green and white cardigan with matching green pants, she sat sipping a ginger ale. One gets the impression that Ms. Christine Marie Evert would sooner commit a double foot-fault at match point than neglect eye shadow or nail polish. The eyes are brown and direct; the long hair framing the oval face is the color of Vermont maple syrup in the sun. "Thoughtful" and "undissembling" are the adjectives that occur first to describe her manner. Ask a question, she takes as long as she needs to turn it over and around. Then: "Yeah," she'll say in unaccented American, and elaborate as the topic merits.

She was asked about the European tour leading up to Wimbledon, when she blew a lead of 7–6, 5–3 in the final round of the French Open and lost to Margaret Court, lost to Evonne Goolagong in the finals of the Italian Open, got creamed by Virginia Wade, 6–1, 6–2, on the grass at Nottingham, England, and finally was beaten by Julie Heldman in the London grass court championships.

"It was pretty bad," she said. "France was the worst because I thought I'd been doing well."

"Yet there was no outward sign that you were discouraged."

"I guess I kept it pretty much inside."

"Considering that you had beaten all the girls who beat you, doesn't it seem now that your trouble must have been mental?"

"Each match has to be considered separately," she said, and left it there. In other words, you couldn't lump all the defeats under a single easy explanation, and who wanted a detailed stroke analysis now?

"Winning from Margaret was a big help," she said. "That was a good match." She meant her smashing upset of the top-seeded Margaret Court at Wimbledon. In the final, however, she caught Mrs. King at her supreme best and was knocked out, 6–0, 7–5.

"I wasn't ready for that match," she said. "Billie Jean and I waited six hours the day before, and it was rained out. I dreamt about the match that night. I dreamt of winning Wimbledon. Then when the match started I was flat, I couldn't get interested. And Billie Jean was great."

"Did you panic after the first set?"

"I made up my mind it wouldn't be love–love."

Chris has been swinging a racquet for thirteen of her eighteen years, but tennis is still fun for her. "I love the game, I really do, although I wouldn't say an hour and a half of concentrating in a hard match is all fun. At first I'm nervous. Then if I win a few games I feel more confident. Everybody asks how long I want to keep playing and I tell them two or three years more, but you can't put a limit on it. I'm enjoying it now, traveling and going out nights and having fun. Forest Hills now—I love New York.

"I keep thinking stars like Billie Jean and Margaret can't go on forever and then maybe—but I don't know. Rosie Casals and others are young and there are so many new ones coming up. I may not be cut out to be number one.

"The most important thing right now?" There was a long pause. "My family is important. I'm away a lot, but I still want to be close to my family."

Turning pro hasn't made much difference. "I was keyed up for my first pro tournament, I liked the idea of playing for money. I won that for $10,000, and it was fun. But the money isn't all that important. I never see it, it just goes to the bank."

So far about $76,000 has gone to the bank this year, income from endorsements probably will match that figure, and first prize at Forest Hills is $25,000, thanks to the "Ban equalizer." This is a $55,000 grant the manufacturers of Ban deodorants have made so women players will not only smell nice, but also stand as straight as men in the Chase Manhattan. Chris is pleased that for the first time, women will compete for the same money as men.

"I don't think I would have fought for it as hard as Billie Jean did," she said, "but it's right. We can't play the men's game, but we put out just as much in competition and we draw as many people."

"How do you feel about Bobby Riggs versus the girls?"

"I think it's good for tennis, but I don't like him putting down women's tennis."

"He's only out to make a buck, Chris. He isn't serious about that chauvinist pig act. He's just found a new gimmick—"

But Chrissie was wrinkling her nose.

TANTRUMS ON GRASS

1981

The Wimbledon championships are under way, that courtly gathering of knights and ladies, the beauty and chivalry of the All England Lawn Tennis and Croquet Club with its strawberries and cream, its white gloves and flowery hats, meticulously manicured lawns and impeccable manners. It is also the stage on which a spoiled brat like John McEnroe can demonstrate just how ugly an ugly American can get.

This is not to suggest that boorishness on the courts is an American monopoly. McEnroe and Jimmy Connors can be as coarse as goats, and they are Americans, but Ilie Nastase has scaled peaks of vulgarity in his time, and he is a Rumanian. However, Sandy Mayer ran Nastase out of Wimbledon in the first round, and Connors has not misbehaved up to now, so the responsibility of making an ass of himself devolves on McEnroe. He is equal to the assignment.

By all accounts, the tantrum tossed by Superbrat during his opening match with Tom Gullikson was up to his unappetizing standards. He smashed two racquets, was twice penalized a point for misbehavior, called the umpire an "incompetent fool," pulled a sitdown strike and addressed an obscenity to the referee.

He should, of course, have been flung out of the tournament onto his ear, but leniency on the part of tennis officials has become something close to vice. We have come to accept this as a fact of life in the United States, but there seemed some ground for hope that a degree of civility might be expected in hallowed Wimbledon. As a matter of fact, the day after his performance, McEnroe was fined $1,500 and warned that another offense would bring a much stiffer fine or possibly expulsion.

Perhaps with the population explosion on the courts, Major Walter Wingfield's genteel game of sphairistike has begun to attract a clientele formerly confined to soccer matches and fist fights. Marvin Hagler, having escaped with his life from Wembley Arena after hammering Alan Minter loose from the middleweight championship, could contribute some thoughts about the gentility of British sportsmen and their marksmanship with bottles, beer cans, and even more lethal missiles.

But in McEnroe's case, he was the culprit, not any of the spectators. They expressed their disapproval with hoots, whistles and slow, cadenced handclapping.

In the United States and many other countries, business concerns put up hundreds of thousands of dollars to sponsor tennis tournaments every week. Naturally the sponsors want the game's uppercase names on the program to provide the publicity their dollars are buying.

Perhaps the sponsor doesn't ask the officials to tolerate loutish behavior by the stars, but the people who run tournaments don't have to be told who is picking up the tab. Consequently the brats have been temporized with until they believe—they know for certain—that they can get away with murder.

They are all pros today, and they compete for loot that makes major league baseball players look like paupers. Monetary fines mean nothing. Penalizing misbehavior by awarding points to the opponent amounts to something less than a slap on the wrist.

The solution is to throw the bums out, and do it on the first offense. The certified members of the Riffraff Club have offended often enough, so there is no longer any point in waiting for a second or third offense in any particular tournament. They should be warned before play starts that the first time they give cause, they will be pitched into the street, and no appeal will be heard.

Enforce such a rule just two or three times, and the slum-clearance job would be completed. If a McEnroe, Connors, or Nastase, or any seeking to emulate them, couldn't compete in the money tournaments, they might have to go to work for a living. True, there is a constitutional guarantee against cruel or unusual punishment, but this would be a case of letting the punishment fit the crime.

Prominent tennis players have been heard to applaud Jimmy Connors because he is colorful, while cocking a snoot at Bjorn Borg because he seldom gives any outward sign of emotion. Perhaps there are officials who feel the same way, and certainly hoodlumism seems to have a distinct crowd appeal.

Anyone old enough to read this has lived long enough to have witnessed growth in the popularity of the game. This was good to see. It was fine when the United States nationals, Davis Cup competition and such escaped from the cramped environs of the West Side Tennis Club and found a new and larger public in Flushing Meadows.

But there are some differences in the techniques and philosophies of a Monday night pro football game in Foxboro, Massachusetts, a bullfight in Mexico City, a fight in the Felt Forum, a Yankees-Red Sox game in Fenway Park and a mixed-doubles match at Wimbledon. The differences should be discernible.

Perhaps nothing can be done to alter the fact that top players who behave like dead-end kids do draw cash customers. It should, though, be possible to teach the whippersnappers a few manners.

7.

Fishing

GRANDPA AND GRANDSON

"Grandpa," the fisherman asked, watching his companion crawl under a barbed-wire fence, "did you grow old or were you made old?"

The fisherman had a little plastic rod and a spinning reel with a bobber on the line. He had dug worms out of a compost heap and now he dunked one in Turtle Pond on Ozzie Fischer's farm near Beetlebung Corner here on Martha's Vineyard. He watched the bobber intently, moving his bait here and there beside lily pads. White water lilies rested on the surface, their petals opened fully. Water striders darted about in cheeky defiance of natural laws. The fisherman noticed a wooden structure floating in the middle of the pond. "The dog has to swim to his house," he said. "It does look like a doghouse," he was told, "but Mr. Fischer built that for ducks in case they wanted to make a nest in it and lay their eggs."

Not even a turtle showed interest in the worm. This may explain why you never see anybody fishing Turtle Pond. However, the swan pond in West Tisbury was only a fifteen-minute drive down island and it is common to see boys fishing there. Probably the proper name is Mill Pond, but in the fisherman's family it is known as the swan pond because a cob and his pen live and love and rear their cygnets there. The couple's only child this year is already half the size of the parents.

The fisherman was thoughtful on the drive. "Do people who don't have a birthday grow older?" he asked.

Yes, he was told, there is one way to avoid that but the method isn't recommended.

"Some people don't have a birthday," he said. "They have to pick July." After a silence he added an afterthought. "Or December. I'd pick July."

"It's August now," he was reminded.

"Yes, but there'll be another July."

"Oh, you mean next July. Yes, there are always two—last July and next July." He thought that over and smiled as if the idea pleased him, but he made no comment.

The swans were at the far end of their pond. On the water beside the road were a dozen or more mallards. Parking, the fisherman's companion asked: "How old are you now?"

At first there was no answer. Then, tentatively: "Six."

"Oh? When will you be six?"

"Tomorrow." His birthday is in September.

Reddish-brown weeds showed a little below the surface. "Throw it where the ducks are," the fisherman said. He laughed when the bobber, split shot, and hook plopped in near a duck, startling her. "Now hold the rod still and watch the bobber," he was told.

"What's a bobber?"

"That red and white thing."

"That's a floater," he said, but not impatiently.

Drawn by curiosity, two ducks swam slowly toward the bobber, eyeing it.

"I have to go to the bathroom," the fisherman said. He saw some tall shrubs. "I'll go behind there." He went off at a trot.

While he was gone the bobber submerged, but the bait was lifted clear before a fish could strip the hook or, worse, get himself caught in the fisherman's absence.

"A fish pulled the floater underwater," he was told on his return. "Be ready to catch him."

In a few moments the bobber broke into a jig. The fisherman cranked his little tin reel. Except for a tiny nubbin of worm, the hook was bare.

"The worms are in the car," his companion said. "Keep fishing with that and I'll get another." By the time he got back the hook was clean.

"Next time the floater sinks," it was suggested, "jerk your rod up first to set the hook in the fish and then crank." In a moment: "There! Good, now crank. No, I'm afraid you're caught in the weeds. Just keep cranking. No! You have a fish. Keep cranking. See him?"

A pale belly flashed right, left and right again. His lips set, the fisherman reeled furiously. He dragged a nine-inch bullhead onto the bank and stared at it.

"Is that the first fish you ever caught?"

"Yes." The tone was hushed.

"Come on, then. We'll take it home and then I'll skin it so your mother can cook it."

"My mommy will laugh her head off," he said. He was jubilant now.

"I'm crazy about my family," he said. "My mother and father and my sister and my cousin Kim, they'll laugh their head off."

TED WILLIAMS' TRIPLE CROWN

BLACKVILLE, NEW BRUNSWICK, 1978

When Theodore Samuel Williams batted .406 in 1941, the Elias Sports Bureau meticulously recorded his 456 times at bat and 185 hits. When he won the triple crown in 1949, baseball's official statisticians took careful note of his 39 home runs, 159 runs batted in and the average of .343 that gave him the American League championship.

Now in the sixtieth summer of his life, Ted Williams is going for another triple crown, and he has to keep his own records. He has caught 1,000 tarpon on a flyrod. He has caught 1,000 bonefish on flies. Next month or maybe in September, he will sink a tiny feathered hook into the lip of his 1,000th Atlantic salmon, turn the fish loose and record the catch in his logbook. No flycaster in the world ever mastered 1,000 of the giants they call the "silver king," 1,000 of those blindingly swift torpedoes that range the coral flats, and 1,000 salmon, the wary monarch of all game fishes.

Ted's salmon count had reached 968 when his camp on the Miramichi was invaded by Bud Leavitt of the *Bangor Daily News* and an accomplice from New York. Ted said salmon coming home to spawn had been moving up the river only in dribs and drabs, though a crew had been here making a film a few days earlier and 17 fish had been taken on camera.

On the first day of the invasion nobody caught anything. Not the tireless and talented host, who can lay out 85 feet of line in cast after cast, hour after hour, covering a pool like a tarpaulin. Not his guide and fishing partner, Roy Curtis, who knows more about salmon than salmon do. Not Bud Leavitt, who is such an authority that the other day a judge in Bangor sentenced three young poachers to study fishing regulations at his knee. Not the city guy, who means well.

On the second day the city guy took a fine salmon. The experience reminded him of Shirley Povich of the *Washington Post*. Shirley is a smallish guy who can't hit a golf ball out of his shadow but once, with one swing on one hole in one round in his life, he outdrove Sam Snead. Catching that salmon when Ted Williams didn't and Roy Curtis didn't and Bud Leavitt didn't, the city guy knew just how Shirley had felt when his ball came to rest beyond Snead's. His glee was unworthy, and secret.

On the third and last day, Ted took two fish, Roy got into one that tore free, and with about half an hour of showery daylight left, Bud Leavitt took one. In the late afternoon an animal was seen swimming across the pool.

"A muskrat, I guess," Roy said. "Could be a groundhog. I guess any animal would swim if he has to. One day I saw what looked like brush floating downstream. It seemed too long for an animal but it was moving across the current toward my side. I slipped down behind some bushes to watch it come ashore, and it was a fox. It was the tail made it look so long."

The muskrat had dived near the rocky island that is an old bridge abutment. Now it reappeared, recrossing the river at top speed.

"He must be late," called Vince Graves, a state of Mainer fishing out of the camp across the river. "He is in an awful hurry."

Later Ted Williams sat on the porch of his camp in a copse of white birch high over the Home Pool. If there had been a designated hitter in the American League in 1960, Bud Leavitt asked, might he have stayed on in baseball a couple of years longer?

"I don't think so," Ted said. "I'd had it. In the winter I kept hearing and reading that maybe I wouldn't be around long. I think the Red Sox were ready to get Yastrzemski started in left field. Anyway, I told Dick O'Connell, 'If you don't want me, I'll retire.'

" 'Oh, no,' he said, 'don't believe what you hear. We want you.' He gave me the same contract I'd had for a couple of years, $125,000. I tore it up and said, 'Now write me one for $90,000.' I took a $35,000 cut because I hadn't had a good year and every time I'd signed a contract before, with Eddie Collins or Joe Cronin or O'Connell, they always asked me, 'Are you happy? We want you happy.'

"During that season Fred Corcoran called me." Fred, the great golf promoter, was Ted's friend and sometime business agent. "He said, 'Dan Topping wants to know whether you would pinch-hit for the Yankees for two years. He wants to hear from you before he talks to the Red Sox. He'll pay the same as you're getting, $125,000.' Even Fred didn't know about the cut. I told him no, I was going to pack it in, and that's the last I ever heard from Topping."

Late that summer Ted announced that the last game of the final home stand would be his finish. He would not make the last road trip with the club. Most of New England moved into Fenway Park to see him hit Baltimore's Jack Fisher for his 521st home run on his last time at bat.

"What were you thinking that last time up?"

"Nothing. I'd had it and this was the end. I wanted to hit the ball and get out of there. Mr. Fisher threw me a fastball and for the only time in my life I didn't know whether I was ahead of the pitch or behind, over the ball or under it. It flashed through my mind, 'This guy thinks he can throw it past me.' Next time he threw, I was swinging."

THE SEWER OF BEAVERKILL

1981

One stormy April night three men rode out of the darkness into the streets of the Catskills village of Roscoe. "Gentlemen," said Sparse Gray Hackle, "remove your hats. This is it."

"This is where the trout was invented?" the driver asked.

"Oh," Mr. Hackle said, "he existed in a crude, primitive form in Walton's England—"

"But this," said Meade Schaeffer, artist and angler, "is where they painted spots on him and taught him to swim."

It was the eve of Opening Day of the New York trout season. It can be said without irreverence that to celebrate Opening Day on the Beaverkill is a little like observing Christmas in Bethlehem. For the Beaverkill is the shrine, the fountainhead, the most beloved and best-known trout stream in America, the river of George LaBranche, Theodore Gordon, Guy Jenkins, and the Flyfishers Club of Brooklyn.

In Roscoe, the willow of the Willowemoc join those of the upper Beaverkill in the Junction Pool, and here the Big River, the main Beaverkill, is born. The Junction Pool is also the birthplace of the beamoc, a two-headed brown trout of vast proportions and agonizing indecision. From the day he is hatched, one head gazes wistfully up the Willowemoc, the other yearns for the upper Beaverkill. Unable to make up his minds, the beamoc lives his life out in the Junction Pool, surviving twice as long and growing twice as big as he could in either tributary.

There are many streams in America more densely populated with trout and productive of more trophy catches than the Beaverkill. There are rivers that are easier to fish. But this is the cradle of flyfishing in America, the treasured stream that draws thousands from all corners of the nation every summer.

It is in imminent danger of becoming a sewer.

Titan Group, Inc., a corporation with headquarters in Paramus, New Jersey, has a 919-acre tract in the town of Rockland that it plans to develop as a 1,000-unit hotel-motel with a trailer park containing 1,000 service hookups, an eighteen-hole golf course, and all supporting facilities. The plan includes a pipeline four and a half miles long to discharge about 550,000 gallons of treated sewage into the Beaverkill every day.

A Sullivan County court has granted Titan the right to condemn private property for construction of the sewer line, and up to now appeals by property owners and conservation groups have been rejected. Among those fighting the project are the Theodore Gordon

Flyfishers, the Federation of Fly Fishermen, Catskill Waters and the Beamoc Chapter of Trout Unlimited.

Property owners and the conservation groups, banded together as the Beaverkill Legal Defense Fund, appealed the Sullivan County Court Condemnation Order but were turned down by the Appellate Division of the State Supreme Court.

They are trying now to find an accommodation that would enable Titan to go ahead with its project without destroying the Beaverkill as a fishery. Failing success there, the fight will be carried on through reargument or appeal to a higher court.

To help the campaign, a "Save Our Beaverkill Fund" has been created under the sponsorship of the Beamoc Chapter of Trout Unlimited, with headquarters in Livingston Manor, New York.

"The Big River," Sparse Gray Hackle wrote, "from the junction at Roscoe to the junction at East Branch (the junction with the East Branch of the Delaware) is a challenge, whereas the Little River is an invitation. It takes stronger legs and longer chances to wade the Big River, a bigger rod and a better arm to cover its waters.

"It is here that the ten- and twelve-pound monsters are taken and the five-pound bass that makes the startled angler think he has hooked into a trout twice as big. Here the stalker can watch an hour, a day, or a week until he sees a great trout feeding and then wade armpit-deep and try to keep sixty feet of line off the water as he works out the single cast which will either raise the fish or put him down.

"Fishing the Big River is a sport but fishing the Little River is a recreation. This dozen miles of the loveliest trout water in America, with the Balsam Lake Club at the top and the Brooklyn Fly Fishers at the bottom, is what the old-timers referred to when they wrote about the Beaverkill, the classic water of the Golden Age."

Little River or Big, the Beaverkill is a holy place, marked by wayside shrines called Foul Rift and Lone Pine, the Deserted Village and Painter's Bend, the Picnic Grounds and Summer House Pool. When they become repositories for man's waste, something special will go out of life.

THE CANOE

There were these two kids in Green Bay, Wisconsin, faithful readers of *Boys' Life* and *The American Boy*. Both magazines carried seductive advertisements for the Old Town canoe, and the kids had a dream. If they had an Old Town canoe they would ship it by rail to the Chain of Lakes country in the northern Wisconsin woods, paddle through the lakes to the source of the Wisconsin River, ride the Wisconsin southwest to the town of Portage, where a mile overland would take them to the headwaters of the Fox, which flows northeast through Lake Winnebago to Green Bay.

They agreed to save their pennies to buy a canoe, "which in those days," Mike Faunce said Wednesday, consulting an old catalogue, "would have required about 3,600 pennies."

"An unreliable memory," one of the former kids told him, "suggests that we had about $1.69 in the treasury when we quarreled about something and dissolved the partnership."

For the first time in his life, the former kid had found himself in Old Town, and had steered directly for the five-story plant where Old Town canoes, kayaks, dinghies, and even rowing shells are built. Old Town is a translation of the name the Penobscot tribe of Abenaki Indians had for an ancient settlement on the Penobscot River. To a faithful reader of *Boys' Life* and *The American Boy*, it is pronounced "Mecca."

"Your canoe," Mike Faunce said, "would have been canvas over a wooden frame, the only kind the company built in those days. We still build them that way but we also have wooden canoes with fiberglass covering, fiberglass canoes and plastic canoes. Today they retail from about $550 to $2,000 or so."

Mike Faunce and Sandy Christensen doubled as guides on a tour of Mecca. Here was the classic wooden canoe.

"The planking is western red cedar," Sandy said. "The ribs are white cedar. The thwarts and decks are ash. On the gunwale, the inner rail is Sitka spruce, the outer rail mahogany. Recently we've gone back to the traditional diamond-shaped head on the bolts holding the thwarts."

"Some people," Mike said, "buy these boats and never put them in the water, just keep 'em in the living room as a work of art."

In the next room Joe Lavoie and John Hardesty were fitting ribs on the iron-bound form of a canoe, which is to a boat builder as a dressmaker's dummy is to a seamstress. John took the cedar strips out of a steamer and together they bent them over the mold and tacked them down. Then, working swiftly before the pliable wood could dry, John fitted on planking lengthwise, securing it with brass tacks temporarily stored in his mouth.

"A visitor asked how many tacks this job took," Mike said. "The man doing it thought that over. 'About twelve mouthfuls,' he said."

Joe said they used to have a man here who could chew gum with a mouthful of tacks. John said there was another who tacked and chewed tobacco. When he wanted to speak he would remove the tacks and put them back in their box. After seeing that, John stopped sharing the box.

When the planking is finished, the stem caulked with a compound and seams closed with wood putty, the canoe gets a lye bath, then is fitted with a top coat of canvas or fiberglass. Two layers of woven fiberglass cloth are bound on with layers of matting for added strength and this surface is sanded four times. Then the boat gets a layer called gelcoat before painting.

A two-year supply of wood is kept in the plant. A one-year supply is in use and a like quantity is drying for a year. Besides the boats, virtually all accessories are made here, including sails.

"Until recently," Mike said, "we had a seamstress in the sail room who was eighty-two years old and had been working here since she was fifteen, with just enough time out to have two children."

"This is the Tripper," Sandy said, pausing before a seventeen-foot plastic canoe. "Maybe you saw the ad."

She referred to a sequence of photographs showing the canoe being flung from the factory roof about sixty feet from the ground. First, the advertisement testifies, "we flooded her and wrapped her around a bridge abutment. Twice. Each time the material's built-in memory allowed the hull to return to its original shape."

"Then," Mike said, "they had to throw it off the roof five or six times so the photographer could get his sequence. The boat is still on display here."

In the office archives are records on every boat the company has sold in this century. If replacements are needed, the files will have a description of the necessary parts.

"Sometimes it would be cheaper to buy a new canoe than restore an old one," Mike said, "but the owner wants the old one."

"It can be a sentimental thing," Sandy said.

BEFORE THE MOUNTAIN ERUPTED

1980

Boiling mud traveling 30 miles per hour overflowed local river banks, smashed bridges, swallowed homes and killed millions of salmon and trout. Some rivers got so hot that fish actually jumped out. . . . The waters of the Toutle River rose from their normal 50 degrees to nearly 90. . . . An estimated 70 million salmon and trout died in the river and in several state hatcheries that were engulfed by the mud flows. . . . At one point along the flooded Cowlitz River, which was jammed with timber carried down from the mountain, people made light of their plight—walking on the logs and scooping up steelhead trout that wriggled on the surface.

Reading of the devastation wrought by the Mount St. Helens eruption in the state of Washington was a wrenching experience, for it was only a few years ago that a small but inept party of anglers fished those very rivers for steelhead and reveled in the wild beauty of that mountain country.

The party included Jack Murphy of San Diego and Will Yolen of New York and was led by Norm Nelson of the public affairs section of Weyerhaeuser, the forest-products giant. A good man and true on his job, Norm was dedicated to the proposition that cutting down trees was good for them. He truly believed that he would never see a poem lovely as a tree on its way to the sawmill.

"How do people feel about Joyce Kilmer?" Norm was asked.

"There is no corporate position on him," he said, "but I sometimes wish he had gone into another line of work."

This was shortly after sunrise on a high, rocky bank of the Toutle River, a tributary of the Cowlitz, which is a tributary of the Columbia. The Toutle was then a beautiful stream of white rapids, great jagged boulders and pale green depths.

Farther down, it plunged through Hollywood Gorge, so-called because of a scene in an old movie entitled *God's Country and the Woman,* starring George Brent. In the film a logging train was derailed on the canyon's lip and the logs plunged into the rapids far below. Now and then people used to try to navigate Hollywood Gorge by canoe or rubber raft, and it wasn't a good idea. One who tried it with an inner tube resurfaced four days later in the Cowlitz.

There was a fisherman every fifty feet or so along the Toutle that day. Most had spinning rods and drifted plastic imitations of steelhead roe along the bottom, hanging up on rocks every few feet. The river banks were littered with tangled monofilament and broken lures.

A man and woman made their way upstream. In each hand he carried a steelhead hooked on a forked stick. She wore a blue bandanna about her head and a studiously nonchalant expression. "She caught 'em," the man said. Later another man came by with two fish. He said only he and the lady of the blue bandanna had scored that morning, but minutes after that a fish came out of the water about five feet from where Jack Murphy stood on the bank. The steelhead had taken a spoon cast by a man a little way upstream.

The Nelson party suffered skunkage, as the late John Randolph used to phrase it, but a day of fishing can be richly rewarding without fish. Nobody else had breathed this mountain air recently. Forests of dark fir climbed peaks outlined raggedly against the spotless sky. The river sang and shouted. Oliver Twist couldn't ask for more.

Next day it was on to the Cowlitz, then the most productive steelhead river in the world. The steelhead, as you know, is a rainbow trout with wanderlust. Hatched in fresh water, he goes to sea as a smolt about nine inches long, ranges widely and eats ravenously. Two or three or maybe five years later, he returns to the stream of his birth with nothing but love in view. At sea the rainbow's pink stripe and blushing fins turn to silver and the head becomes steel gray, but after a time in the river his color returns.

In 1972 anglers took 46,000 steelhead from the Cowlitz and in the record month of December 1971, the catch was 19,000, which is greater than the annual yield of Washington's No. 2 River, the Skagit. The Cowlitz was a wide, tossing torrent, too big to wade. Four guys from the Washington Department of Game provided boats, expertise and companionship. They used casting rods and their lures were little wads of wool yarn in two tones of pink. Steelhead, like the Atlantic salmon, do not feed actively during the spawning run, but small bright morsels seem to catch their attention. Eight of ten steelhead interviewed thus far said they had mistaken these morsels for shrimp or roe.

For a stranger, the river was impossible to read but Dave Gufler and Jim Briscoe of the Game Department knew where the pools were. They would anchor at the head of a pool and let the current roll their lures over the rocky bottom. Their companion, using a flyrod, took three jack salmons on the surface. None weighed more than a pound but they all had a terrible temper. The jack is a precocious king salmon who comes back to the river ahead of his age group.

A steelhead took Gufler's tuft of yarn, leaped in a twisting frenzy and took off. Briscoe made three passes with the net before he came into the boat. Then Briscoe fought and outpointed a leaping silver torpedo.

"Would you let me try that flyrod for a while?" Briscoe asked the guest. He handed over his casting rod, which he had surreptitiously rigged with a green Hot Shot. This lure, a comparatively new development at that time, was a plastic minnow that a retarded chimpanzee could fish successfully. You just dropped it in the current and it went and found steelhead. It found two for the guest, beautiful, leaping, gallant adversaries.

Today these grand rivers are fouled with mud, choked with debris. Thousands of acres of Douglas fir lie flattened by the blast. President Carter surveyed an abomination of desolation from a helicopter. "The moon," he said, "looks like a golf course compared to what's up there."

ASSAULT BY A FISHERPERSON

ILE D'ANTICOSTI, QUEBEC, 1976

We hold these truths to be self-evident: that if God had intended man for racing, He would have given him four legs like a horse; and that the only sensible way to travel is in a yellow convertible with the top down. With Montreal heaving and panting with foot-racers in this second week of the Olympics, it was obviously the right time to put children's games aside and come off to Anticosti Island to kill a salmon. Anticosti lies in the Gulf of St. Lawrence northeast of the Gaspé Peninsula and men have been making war on salmon here since Frontenac, the governor of New France, granted it to Louis Joliet in 1680 as a reward for discovering the Mississippi and Illinois rivers. (To be sure, DeSoto got to the Mississippi first, but he was a Spaniard and the French had never heard of him.) After almost 300 years of hand-to-fin combat, the human population of the island has grown to 235 and the fish are reduced to a few million.

To reach Anticosti you fly Quebecair from Montreal to Quebec to Baie Comeau to Sept Iles, then change to a subsidiary airline called Les Ailes du Nord (Wings of the North), which serves the island metropolis of Port Menier in leisurely fashion. You can get to the island in about four hours and get off in less than a lifetime, fog permitting. Your luggage takes a little longer—say about three days.

Joliet built a fort here and established cod and seal fisheries. After a century or so the island passed to other ownership and in 1895 it was bought by Henri Menier, the French chocolate king. He stocked it with elk, buffalo, and other fauna and built a chateau that burned down in 1952. He also evicted several hundred squatters who were doing a lively business in salvaging goods from shipwrecks. Since

Jacques Cartier discovered Anticosti in 1535 it has been the scene of more than 400 wrecks with loss of 4,000 lives, but not all were purposely arranged by the squatters.

In 1926 the Consolidated Paper Company bought the island from Menier's heirs. Until two years ago the company continued to lease fishing rights on salmon rivers where Menier had built camps. Then the province of Quebec bought Anticosti as a provincial park. There are now three camps accommodating four fishermen each (or hunters in deer season) for $125 a person for a minimum of two days and three with eight beds each at $1,000 or $1,600 a person for six days. All rates include meals and guides.

When the Wings of the North sat down on the gravel landing strip at Port Menier the cargo included Pierre d'Auteuil of the Ministère de Tourisme de la Chasse et de la Pêche, one fisherman, one fisherperson and no luggage. Ah, well, said Pierre, who is young and hopeful, there would be clothing, boots and fishing tackle at Rivière à la Loutre (Otter River). He introduced Paul Boulet, who would guide the party. Paul is ruggedly handsome, dark, with curly black hair and deep, lustrous eyes. He has been guiding for ten years. Mario Andretti should have his way with a Ford pickup truck.

In Quebec, Harold Martel of the Ministry of Tourism of the Hunt and of the Fish had said the streams on Anticosti were so low the salmon were committing hara-kiri on rocks but Paul reported that a good rain two nights back had raised La Loutre a couple of inches and started fish moving. La Loutre was 55 miles away, he said, on the south shore.

It was only a mile or so as the pickup lurches before the fisherperson spotted a deer in the evergreens beside the road. Paul said the island, about 150 miles by 35 at its widest point, had a deer population of 60,000. They are descendants of 150 bucks and does imported in 1897.

Moments later the fisherperson saw a second deer, a second doe, then a fawn. Around a bend, the truck startled a fawn in the road posing for a calendar. He made for the woods where his mom waited. Farther on a mother and child made way for the pickup, the fawn leaping to safety, the doe taking her time. Paul turned off on a side road where a buck was just leading a doe out of the forest to show her his etchings. Finally, beside a stream near journey's end, Pierre saw still another deer, the tenth of the drive.

The lodge at La Loutre is a simple frame house on a rise beside the river about 300 yards from its mouth, commanding a view of forest and sea. It is the oldest of the camps, opened in 1918. Paul said that before there were roads, fishermen reached it by boat and rode horseback to the pools. A stove in the living room burns bottled gas and on a wall is a color photograph marked "Wilson Pool, July 1967." It shows thirty salmon abreast in clear water.

With a couple of hours of daylight after dinner, Paul drove to a pool he called Quatorze (Fourteen). Here the stream runs swiftly between low gravel banks and turns square left against limestone ledges with a big eddy to the right. Paul stationed Pierre and the fisherman at the head of the riffle, the fisherperson near the tail. The fisherman worked the riffle once without result and was walking back upstream, towing his fly, when he felt weight on the line. A brook trout of about fifteen inches was trying to eat the Black Ghost. The trout was for breakfast.

Pierre's rod tip bent and a shaft of silver shot out of the darkening pool. The fish leaped three times before Paul got a landing net under it. It was a young salmon, a grilse. On Anticosti, Paul said, salmon run from three to ten pounds and those under four are considered grilse. "Paul said the fish I catched was about three and a half pounds," Pierre reported later.

Since arrival at Quatorze, each visitor had worn a halo of tiny black flies, aggressively carnivorous. They concentrated on ears, bald spots, temples and necks, and wherever they hit they drew blood. A hat would have been some protection. In the missing luggage were two hats.

"Why don't they bite you, Paul?" the fisherperson asked as twilight came on and the clouds of insects thickened.

"They are used to me," Paul said. "We get along."

By bedtime, each bite had raised a lump the size of a hickory nut. The fisherman had often been called a knucklehead. This time it fit.

THE BRAKES GOT DRUNK

LAGUNA DEL MAULE, CHILE, 1953

This typewriter is being beaten with fingers whose knuckles are bleeding and nails broken after hand-to-fin struggles with trout exactly the size, shape, and disposition of Tony Galento. Up here in the Andes fishing is a more perilous game than Russian roulette. If you survive the mountain road, there are rainbow in Lake Maule ready and willing to eat you for bait. Nothing is impossible to fish that live a mile and a half up in the sky.

Lake Maule perches on the Chilean-Argentine border about twenty kilometers and two thousand feet above the sparse grove of maytenus trees at timberline where camp had been pitched the evening before. The last drop of fluid had drained out of the brakes of the old Chevrolet truck during the journey to campsite, and there are no filling stations along the narrow, twisting shelf that serves, more or less, as a road.

Herman, the driver, halted trucks that passed camp occasionally with construction crews working on a dam at the lake. They told him oil would ruin the brakes, but said wine could serve as an emergency fluid.

"Because it contains alcohol, eh?" said Captain Warren Smith, of Panagra. "We can do better than that. Where's the Vat 69?"

The Chevrolet scrambled up to the lake with a boiling radiator and a full brake cylinder, not the best truck in Chile, but by all odds the happiest.

Maule straddles a pass in mountains entirely devoid of vegetation. They are bare peaks of volcanic rock crumbling into gray dust under the wind that blows eternally up this gorge from the west, making even these midsummer days uncomfortably cold. A little way out from the shore there is a belt of seaweed just under the surface where the trout lie and feed on a small pink crawfish called *pancora*. This shellfish diet gives the rainbows their majestic size, but it is the barren landscape that gives them their evil temperament. In all this desolation they brood.

Captain Smith and his North American burden rode by outboard to the east end of the lake, where snow touched the Chilean mountains rising from the water's edge and Argentine mountains showed just beyond. They started casting over the weed beds, using a small-ish bronze-finish spoon of scarlet and orange. Almost immediately there was a grunt from the captain and wild splash. Something dark and shiny and altogether implausible came out of the water and returned. It looked like a trout, but not like the sort of trout people ordinarily see when their eyes are open.

"You go on fishing," Captain Smith said. "I'll be awhile with this fellow."

His rod was a bow and his line hissed through the water. The fish was in and out of the lake, in and out, and then it was in the boat flopping on a gaff, a pink-striped brute of black and silver. "He'll hit about nine pounds," the captain said calmly.

Thereafter the captain cought fish and his companion caught back-lashes and weeds. So intense, however, is the dislike these trout have for people that even the least proficient angler is bound to be under attack.

Between backlashes, a distant relative of Primo Carnera sprang up for a look at the latest New York styles in outdoor apparel, made a face of hideous disapproval, and spat out the spoon.

Another grabbed the same spoon and went into a terrifying rage.

Four times in quick succession he stook up on his tail, snarling and shaking his head and cursing horribly. On the fourth jump he snapped the leader.

Then Captain Smith had one that broke the leader and departed. Then it happened again to the amateur, but not before the whirling reel handle had smashed fingernails and stripped skin off awkward knuckles.

By now half the population of the lake had taken a passion for collecting hardware. Six leaders were snapped and six spoons confiscated by force before it was decided that the fifteen-pound test nylon was faulty. There's an awful lot of trout in Maule going around with their faces full of painted metal with nylon streamers. Maybe the style will catch on, like nose rings in the cannibal islands.

With the spoon tied directly to the casting line, anybody could catch fish. Practically anybody did. The outboard would take the boat upwind to the lee of a point or island; then the wind would drift it swiftly over the weed beds. Duck and geese and tern and grebe swam on the water. Except for one other fishing party, the place belonged them and the fish.

"Let's take one more drift," the captain suggested, "and call it a day."

Half a moment later his companion screamed. The reel handle was snatched from his grasp and the drag sang. A trout leaped, fell back on his side. He looked six fet long. He dived, wrenching off line. The boat drifted on, but he wouldn't come along. Twice the captain ran the boat upwind, cautiously undoing knots the fish had tied around weeds. At length the sullen beast came aboard.

He was a good twelve pounds, broad-shouldered, magnificently colored, and splendidly deep, like Jane Russell.

BASS DERBY

MARTHA'S VINEYARD, MASSACHUSETTS, 1950
The rain which had been falling in sudden sullen bursts all day backed off just before the arrival of Mr. Al Brickman, proprietor of Vineyard Haven's popular stores, Abercrombie & Brickman and Bergdorf-Brickman. Mr. Brickman had contracted to show an ignoramus a thing or two about fishing in the annual Martha's Vineyard striped bass derby, a month-long competition in which anglers who snatch the largest comestibles out of the oceans are rewarded with automobiles, cruisers, fishing tackle, etc.

Mr. Brickman was accompanied by Stan Bryden, an island man, and General Charles W. Ryder, who recently switched his address from one island, Japan, to another island, Martha's Vineyard. On the drive down to Menemsha Bight, all three explained that experience of surf casting was not essential to a derby candidate.

"That boy Drake," said Stan Bryden, "whose forty-pounder is leading the field right now, never caught a bass before he hooked this one."

"One day," said Al Brickman, "there was an off-island kid over here on his honeymoon, borrowed some tackle and made one cast and got a backlash. While he was untangling the backlash, a bass took his plug. He couldn't reel in so he just backed up inland and dragged the bass onto the beach. He lost the plug, and that night he come down to my store, bought another plug, went back and caught another striper."

At Menemsha Bight the bass-slayers got into hip boots and rubberized overalls and waterproofed parkas and lugged their tackle down to the beach. The tide was rampaging out through a narrow cut and there were perhaps half a dozen fishermen casting into the current from the rock jetty, with a dozen or so more strung out along the beach flinging their feathered jigs into the surf. The jigs, or plugs, or tin squids, are cigar-sized gobbets of lead with feather tails which, it is optimistically hoped, will look edible to large stupid fish.

Either there weren't any large fish or they weren't stupid enough. The anglers kept heaving their jigs out to sea and reeling them in and nothing else kept happening. Nobody worked too hard. A guy would make a few fruitless casts, then thrust the butt of his rod into the sand and go light up a cigarette and tell some lies.

"When I was a kid," Al Brickman was saying, "a buddy and I used to camp down here in two pup tents and go fishing, and the things we'd catch you wouldn't believe. Ever see a goose fish? They have two feet on 'em webbed just like geese."

"See old Levi Jackson fishing down the beach there?" said Ted Henley, an island man. "Every time I see him I think of one time I saw him with a monkfish, which are as fat as this with a mouth that big. He'd stuffed this monkfish full of rocks and old scrap iron and all sorts of heavy stuff and then I saw him sewing up the fish's big mouth. I watched, wondering what in the world he could be doing.

"Well, he finally got the fish sewed up and then he picked it up like this and threw it overboard. I heard him say, 'There, you slob. You've torn up my nets enough. You'll never do it to anybody else.' "

A gull flew in from sea, wobbling crookedly, with something dangling from its claws. The bird alighted on the jetty close enough so you could see it had a surf-casting plug looped to one foot. Apparently it had been stupid enough to think this gadget of lead and feather was a fish.

"I'm going to get that jig," Ted Henley said, and he picked up a stone and crept toward the bird. When he got close he threw the rock. It missed, but the gull took flight with a scream and the plug shook free and Ted recovered it.

The tide was changing and bluefish were breaking water in the rollers out beyond the reach of the beach casters. Now one of them hooked into a fish and a man beside him shouted, pointing, and all the yarn-spinners snatched up their rods and rushed to the water's edge and began casting relentlessly. Nobody got anything, except the one man who had brought in a bluefish.

As evening came on, more cars rolled down to the beach and more fishermen went to work. When the setting sun broke through clouds on the horizon there were about twenty-five anglers strung along the beach casting earnestly. Some of them would keep at it all night.

Al Brickman's party stowed tackle and started for home. General Ryder was telling about bass-fishing in the spring in Menemsha Pond during the spawning run of herring. The herring, he said, come through a cut from the ocean and go into the pond to spawn and the stripers follow them in.

"You net some herring," he said, "and put one on your line for bait, hooking it through the fleshy part of the back. Then you toss him out and teach him to swim. A bass comes along and slaps the herring, stunning him. You wait, because the bass will then go around and try to eat him head on. When the bass takes the herring in his mouth and starts swimming away, you tighten your reel and you have him.

"The gulls, though, they come in with the bass and they hang up there waiting. When a bass stuns a herring, the gull dives and grabs the stunned bait. Then you've got a gull in the air on the end of your line, and that's something."

"Did you see cormorant fishing in the Orient?" the general was asked.

"You mean where they have a cormorant with a ring around his neck so he can't swallow the fish, and they send the bird out fishing and he grabs the fish and they take it away from him? Yes," the general said, "I saw it and the cormorants love it. They get to eat the little fish, which slip down their throats.

"I have also," the general said, "netted ducks in the private preserves of the Emperor of Japan. You use a long-handled net and catch the ducks on the wing. That's quite a sport too."

That's what a bass derby is like. No bass, but much education.

JUNIOR EAGLE

GREENOUGH, MONTANA, 1964

A golden eagle soared in lazy circles, gazing down with ill-concealed contempt at the fishermen who wallowed up to their navels in the Blackfoot River. Chances are he had never seen anything sillier than grown men threatening the indifferent trout with those long, skinny sticks when anybody knew the way to get fish for dinner was to plummet out of the sky and sink your talons into one.

"That reminds me," Skipper Lofting said, dropping his dry fly at the head of a riffle, "you must meet Junior. Chances are you'll want an interview with him."

Junior is a baby bald eagle hatched this spring in the top of a huge ponderosa pine a couple of miles up the Clearwater River from the E-Bar-L Ranch. Perhaps someday he'll grow up to pose as the majestic symbol of American might, with a quiver of arrows in one clutch of talons, an olive branch in the other, and a necktie reading *E pluribus unum* under his aquiline face. But right now he's a loafer sponging off his folks.

"He's not very bright," Skipper said. "He's been taking preflight training and his groundwork is awful. Can't seem to get the hang of aerodynamics. He'll climb up on the edge of the nest and spread his wings till an updraft lifts him about eighteen inches. Then plotch, down in the nest, and he's all tuckered out. Lies down like a dog stretched out on his side."

A fellow didn't like to say it, but Junior is a lousy name for an eagle. He could have been called Sonny, after the Eagles' quarterback, or at least Young Bednarik. But Skipper found him and named him Junior, and that's that.

Mellow evening sunshine was like honey on the green valley of the Clearwater as Skipper drove up the bumpy, meandering trail. Long shadows mottled the lovely landscape. Skipper led a party of six, including Shammy, a genteel Labrador retriever the color of a vicuna coat.

"There," he said, pulling up at the base of a tall cone-shaped hill, "in that telephone booth." He pointed to a great, untidy tangle of sticks and debris about halfway up the hill in the scraggly top of a ponderosa. It looked like a poorly constructed outhouse and it was deserted. Suddenly from farther up came the sound of a rusty hinge on a swinging door.

"That's Mama," Skipper said, though this was plainly ridiculous. That discordant screeching bore no resemblance to the distress call of Eagle Patrol, Troop Five, Boy Scouts of America, Green Bay,

Wisconsin, which was a clear, prolonged cry of "Kreee!"

"Mama never read the Scout Manual," Skipper said apologetically, "so she doesn't know how an eagle's supposed to scream. Come on."

Now he was no longer Colin M. Lofting, steeplechase jockey, author, artist, cowboy, bucking horse rider, guitar player, angler and dove shooter. He was Sir Edmund Hillary leading his Sherpas in an assault on Everest.

"Here's Junior," he called from the crest. "Do you want that interview, or don't you?"

The answer from below was a labored gasp. "Sure (puff), but he'll (puff, puff) have to ask the (puff) questions."

Junior was a disheveled glob of feathers in the topmost branches of another ponderosa. His perch was level with the summit, enabling the climber to look him square in the eye at a forty-foot range. Obviously he had soloed to this point from the nest and he wasn't about to trust himself any further to the insubstantial air.

Shrieking imprecations, Mama wheeled great loops, her head and fantail gleaming white. Someday, no doubt, Junior would be an equally dressy bird, but now he was a shabby dark brindle from crown to ankle. He was a hell-of-a-baby, as big as Bobby Ussery, with a Durante nose. How he was ever packed into an egg is one of nature's mysteries.

"Wonder where the old man is," Skipper said.

"Probably this is his night to go bowling."

"I don't think so," Skipper said. "Mom and Pop are hardworking peasant stock. Scrimp and save, and nothing too good for their son. First time I saw 'em, I was fishing the pool down there and one of 'em came in about six feet over me. It was like a storm shutter sailing over my head. Grabbed a squawfish and flew off and was back in a matter of seconds, just working and slaving to feed this moocher."

"What does he need with fish?" somebody asked, slapping. "These mosquitoes are big enough to make a full meal."

"You going to interview him or not?" Skipper said.

"Okay. Junior, what do you think of the Wright brothers? Think they'll ever get it off the ground?"

Junior shook his head. It was the considered opinion that if the Creator meant eagles to fly, he'd equip them with Pratt-Whitney motors.

CANNON FODDER

1946

Mr. Jimmy Cannon, a Florida tourist who dislikes bloodshed, came upon the cadaver of a small fish "untimely ripp'd" from Tampa Bay the other day and the sight moved him to such a paroxysm of compassion that he devoted his entire column in the *New York Post* to a cry for vengeance upon all fishermen.

"Cruelty disguised as a sport!" Mr. Cannon raged in type that quivered on the page. "Fishing is the vice of the shirker and the rummy. No-works, ashamed of their laziness, cover it up by doing their loafing with a fishing line in their hands, while the honest man who spends his time on the couch, the porch or the street corner, is insulted for his indolence. Fishing is also used as an alibi by a lot of cowardly rum-bags. . . ."

For reasons that must be obvious to the regular reader, this agent —who, by the way, never has been insulted on a couch—should be the last guy in the world to complain about anyone else popping off without knowing what he's talking about. Therefore, not one hint shall appear here to suggest that Mr. Cannon is a habitué of the kippered-herring belt who wouldn't know a gudgeon from a parr if he ever had to rub fins with a live fish.

Furthermore, it is a scientific fact that all of us fishermen are gentle, patient, cheerful, devout, and virtuous. As the milkmaid's mother told Mr. I. Walton, "My Maudlin shall sing you one of her best ballads; for she and I both love all anglers, they be honest, civil, quiet men." We can take a sneak punch without yelling that the guy who threw it is a cad and a bounder who has libeled the noblest body of men outside a seminary.

Mr. Cannon, however, needn't think he can get away with putting the slug on rummies. There is altogether too much loose talk against lushes, who are, as a group, full of sunny generosity and good works, as Salvation Nell would testify after any night's tour of the gin mills with her tambourine. Mr. Cannon himself is off the juice, and it is well known there are none so intolerant as the dehydrated bibber who goes around with his tongue cleaving to the dry roof of his mouth unable to make any sound except "Tch, tch."

The belief that fishermen never go fishing without medication is erroneous. Before the war three of us were up in the Laurentian Mountains. Coming back to camp parched and weary after the first tough day of beating off voracious trout with a large, knobby club, we made a sudden and scarifying discovery.

"Hélas!" said M'sieu Roy, manager of the camp. "Nom du chien du cochon! Sacré bleu! Often have I seen the gentlemen, les pêcheurs, to come and forget the rods, forget the lines, forget the flies and forget the reels. But parbleu! Never have I seen them to forget the whiskey!"

He was aghast and so was the provincial government of Quebec, which, notified by telephone, sent a courier with a couple of imperial quarts pell-mell through the wilderness as though he were rushing serum to Nome. Which proves that we'll never go to war against Canada.

Thereafter we were equipped to while away evenings in the traditional manner of anglers as described by St. Izaak: "To tell tales, or sing ballads, or make a catch or find some harmless sport to content us, and pass away a little time without offense to God or man."

In his diatribe, Mr. Cannon exempts "the guys who go after marlin and barracuda and other big fish that have a gambling chance to jerk him overboard." Which proves that all Mr. Cannon knows about deep-sea fishing is what he reads in Zane Grey. The deep-sea fisherman takes his sport on a padded deck chair on a powerboat and wrenches his prey out of water by means of a block-and-tackle rigging supported by a sort of derrick built onto the craft. It is strictly no-contest, the whole purpose of this mechanized slaughter being to round out the cast for a snapshot which the angler will mail home with the inscription, "That's me on the left."

The true sportsman among anglers is the trout fisherman, who wades right into the fish's territory and battles it out hand to hand, taking an honest man's chance of being swept down the rapids and bashed against the rocks.

"I have," says Mr. Cannon, "done a little research with waitresses, bellhops, and bartenders. The waitresses say fishermen abuse them most and tip with a miser's caution."

Well, if Mr. Cannon says he has done research with waitresses, nobody has the right to dispute him. But if he talked fishing with 'em, it was the biggest form reversal since Jim Dandy won the Travers.

This is all we have to say in the matter, except to recall that Mr. Walton mentioned a Sir George Hastings, "an excellent angler, and now with God." This is documentary evidence of what happens to fishermen when they die. Does Mr. Cannon hope to do better?

FISH IN HER PANTIES

STURGEON BAY, WISCONSIN, 1974

Early in the morning the commercial fishermen put out from the east shore of Door County to visit their pond nets. Door County, sometimes called Swinging Door County, is a jagged spear of limestone that divides the waters of Lake Michigan on the east from those of Green Bay on the west. This was the doorway to New France almost two-and-a-half centuries ago for men like Jean Nicolet and Jacques Marquette, who came by canoe up the St. Lawrence and through the Great Lakes to dicker for the skins of beavers and the souls of Indians. Today the area is visited mostly by sportsmen bent on piscicide, for the coves and bays that notch both sides of the peninsula provide smallmouth bass fishing that is sometimes spectacular.

Twenty years ago commercial fishing here was dead and partly decomposed. The lamprey eel had wiped out Lake Michigan's whitefish and lake trout. When, at last, these predators were controlled, alewives became a plague, so coho salmon were introduced to eat them. Coho throve mightily, Chinook salmon and steelhead have been added to the fishery, and the trout and whitefish have made a great comeback.

Making the rounds of their pond nets, the commercial men clean their catch as they go, attracting a cloud of screaming gulls. Each day at almost the same hour, an osprey takes flight from his nest above a bluff on the Lake Michigan shore and bears down on the boat.

His target is not the craft itself, but the gulls in its wake. Invariably in his swift flight he picks out one bird that is making off with a kingsized serving of fish. Finding himself under attack, that scavanger accelerates in frantic flight but in a race the fishhawk can give a herring gull twenty pounds and catch him at any pole.

The gull keeps trying, though, until the last few seconds. Then with a scream of terror he drops his blue-plate special and flees. The osprey dives, scoops up his breakfast, and makes his leisurely way back to the table.

This green thumb of Wisconsin is the pleasantest part of the state, though it is not so widely known as the Chain of Lakes country around Eagle River and Rhinelander or Lac du Flambeau and the Brule River, where they used to keep big trout tethered so Calvin Coolidge, wearing a high starched collar and a bloodless expression as he fished, could pleasure himself on vacation from the White House.

For years before the arrival of the coho, Chinook and steelhead, the tenant in this literary flophouse came to Door County annually to commit piscicide. From Sturgeon Bay to Death's Door, from Moonlight Bay to Mink River, he made war against smallmouth, barred yellow perch, and an occasional great northern pike.

This visit is a brief one, allowing no time for angling but plenty for reviving memories. It is a privilege to report that fifteen years have not disturbed the pure and sparkling peace of North Bay; that Peninsula State Park between Fish Creek and Ephraim has preserved its scenic purity in spite of a camper explosion; that the Strawberry Islands remain flawless emeralds on a background of blue satin; and that the remarkable seiche of Rowleys Bay still oscillates from flood to ebb tide to flood every twenty minutes.

These are not, of course, the only attractions of this region. If and when the Green Bay Packers reopen for business, their fans in Sturgeon Bay can get down to see them play in less time than a New Yorker needs to follow the Giants to New Haven. Nor is the drive to Milwaukee any hardship for the baseball fan who wants to catch Reggie Jackson's or Gaylord Perry's act.

At a dozen or more points between here and Green Bay, Highway 57 crosses brooks that are dry now in mid-summer, but carry a fair flow in late winter and early spring. A motorist traveling the road after dark in that season is puzzled now and then to see dozens of cars parked on both shoulders of the highway, as though the whole population of Dyckesville or Brussels or both were gathered for a country wedding or a fish boil or maybe a chicken booyah. The puzzling thing is that there will be no light showing anywhere, no house or saloon where a party could be going on.

It may take the newcomer a night or so to realize that the spawning run of smelt is on and these little streams that empty into the bay are jelly-thick with tens of thousands of small, delicious fish working up the creeks to make love. That explains the parked cars; their owners are lined up along the banks scooping smelt into buckets.

In some years during a good run it is possible to back a truck down to the water and shovel it full of fish. Twenty miles across the bay from here, the Menominee River marks the border of Wisconsin and the northern peninsula of Michigan. Near its mouth a bridge connects Marinette, Wisconsin, with Menominee, Michigan.

One spring there was frenzied activity on and near the bridge. Smelt were coming upstream by the millions and gourmets were scooping them up with any equipment they could lay hands on. One caught everyone's attention, partly because of her ample dimensions and partly because of her ebullience but mostly because of her imaginative fishing tackle:

Rigged on a hoop attached to a stout cord, she had a pair of lady's bloomers, weighted and tied shut at the knees. From her perch on the bridge she lowered her lingerie into the river, let it sink and then, whooping with triumphant laughter, hauled up panties wriggling with smelt.

YOUNG MAN WITH FLYROD

1951

Vacation was almost over when Mr. Sparse Gray Hackle called and said how about a weekend of matching wits with the trout that live in the Neversink River. Frankly, it looked like an overmatch from the beginning, but it had been the sort of vacation that cried aloud for relief.

A task force of three was made up swiftly. It included a young man of twelve, going on thirteen, who had never before attempted to mislead a trout with a tuft of feather and barb of steel. He had, however, shown an encouraging spirit several summers earlier when he was eight or nine and used to accompany his parent on forays against the smallmouth bass of Wisconsin. The pair would angle lazily through the mornings from a rowboat until the noonday sun drove them ashore. Then they'd seek out the nearest crossroads tavern, where each would satisfy his appetite according to his needs.

On one such day the young man stuffed his face with a ham sandwich, slaked down the mess with a Coke, and observed: "Gee, Dad, this is the life, ain't it? Fishing and eating in saloons."

There was to be no eating in saloons on the Neversink expedition. Mr. Hackle had arranged for accommodations with Mrs. George Stailing, a patient and gracious lady whose farmhouse near Claryville offers immaculate lodging and prodigious fodder and commands a tempting stretch of river. Adroitly dodging thunderbolts that came crashing down out of the Catskills, the car crept through the rainy darkness and made bivouac there.

At least one member of the party had a sleepless night and admitted it next morning, shamefaced, because it does seem childish to get so keyed up on the eve of a day in a trout stream. Always happens, though.

The young man and Mr. Hackle had slept soundly and they set a punishing pace on the mile-and-a-half hike into the water formerly held by Mr. Ed Hewitt. This is open water now, soon to be converted from river to lake when a dam, in construction, creates a new reservoir so that New Yorkers may have water to emasculate their Scotch. It is beautiful water that comes boiling down out of the great, greenish Camp Pool through a long, rocky run; it was still perfectly clear after a night of rain and, said Mr. Hackle, who knows the river, it was low.

Mr. Hackle set one of his company to floating a dry fly into the broken water at the head of the run. The fly was a big White Wulff, and as it rode the wavelets tiny brook trout slapped at it impudently. They came to no harm. Perhaps they only flicked it with their tails, not actually trying to bite the fly. Or maybe they took sample nibbles, said "Pfui," and spat at leisure, properly confident that the dope holding the rod couldn't get his reflexes working in time to sink the barb into their sassy faces.

Meanwhile Sparse had tied a wet fly to the young man's leader and led him to the middle of the run and watched as the first cast was made. The first cast took a fish. Details can be distasteful. If it was a very young and very small and very inexperienced fish, there is no point in mentioning that. The young man was young and inexperienced, too.

The point is, the young man made one cast and got a rise and set the hook and got the trout home and then sent him about his business with a sore lip and, presumably, greater wisdom than he had possessed before.

Mr. Hackle, who realizes that the great teacher is the one who knows when to let well enough alone, retired to the tail of the run, where he caught and released a couple of juveniles. His pair and the young man's singleton were the only fish hooked that day. That didn't matter; there'd be another chance the next day.

"It's sure got it over bass fishing," the young man said. When he was reminded that he had drawn blood on the first cast of his life, he had the grace to smile in deprecation of the size of his catch. He did not remark that there was, really, nothing difficult about this game.

When it was mentioned that he was the only member of his family to catch a trout in 1951, he laughed with pleasure and made no comment. No intelligible comment, anyway. He was down on all fours in a bramble patch at the moment and his mouth was full of wild raspberries.

8.

Offbeat

THE STUDENT ATHLETE

Some edifying words about student athletes were heard on the air over the weekend: Whenever a college football game is on radio or television, it is accompanied by edifying words about student athletes, about the importance of intercollegiate athletics in a rounded educational program and about the vital role played by the National Collegiate Athletic Association. The edifying words are composed by writers for the N.C.A.A.

Student athlete is a term susceptible to various definitions. It can mean a biochemistry major who participates in sports, or a Heisman Trophy candidate who is not necessarily a candidate for a bachelor's degree. Some student athletes are more studious than athletic, and vice versa.

There is at hand a piece written by a student athlete in his senior year at a major university that has been polishing young intellects for more than a century. He is an attractive young man, short months away from graduation, the best wide receiver in the school. One of his professors, who happens to be a football buff, asked him why his teammate, John Doe, never played first string although he was a better passer than Richard Spelvin, the starting quarterback. The young man said he would write the answer "like it was a quiz."

What follows is an exact copy of the young man's answer. That is, it is exact except for the names. The quarterbacks are not really named John Doe and Richard Spelvin and the university's athletic teams are not known as the Yankees.

People (Some) feel that Doe did not have the ability to run the type of offense that the yankys ran. He also made some mistakes with the ball like fumbling.

As a wide receiver it didn't make me any different who quarterback. But I feel he has the best arm I ever saw or play with on a team. Only why I feel the I do about the quarterback position is because I am a receiver who came from J.C. out of state I caught a lot of pass over 80 and I did not care a damn thing but about 24 in one year.

Spelvin is my best friend and quarterback at my J.C. school. Spelvin has an arm but when you don't thrown lot of half the time I dont care who you are you will not peform as best you can. Spelvin can run, run the team and most of all he makes little mistakes.

So since they didn't pass Spelvin was our quarterback. But if we did pass I feel Spelvin still should of start but Doe should have play a lot. Tell you the truth the yanky's in the pass two years had the best combintion of receivers in a season that they will ever have. More—ask to talk about politics alum Doe problems just before the season coaches hate?

The last appears to be a suggestion that alumni politics may have played a part in the coaches' decision on which quarterback would play first string. However, the professor who forwarded this material did so without comment or explanation.

The importance of disguising the names of these student athletes and the identity of the university is obvious. It would be unforgivable to hold a kid up to public ridicule because his grip on a flying football was surer than his grasp of the mother tongue. He is only a victim. The culprit is the college, and the system.

The young man's prose makes it achingly clear how some institutions of learning use some athletes. Recruiters besiege a high school senior with bulging muscles and sloping neck who can run 40 yards in 4.3 seconds. The fact that he cannot read without facial contortions may be regrettable, but if his presence would help make a team a winner, then they want his body and are not deeply concerned about his mind.

Some colleges recruit scholar athletes in the hope that the scholar can spare enough time from the classroom to help the team. Others recruit athletes and permit them to attend class if they can spare the time from the playing field. If the boy was unprepared for college when he arrived, he will be unqualified for a degree four years later, but some culture foundries give him a degree as final payment for his services.

One widely accepted definition of the role of a college is "to prepare the student for life after he leaves the campus." If the young man quoted above gets a job as wide receiver for the Green Bay Packers, then perhaps the university will have fulfilled its purpose. However, only a fraction of college players can make a living in the National Football League. Opportunities are even more limited for college basketball players, for pro basketball employs fewer players.

Where outside of pro football can our wide receiver go? He can pump gas. He can drive a truck. He has seen his name in headlines, has heard crowds cheering him, has enjoyed the friendship and admiration of his peers and he has a diploma from a famous university. It is unconscionable.

TEA'S A DAMNED FINE DRINK

1939

It seemed that a fellow living in a city surrounded by a Germantown Cricket Club, a Philadelphia Cricket Club, and a Merion Cricket Club ought to make it his business to know something about the great game that is not played at the Merion Cricket Club, the Philadelphia Cricket Club, and the Germantown Cricket Club.

So this week we went out to Haverford College to see the all-star team from Chicago play Philadelphia's General Electric cricketers, who, you doubtless will be pleased to know, are champions of the East. We were moderately pleased to know it until we saw the Chicagos polish off the Electrics with an ease that suggested being champions of the East was something like winning the first-half pennant in the Three-Eye League.

This impression was strengthened when we asked how the cricketers more or less in action before us would compare with the better teams in England. The inquiry brought well-bred shrugs which seemed to infer that none of these chaps could carry the bat of a player on one of England's county teams.

Still, it was possible, by watching closely and listening attentively to Mr. K. A. Auty and Mr. J. H. Grudgings, to gather sprigs of information about this delightfully desultory, ingratiatingly indolent sport.

Mr. Auty is president of the Illinois and Chicago Cricket Associations and the United States Rugby Association, and Mr. Grudgings is president of the General Electric Cricket Club and when they were young in Loughboro, they used to go sparking with the same girls. But they never met until this week.

Like Mr. Auty and Mr. Grudgings, practically everyone on the sidelines and all but one of the players were of English birth. The exception was O. R. Jones, the Electrics' wicket-keeper, or stumper, or, to use a baseball analogy, catcher.

As a matter of fact, Mr. Jones used to be a baseball catcher, and a lefthanded one at that, which possibly accounts for his taking up cricket. From old habit he wears only one glove, on his right hand, instead of one on each hand, as most stumpers do.

Baseball analogies come readily to mind because, quoting Mr. Auty, who writes books about it, cricket is "polite baseball." By polite he means nobody hurries very much and they take time out for tea and there's no swearing at the umpires or fighting and players can stay in the game up to the ripe athletic age of seventy-odd.

Indeed, players can reach a fairly ripe age in a single match, although the series of "friendlies" the Chicago club is playing in the

East are piddling little one-inning matches played out practically like a flash in five or six hours.

We hadn't intended to bring up the matter of the tea, thinking the gentlemen might suspect us of sharing that slightly condescending attitude of many Americans toward the English fondness for the beverage. But Mr. Auty brought it up while talking about how tired a fellow gets playing all afternoon in the hot sun.

"That's why we drink tea," he said. "It's refreshing and invigorating and one shouldn't take cold drinks when he's all heated up. Tea, it's a damned fine drink."

And sure enough, we had a dish between half-innings and it was good, although personally, as a health measure, we have always leaned toward bourbon and away from these fancy drinks.

Well, anyway, cricket is played on a crease, which is a 66-foot strip of lush, smooth turf in the middle of a great big field. When the Merion and such creases were laid out, shiploads of special turf were brought from England. That's why the local cricket clubs have such elegant lawn tennis courts; they used to be creases.

Because the Haverford turf isn't smooth enough, a long mat of coconut fiber just like a 60-foot doormat was used. At each end was a wicket, constructed of three slender sticks about 16 inches tall stuck insecurely into the earth with two smaller sticks, or bails, laid across the top.

The batsman stands in a chalked-off space in front of the wicket, wielding a 28-inch flat bat of seasoned willow that costs 12½ clamshells, or fish, as we say in England. He wears hobnailed boots of buckskin that cost about 35 smackers and whatever other clothes appeal to him, and tries to bat a hard cowhide-covered ball that costs three bucks and a half. Fearful of appearing crassly American, we didn't find out the price of the shin protectors and gloves batsmen and stumpers wear.

The bowler stands well back of the far wicket, takes a running start and delivers the ball with a stiff-armed, overhand motion, completing his delivery before his rear foot passes his wicket. He is not required to bounce the ball in front of the batsman but he almost always does because this enables him to bowl hooks; the English he puts on the ball takes effect on the bounce.

If the batsman misses a strike and lets the ball knock down the wicket behind him he's out. If his bat knocks the wicket over he's out. If he hits a fly to a fielder he's out. If he protects the wicket with his leg he's out on a "leg before," or l. b. w. If he strides out of the batter's box and doesn't get back with a foot or the end of his bat before the stumper tags the wicket with the ball, he's out.

If a hit eludes the fielders, the batsman and the nonstriking batsman, who'll be standing near the other wicket waiting for his turn with the shillelagh, race back and forth from wicket to wicket, scoring a run each time they exchange wickets.

If a fielder throws the ball back and hits the wicket, or throws to the stumper who tags the wicket, before a batsman "makes his ground," the batter's out. Making his ground means getting safely to the batting box.

Even with all these ways of retiring 'em, it's pretty hard to get a good batter out. That's because he needn't run except when he is sure it's safe. The only time he can score runs without running is on the equivalent of a home run. If his hit rolls over the boundary of the field he gets four runs automatically; if it lands on or beyond the boundary he gets six. Or in case of an illegal delivery or a "wide," a ball bowled beyond his reach, he gets one run automatically.

There's no such thing as a foul ball and the best hits, or shots, are those sliced adroitly past fielders in what would, in baseball, be foul territory. When a batsman comes up with a good one of these, the spectators call, "Nicely, nicely."

They say one of the slickest "bats" of all time was the Maharajajam-sahib of Nawanagar, better known as Prince Ranjitsinghi, or just Ranji for short. He used to squirt hits all the way to the boundary behind him, which is about like slapping a foul tip into the bleachers. Ranji could, and did, bat two double centuries in a single match on a single day (smack in 400 runs in a game) and 3,000 runs a season was an old story to him.

When a sequence of eight balls has been bowled to one batsman that constitutes an "over," the fielders shift positions and the other batsman is up. Maybe the same bowler will serve to him or maybe he'll go into the outfield and some fielder will take a turn at bowling. There are likely to be as many as eight bowlers on a team, all playing the outfield when not bowling.

"Bowling a maiden over," means, no matter what you think, bowling a runless sequence of eight balls.

We won't go into the origin of the names of fielding positions. Suffice to say they're called first slip, second slip, point, coverpoint, midoff, midon, long on, square leg, and such.

Sometimes a batsman scores, say 50 runs, and decides to quit and give someone else a chance, even though he hasn't been put out. "That," Mr. Auty explained, soberly using a familiar expression, "is considered cricket."

Umpires never make decisions except on appeal. Should a batsman helpfully pick up the ball and return it to the bowler and a member of the team afield were to appeal to the umpire on the technicality that rules forbid a batsman touching the ball with his hands, the batsman would be out. But such a picayune appeal wouldn't be cricket, sir.

In the match we saw, one gentleman, who has varicose veins, asked for a pinch-runner. That didn't mean he had to leave the game. He just had a teammate stand beside him and do his running for him.

The gentlemen generally seemed just a wee bit disdainful of the talents of our professional ballplayers. Nevertheless it seemed to us a cove like Jimmy Foxx or Joe Medwick could, with a little practice, whip the socks off the ordinary cricketer.

But then Arthur Brisbane's gorilla probably could whip 'em all.

RENDEZVOUS WITH DANGER

INDIANAPOLIS, 1948

A fat, jovial man is sitting on the tailboard of a small enclosed truck inside the first turn of the Indianapolis Motor Speedway. His machine is four rows back from the rail, one among thousands and thousands of cars that stand, glittering under the sun, almost as far as the eye can see across this clamorous, hideous cauldron of noise and speed and reeking oil. On the truck's floor is a bed of straw with tangled blankets and mussed pillows. The man says he and two friends— "three bachelors from Gary"—drove over yesterday and pulled up in line maybe half a mile outside the gate about eight o'clock last night

"How was the sleeping in here?"

"Fine. We had a great time. Left the truck in line and went into town and drank coffee all night. The line started moving in at five this morning. Have a can of beer?"

At his feet, a metal box holds beer cans in melting ice. He has a box of crackers open at his knees, a beer in his hand, and around him are paper parcels of food.

"You're pretty well stocked. Can you see the race from the truck top?"

"Not so good. We were over by that gate awhile. Couldn't see anything from there, either."

"Kind of a long drag, wasn't it, waiting all night and not seeing much now?"

"Yes, but it was worth it. Sure you won't have a beer?"

This particular area, where the infield crowds fight for position near the turn because the turns are the danger points in the annual five-hundred-mile race, offering the likeliest opportunity to see a man untidily killed, is an indescribable place, a grassy slum of gay squalor.

Here a fat woman in halter and shorts sits sunning herself on a camp stool. There a girl in slacks lies sprawled in sleep beneath a truck. The car tops are cluttered like windowsills along the Third Avenue El, covered with mattresses and blankets and seat cushions and homemade platforms supporting boxes, chairs, folding stools.

The car interiors have the homey, lived-in look of beds that haven't been made up for three days. Some have blankets or newspapers hung over windows and windshield for protection from the sun and a smidgen of privacy. The men are virtually all coatless, for it's a warmish day, and many are peeled to the waist. There's one shaving in front of his rear-view mirror. When a luggage compartment is opened, it generally reveals a washtub of iced beer.

There is a skeleton skyline of scaffolding, mostly unpainted two-by-fours set up astraddle the automobiles and supporting an observation platform perhaps fifteen feet high. Some are professional jobs of structural steel, bolted together and rising as high as twenty-five feet.

One of the tallest and certainly the most precarious looking consists of two double-length painters' ladders propped up in an inverted V. Two or three planks thrust between the upper rungs make unsteady perches against the sky.

The earth is a vast litter of crushed lunch boxes and tattered paper and beer cans and whiskey bottles and banana skins and orange peels and the heels of used sandwiches and blankets and raiment and people. Over everything is the reek of burning castor oil, the incessant, nerve-shattering roar of racing motors.

This is the Indianapolis "500," a gigantic, grimy lawn party, a monstrous holiday compounded of dust and danger and noise, the world's biggest carnival midway and the closest sporting approach permitted by the Humane Society to the pastimes which once made the Roman Colosseum known as the Yankee Stadium of its day (cars are used in this entertainment because the S.P.C.A. frowns on lions).

The speedway is a rambling, ramshackle plant enclosed by two and a half miles of brick-paved track and the only space not jammed is the nine-hole golf course in the remotest part of the infield. Through binoculars from the press loft, couples can be seen reclining in comradely embrace beneath the trees on the links, but there seem to be no golfers.

It is said there are 175,000 people here, although gates started to close half an hour before race time. At that morning hour the Purdue University band was on the track giving brassy evidence of the advantages of higher education. At length these embryo Sammy Kayes tied into the national anthem and followed with "Taps," just in case. Bombs went off. Rockets burst in air, making a heavy flak pattern below cruising planes. James Melton sang "Back Home Again in Indiana" slowly, a full four seconds off the track record.

The cars had been pushed into place, three abreast in eleven ranks. Their drivers, goggled and helmeted, looked like Buck Rogers cut-outs. The flying start was a burst of thunder, a blur of colors. Since then, it has been an unceasing grind, hour after hour, making the eyeballs ache, the temples throb. Every car has a different voice, none soothing. There is a twelve-cylinder Mercedes said to have been built for Adolf Hitler; it runs with a scream like Adolf's conscience.

Now, late in the race, the favored lane near the outside, which is called "the groove," has been blackened with oil. Coming down the straightaway, the cars skitter nervously on this slick, swinging their hips like Powers models. Most of the thirteen drivers still in the race steer to the cleaner bricks inside the strip.

Duke Nalon stays in the groove, though, and is leading with only fifteen of the two hundred laps remaining. He has the fastest, most powerful brute of a car ever put on this track, but its speed requires a special fuel which gives poor mileage, and now he pulls in for refueling. The crowd gives him a yell, the first time its voice has been heard all day. The pit crew works swiftly, finishes, can't get the motor started again. The car starts once, dies, and must be pushed back to the pit for more feverish seconds. This is the day's most exciting moment.

When Nalon finally goes away, to another small cheer, Mauri Rose and Bill Holland are ahead of him. The race is over; it was lost there at the gas pump.

BICYCLES IN THE ALPS

GAP, FRANCE, 1960

From the summit of the mountain called Col de Perty, misty Alpine peaks stretched away in wave after gray-blue wave, as far as the eye could reach. The morning had been hot in Avignon in the soft valley of the Rhône, but up here, 4,000 feet in the sky, a fresh wind was blowing, stiff and chilling. Col de Perty is a barren knob not close to anything or anybody, yet it looked like the bleachers in Yankee Stadium on a good day with the White Sox.

From somewhere, by some means, they had come by the hundreds —wide-eyed kids and old pappy guys and wizened peasant women and young guys and exuberant girls waved at the press cars whirring by. A smiling doll had a counter of plain boards set up, where she sold razor-thin salami in yesterday's bread, and nearby was another hutch offering soft drinks and beer.

They had been waiting for two or three hours, perched on rocks or camp chairs or just meandering about. Now a sense of expectancy came over them all as a squadron of cops on motor bikes came around the shoulder of the mountain. Then from the crowd on the highest slope came a buzz that grew into a hum and finally a babble.

Bicyclists in bright jerseys emerged from behind a rocky promontory. They came straining bitterly, leaning on the pedals, teeth clenched, shaved limbs glistening with sweat—a little group of leaders in single file, then a gap, then a long cluster, then the laggards.

This was the Tour de France topping the first challenging peak of the Alpine section of the course. There would be more and tougher heights to scale later, but this was enough to split out the men from the boys.

The Tour de France, now being contested for the forty-seventh time since 1903, is an annual bike race of 2,600 miles around the perimeter of France, over the Pyrenees and over the Alps. Some of the roads are terrifying in a car, but these characters go pumping a hundred-odd miles a day at something like twenty-five miles an hour.

There is nothing in America even remotely comparable with it. We think the World Series claims the undivided attention of the United States, but there is a saying here that an Army from Mars could invade France, the government could fall, and even the recipe for sauce Béarnaise be lost, but if it happened during the Tour de France nobody would notice.

Today's leg was the fifteenth of the course that began June 26 at Lille in the North, took the riders up into Belgium through Brussels and down the west coast, then east to this corner near Italy and Switzerland. Of the 120 starters, 88 had made it into Avignon last night, hoping to reach Paris on July 17.

In that ancient walled city which once was the seat of popes, there was festival last night but there was also mourning for the loss of a favorite, Roger Rivière from the French team. On yesterday's run he had plunged off the road, hurtled through a gap in the retaining wall and plummeted seventy-five feet, winding up in the hospital with a broken vertebra and a highly intelligent statement: "You shall see me no more on a bicycle."

In the overall time reckoning, he had been second, only one minute thirty-six seconds behind Italy's Gastone Nencini, who set off again this morning in the yellow jersey of the leader, probably the most coveted, and sweatiest, piece of apparel in Europe.

This is the order of march in this implausible parade: an hour before the cyclists start, the "publicity caravan" departs, a great parade of sound trucks and shills advertising commercial products. Then a platoon of motorcyclists clears the road for the racers, who are followed by a control car and then a double file of press, radio, television, and team cars carrying the team managers and spare parts for broken bikes.

Out of Avignon it was fairly level going for a while, with the whole field pumping along in one great clot. In every village, streets were jammed. All along the country roads there were family groups waving and cheering.

For the first 50 miles of this 110-mile leg, the road climbed gently toward the foothills of the Alps. Then the high hills began, capped here and there by fortifications left over since the Roman Empire. Past a village named Pierrelongue, Albert Geldermann of Holland went into a ditch, crawled out with blood streaming down his left leg, swiftly replaced a bent wheel, remounted, and pumped hard to catch up with the pack. (There is shortwave radio control that brings up a team car or the race's attending doctor on quick notice.)

As the narrow road wound through a gorge, a Belgian named Louis Proost crashed against the retaining wall. He remounted but he was badly knocked about, and in a mile or so he had to give up. He wobbled over against the wall and sagged there, crying like a child.

They went sweating up Col de Perty, went ripping down the far side at a bloodcurdling fifty miles an hour, and now the field had stretched out, with five riders in a cluster about a mile ahead of the main pack. Behind the latter were the stragglers, followed closely by a car that is called the *camion balai,* the "broom truck," which gathers up the debris.

Then it was up again around devastating hairpin turns to Col de la Sentinelle and finally down to this village, with a wild sprint down a tree lined street with Belgium's Michel Van Aerde beating a Dutchman named Van den Borgh by inches for the day's lap prize. The villagers milled and swooped and cheered and a dozen radio announcers babbled and a truck rolled by advertising bananas, "the fruit in the yellow jersey."

IN THE DOGHOUSE

1948

According to the best contemporary literature, red, raw courage is stock equipment in Madison Square Garden, the nation's most celebrated blood pit. Never was the truth of this brought home more effectively than when the intrepid management covered the entire Garden floor with an expanse of pale green carpet for the Westminster Kennel Club show. This, of course, is written from the viewpoint of one who recently entered the service of a puppy.

A visit was made to the Garden for the dual purpose of schneering at the other dachshunds and admiring the ladies who are led across the ring by the toy breeds. It is a scientific fact that the ladies tethered to the tiny toys are invariably the most magnificent members of the species. No exception was taken in this case; the smallest pooch noted was towing the largest handler, a celestial creature measuring seventeen and a half hands at the withers, deep of chest, with fine, sturdy pasterns.

Apparently the dog business, like any other, is a matter of ups and downs. For example, Walter Foster, who used to handle the imposing boxer, Ch. Warload of Mazelaine, winner of best of show last year, showed up in the toy class this time as handler of a pug named Abbeyville Personality, which wasn't even a ch. Whether going from boxers to pugs represents progress or decline is a matter of opinion.

Strictly speaking, dog show fans are not sport fans at all, but claques. Thus a terrier man will beat his palms raw when the Boston, Ch. Mighty Sweet Regardless, is in the ring, but would die before he'd emit a peep of applause for any other breed. The lady customers are less discriminating. They squealed with joy over all the toys and strained their stays for a Yorkshire named Ch. Little Boy Blue of Yorktown, whose weeping-willow coiffure suggested a set of old-fashioned portieres.

There was also considerable enthusiasm when a lady working a large white poodle rushed back and forth across the ring at a pace which ladies usually reserve for catching a bus. With the puffball of ermine keeping pace at her heels, she looked like somebody fleeing an avalanche of snow.

A personal favorite in the nonsporting group was a bulldog named Ch. Michael Pendergast, who looks exactly like Babe Ruth in his prime, even imitating the Babe's jaunty waddle. However, spectator sympathy was clearly with the defending champion, Mighty Sweet Regardless, and there was no denying that this is a comely bone-polisher with the strut of a drum major.

Chances are the judge makes up his mind the first time he runs his eye over the group and goes through the interminable mumbo-jumbo which ensues just to get the crowd wheed up and to prevent the also-rans from hollering that he gave their pets the brush.

In this respect, the judge of the nonsporting group, a Dr. M. Ross Taylor, proved himself a ch. among chs. He was imperious; he was painstakingly studious; he was profoundly authoritative of mien. He had splendid conformation—broad shoulders, white hair and an erect carriage—and was beautifully turned out in an ensemble of rich brown.

One was inclined to hope that he would, in the end, award first prize to himself. But after what seemed a positive fit of indecision he gave the duke to Mighty Sweet, whereupon the crowd howled approval and a phalanx of photographers rushed forward, flash bulbs popping. At this point a tour of the basement was begun with a guide who knows about dogs. All contestants are housed downstairs in stalls awaiting their appearance on the show floor. The guide paused before a stall occupied by a dog and a slight, sandy man wearing a loud sports jacket.

"This," the guide said, "is a liver hound with a light chestnut horse player."

"Afghans," the guide said, gesturing down a row of stalls containing gray, furry, floppy things sprawled out and dozing. You could see why they're called Afghans. They look just like those knitted businesses which wives keep folded on the couch for taking afternoon naps under.

The guide was pleased to come upon a dog voraciously eating a copy of the show catalogue, price $1.25. "Very rare breed," he said, "called a comma hound, or copyreader. Look what he's done to that first paragraph."

JAPANESE BOMBARDMENT

SANTA BARBARA, CALIFORNIA, 1942

The Japs knew exactly what they were shooting at when they shelled the Elwood oilfields near here last night.

Those weren't token shells fired at random just anywhere along the coast merely to furnish an audacious punctuation of President Roosevelt's radio address.

It was not blundering accident that led the submarine into the little cove below the bluff where derricks, storage tanks and the Barnsdall absorption plant stand.

That is old, familiar ground to the enemy. For years before the United States embargoed oil shipments to Japan, Nipponese tankers used to put in there and take on cargoes from the loading platform.

It was only because of the gunners' bad aim that no damage was done.

All this was common gossip today among eyewitnesses.

"I'd been expecting it, of course," said matronly, fifty-five-year-old Mrs. Hilda Wheeler, who watched from her backyard as shells exploded three hundred yards away.

"You see, when the soldiers were here everyone talked about the possibility of an attack. The boys said the one thing they wanted most was to get a Jap sub, and then, of course, we all knew the Japs had been coming in here all those years."

English-born, Mrs. Wheeler and her husband, Laurence, operate a restaurant on the shore side of El Camino Real, California's main coast highway about a half mile from the craggy beach at this point. The kitchen window looks out upon the wells and tanks.

Today Mrs. Wheeler stood in the kitchen, her hands folded across her print apron, patiently struggling to help prepare meals for the customers while newspaper men and photographers clamored about her. Her attitude was one of pleased yet quiet excitement as she told her story.

She had been working in the kitchen when the first shell burst. A deep, heavy boom accompanied by the rattle of gravel against the nearest oil tank. Then the whine. Then the slap of the gun's report.

"I saw earth fly up in a sort of fan. Then I realized it was the Japs. I ran out back there to watch."

"Weren't you scared? Didn't you think of ducking for cover?"

She smiled.

"Would you, with all those fireworks going on? It was fascinating. You kept wondering where they'd hit next. I could see the flashes and I thought, 'Oh, they're aiming for the tanks and the plant.'

"There must have been a dozen, maybe more. I heard one whine over the place here. I believe it landed up there in the orange groves toward the hills.

"I remember that when it stopped I thought, 'Why hasn't Papa come outside?' No, I wasn't scared. Just a little queer feeling here."

She pressed a palm against her waist.

"Hotcakes, mother," her husband said, shouldering in from the dining room.

"Please," Mrs. Wheeler protested, "no more pictures. I just have to make hotcakes. Why don't you get someone who's prettier?

"No, please, I have a very intelligent son, and he and his wife saw it all and I'm sure they can tell you anything more—

"Oh well, yes, I had a fine sleep last night. As soon as I knew the soldiers were here, I felt perfectly safe."

As she talked, others were telling what they saw. Gerald Otto Brown, forty, a wispy little tractor operator for the Signal Oil Company, had driven up from Los Angeles about half an hour before the attack.

"I was sitting in my car on the company lease near the beach," he related, "listening to the President's talk. He just got to the point where he said:

" 'We have most certainly suffered losses—from Hitler's U-boats in the Atlantic as well as from the Japanese in the Pacific—and we shall suffer more—'

"He just reached that when I heard a shot. I asked the caretaker if it was artillery practice and he said no, there wasn't any here. So I ran up to the edge of the bluff where I could see.

"I was out on the north point of the cove, about a mile above the sub. I'd judge the Japs were a mile offshore. It was just getting dark, but I could see the gun crews working. There were two of them.

"Most of the shells seemed to hit the cliff face. I kept thinking what a swell target the sub would have made, just lying there on the surface broadside to the shore.

"I saw the sub turn and move away. When it got too dark for me to see, it was still on the surface.

"Afterward I heard a funny thing in Wheeler's place. It seems there were some customers there listening to the President and they didn't all run outside. One woman said:

"'Well, the President doesn't seem excited. Just keeps talking through it all.'"

Some of the nicest people of lovely, wealthy Santa Barbara drove up the coast today to see the shelling. The soldiers spoiled all the fun, though. Wouldn't let anybody onto oil company land to see the craters.

Still, it was a lark. Exciting. Something to talk about. That's the way the residents of this strip of coast took it; sat through a four-hour blackout when all civilian movement was halted, then went to bed when all-clear sounded at 12:20 A.M.

Many had no idea what happened. At 5:00 A.M. a tall, young man was encountered in the Southern Pacific Railroad station here. His eyes grew wide when he was shown a newspaper.

"Well, my gosh," he said slowly, "now that's getting right close to home, isn't it?

"I heard the blackout whistle and went outside to listen, but I couldn't hear anything. I had to go downtown at four o'clock today to get my uniform, so I went to bed early."

Uniform for what?

"I go in the Army today. They kind of gave me a sendoff, eh?"

GORGEOUS GEORGE

1948

The announcement which came through the mail bore the return address of Mr. Toots Mondt, the rassling tycoon. It read:

"The most sensational wrestler of all time—the man who has swept the national (sic) with his personality and color and the fact that he is different—Gorgeous George is here at last! You are cordially invited for cocktails and the first New York appearance of Gorgeous George in New York at Marye Ward, Hair Stylists, 356 East 57th Street. The pride of Hollywood and everywhere else he's appeared is scheduled for a hair marcel and will then play host to the Press of New York whom he's been most anxious to meet. Don't miss it!"

Well, the back room of this ladies' barber shop was pretty well jammed when Gorgeous George arrived, wearing long blond curls and somewhat formal afternoon attire—black coat with mother-of-pearl buttons on the sleeve, soft white shirt with nine-inch points on the collar, striped trousers hung on braces. Ahead of him came a valet spraying the joint with an atomizer.

"That's George No. 4 in the atomizer," said a man with curly black hair and a fairly fancy suit of a small, checked pattern. "He never enters a ring that hasn't been sprayed with it first."

Gorgeous George sat in front of a mirror and a couple of barbers with curly black hair took down his hair and started putting it up in little metal gimmicks. Gorgeous George has a thick red neck and the features of a Roman senator.

A rather awed crowd clustered around Gorgeous George, talking. From the background, only an occasional phrase could be heard. Once George said, "In other words, allus I do is what I please and nobody stops me." Somebody else suggested the hairdo was decidedly feminine and George flew into a noble tizzy, shouting about George Washington and other distinguished characters who wore long hair.

In the background, the man in the checked suit was talking. He said he was a rassler himself and George's business manager, name of Sammy Menacher. He displayed a program of some shindig run by a thing called a Coiffure Guild in Hollywood.

"Each year," he said, "they pick a Coiffure Queen out there. See? Here's a picture of this year's queen, Frances Langford. This year, for the first time, they picked a Coiffure King. See? Here's a picture of Gorgeous George. 'Our King,' it says here. The hairdo he's got, that's the Gorgeous George Swirl."

"Has this critter a name?" Mr. Menacher was asked.

"Gorgeous George is his legal name."

"What's alleged to be his history?"

"He started wrestling nineteen years ago," Mr. Menacher said, "when he was fourteen. About six years ago he started letting his hair grow. It was black. Then he had it bleached, the way it is now. No, that's not platinum blond, or even honey blond. It's Lana Turner blond.

"He's got fifty-nine dressing gowns and the sixtieth is being made. One has an ermine cape. No, not quite a stole, more like a collar. He never wears the same dressing gown into the same arena twice. His valet keeps a chart."

"Is he a fiend in the ring," Mr. Menacher was asked, "or an All-American Boy?"

"He is savage," Mr. Menacher said. "He is a rough customer in there. That's the amazing thing, the way he changes."

"Amazing to whom?"

"To the public," Mr. Menacher said.

"It's the worst corn I ever saw," said Mr. Mondt, whose orange hair is worn only across the back of his thick neck. "But he sure draws the customers. When he struts down that aisle with his chin in the air, he looks the queen of a carnival midway.

"The closest thing I ever saw to him," Mr. Mondt said, "was a guy they called the Wrestling Minister. He looked like a blinkety-blank parson and he dressed like a blinkety-blank parson and he walked like a blinkety-blank parson. And he was the biggest blinkety-blank scoundrel I ever knew."

After a long while they took the drier off Gorgeous George's skull, brushed him up, and he arose, his head a mass of lovely, soft curls.

"Now I feel more relaxed with my hair done," he said. "I allus feel such a mess before."

Mr. Menacher had a gold bobby pin in his lapel. So did the valet.

"In Hollywood," Mr. Menacher said, "everybody wears one. Have you heard the new song hit 'Gorgeous George Is the Man I Mean'? "

He spoke to an almost empty room. A large number of guests had departed, looking a trifle green about the gills. Too much whiskey, no doubt.

STRICTLY CHICKEN

1948

Only a few strands of light escaped from the whitewashed stone building under the trees and you had to get almost to the door to hear the roosters crowing. Inside there were probably two hundred men seated and standing on wooden bleachers around the cockpit, a patch of hard clay twelve feet square, within low board walls.

A red cock and a gray—that is, one with a cream-colored hackle on which a crimson stain was spreading—were in the pit. The gray obviously was losing. His legs wavered and he tottered in small, blind circles like a helpless prizefighter. Now he collapsed, a shapeless mound of damp, soiled feathers. But when the other bird closed with him he fought back, pecking at his enemy's head and lashing out with the inch-and-a-quarter steel gaffs curving upward from his natural spurs.

"The gray'd kill that red if he could find him," a man muttered.
"He's got the wallop," another agreed, "but he can't connect."

As they fought, a man wearing a duck-hunter's cap explained the rules, which vary from state to state and pit to pit. While the birds are fresh enough for an outright kill their handlers let them fight, breaking them only when they are hung (when one sinks a heel into the other's head or wing or body). Then the referee says, "Handle," and starts counting.

The handler has fifteen seconds to work on his bird, rearrange his feathers, clean head and bill, breathe on his head and back to warm or cool him as the need dictates, walk him briskly around holding him by the tail. After counting to fourteen the referee says, "Down cocks," or "Pit 'em," and the chickens are set down in diagonally opposite corners.

If they fight until too weak for a kill, one handler will say, "Gimme a count," provided his bird has struck the last blow with beak or gaff. If the other bird doesn't peck or kick in retaliation before the referee counts off ten seconds they are parted for another fifteen-second rest. When one cock has scored two unbroken counts of ten in succession, they are breasted—pitted head to head in mid-ring—and after the bird owning the advantage has kicked at the other, he can win with a count of twenty. The loser can break the final count only by kicking, not pecking.

By the time this exposition was finished, the red had scored two consecutive ten-counts. When they were breasted, the gray's head sank slowly to the earth and he lay inert through the long count while the other slashed at him.

"The gray was the best cock," the man with the ducking cap explained, "but he lost an eye and got hit in the brain early and he couldn't see."

"He's dead now?"

"As good as. Sometimes you can save a beaten bird, but they'll kill this one."

Spectators paid off bets while another pair was brought in and weighed. Then a tumult of wagering arose for the next event. "A hundred on the spangle." "It's a bet." "Twenty-five the red." "Make it fifty." "Bet." Wagers ranged from $5 to $100. This was a $300 derby in which each owner put up $300 and entered eight chickens. Ordinarily there'd be upward of ten entries and the stake money of $3,000 or more would be split, sixty-forty, between the cocker winning the most fights and the runner-up.

However, this derby had drawn only four entries, or thirty-two birds, so it was winner-take-all the $1,200. In addition, owners are expected, but not required, to make side bets, generally $50 or $100, on each of their eight fights.

As the next event started, handlers "billed" their cocks, holding them aloft head to head so they would discover and peck each other, then pitted them in opposite corners. The cocks tore into each other, meeting in midair on each fly, uppercutting savagely with the flashing gaffs. They went down with a heel deep in the spangle's head. Next time his handler put him down, the spangle held his head cocked to one side.

"He's been brained," said the man with the cap. "See, he's a little wry-necked. Sometimes that don't matter, just affects a nerve center a little while."

"That fellow," he said, indicating the spangle's handler, "has good cocks. But he won a derby about six weeks ago and he's fighting the same cocks back tonight and I think they're a little tired. See how the other chicken's comb is a brighter red? He's got better condition."

The red killed the spangle without a count. A Wisconsin Red Shuffler was pitted with a white chicken, which made a few flies and then fled in circles like Jersey Joe Walcott in the fifteenth round with Louis. The crowd jeered.

"There he goes! Give 'im room! Open the door, Richard!"

"Those wheelers are dangerous," a man said. "I don't like 'em, but just when you think you've got 'em on the run they come back and wallop you."

The thing degenerated into a long "drag" fight, with innumerable ten-counts alternately broken. The cocks were taken to the "drag" pit, a smaller square where such fights are finished when a fresh pair is ready for the main pit. Ultimately the white "wheeler" won. Good-humored growls of disgust saluted his victory.

The crowd was almost universally good-humored, winning or losing. Once a handler accused another of roughing up his chicken while separating them, but as they began to bicker the spectators shouted, "Fight the cocks!" Another time, a chicken began to squawk whenever hit, and there were more jeers.

"The sucker's got donkey in him, Mike," a man said.

Mike agreed. "Sure, he's a donkey."

Donkey, or dungie, means a cock with a strain of cold blood. Besides the sixteen fights in the derby, there were several "hacks," independent fights arranged by the owners. In one of these, a cock was hit and flew right out of the pit, not once but three times. That ended the fight.

"Wring his neck," somebody yelled, and the bird's handler thrust his chin out.

"You do it," he challenged. Nothing happened.

RODEO HEADMASTER

1963

Jim Shoulders walked into Toots Shor's and set his wide black hat on its crown on the checkroom counter. The girl scooped it up with somebody else's overcoat—the cowboy wore none—and Jim's hand shot out in polite haste. "Please," he said, turning the crown down to preserve the expensive curl of the brim.

There was a time when the price of a hat like that . . . well, at fourteen Jim was a scrawny kid slinging a pitchfork as a harvest hand in Oklahoma. He rode over to Oilton in Creek County, where the Cimarron snakes up toward the Osage Reservation, and won $18 in a bush-league rodeo. That was about what a field hand could clear in a month. Jim never looked back.

It was the dinner hour, but the king of cowboys said no, he'd just have a Jack Daniels. "I ate once already today." He was due at CBS to help edit film for a sports spectacular on rodeo. Twenty-four hours later he would be aboard an angry Brahma bull in San Antonio, an ill-tempered beast that would try to buck him off and hook him before he lit.

"And I'd deserve it," he said. "You buck off, you deserve to get punished. You'll try a little harder next time."

After eighteen years, Jim says, arena floors are getting harder, bulls and bareback broncs taller, the travel jumps tougher. "I don't haul so good anymore." You wouldn't know that to look at him, slight, smallish, with a curiously catlike springiness even in the way he sits in a saloon.

You might put his age at anything between twenty-five and thirty. He is thirty-three, going on thirty-four. "Old Boney," the cowboys call him. They have called him other things, especially during the decade of 1949–59 when he shattered all records with sixteen championships, seven in bull-riding, four barebacks, five all-around.

Over those years there may have been two or three major-league ballplayers and half a dozen jockeys who topped his average income of $37,827. His 1956 total of $43,381 still set a record.

Now he has a side interest—a rodeo school on his ranch at Henryetta, Oklahoma, offering six-day courses for beginners in bull-riding, barebacks, and saddle bronc. He limits classes to sixty in each event and puts up pupils in a bunk house which he calls, with graphic candor, the boar's nest.

"We started last year," he said. "Had one boy from Hawaii, two or three from Canada, one from Brooklyn, three from New York, kids from all over that want to ride rodeo. The youngest was fifteen and the oldest thirty-four.

"You see there ain't any place a kid can get stock he can ride and instruction in fundamentals; he cain't buy buckin' horses and bulls and build an arena. Even the smallest local rodeos cost him entrance money and he's got to draw for stock.

"He might draw a bull that'll pitch him leaving the box and maybe hook him, too. He can't learn nothin' that way except how to git up and run for the fence. And maybe, learning, he wants to change his rigging or something, but with $100 entry money up, that's no time to change. He's tryin' to win something."

"Can a boy learn enough in six days to give him a start?" Shoulders was asked.

"He can learn one thing quick—whether he's got any business in rodeo. And, of course, most of 'em don't. I had this nice kid from Kentucky—"

Jim chuckled at the memory. "He was enrolled for bulls and bareback, and he's never been on anything before. He froze on his first horse. I blew the whistle right away and got him down. He watched the others awhile and I kept saying, 'Want to try one now, Gary?' 'I think I'll just watch awhile,' he'd say. Finally, I put him on a Hereford bull that just walked out and stood. I got the kid to loosen up and relax his back and move around a little, but he said he guessed he'd wait till tomorrow to ride anything else.

"Next morning he pulled me aside. 'I don't want you to think I'm chicken,' he says, 'but I guess, by God, I am.' I told him, 'Gary, I don't know what makes a man right for rodeo any more than I know why Mickey Mantle can hit better than somebody else just as strong and fast as him, and in better health. Don't worry about it, because like I told you all yesterday, hardly anybody's going to make it.' But he was such an honest kid I had to laugh."

"Did you have any boys who looked good?"

"There was one showed some promise on bulls and one looked real good riding bareback. Try? He was on thirty-seven head of bucking horses in six days. One bucked him plumb over the fence out of school.

"I told him, 'Now you know what it means to get your tail pitched out of class.' He got up laughing."

THE BOAT RACE

1970

In many American newspapers, the most absurdly overplayed event in sports is the "competition" for the America's Cup. This is a boat race in the horse player's sense of the term. Under the terms dictated by the New York Yacht Club, it is almost totally devoid of competition. It is frequently deficient in sportsmanship. A dentist filling a tooth offers livelier entertainment for spectators. It commands substantially less reader interest than the Treasury's statement of gold balances.

Still, there are papers that assign one or more staff men to the story for an entire summer, publish lengthy daily accounts of the trials leading up to selection of a challenger and a defender, and devote six or eight columns of space to the predictable results while the races are underway.

Perhaps the gazettes are motivated by a mistaken notion that national pride and prestige are somehow involved in the fortunes of *Intrepid* or *Gretel II,* or maybe publishers are impressed by the staggering cost of these sleek and comfortless craft. At any rate, the trivial adventures of a few millionaires getting their bottoms wet at play are reported with a respectful solemnity that borders on servility.

The first race of the current challenge series was sailed in rain and cold and controversy and frustration. When it was over, only the race committee knew who won, and the committee wasn't telling. After preliminary jockeying for position, both yachts went over the starting line with protest flags flying, but the nature of the objections was not disclosed and the skippers were instructed not to talk.

Fans and readers, if any, owners of the boats and their crews had to wait until the next day to learn that *Gretel*'s protest had been rejected and the Australian challenger had indeed been walloped by almost six minutes. The authorities were right there on the committee boat when the protest flags were broken out. If the evidence of their own eyes wasn't sufficient, the committeemen could have talked with the skippers and issued a ruling immediately after the finish. But the New York Yacht Club doesn't work that way.

Not that anybody expected the committee to uphold a foreign protest. For 119 years, the New York Yacht Club has applied the rules with the single aim of keeping the America's Cup right where it is, bolted to a heavy oak table in the trophy room on West 44th Street. You'd think the old ewer was the Kohinoor diamond instead of a singularly ugly pitcher with a hole in its bottom, not fit to hold a pint of beer. The tiger mother protecting her young is a gentle old tabby compared to the New York Yacht Club in defense of its hardware.

After the rakish schooner *America* won the mug by whipping fifteen British boats in a race around the Isle of Wight on August 22, 1851, the custodians of the trophy took steps. The first challengers were required to sail against a whole fleet of defenders, and for years the races were conducted over the "inside" course in New York harbor, where familiarity with local conditions was an overwhelming advantage. "A penny show in a puddle," was how the late William P. Stevens, yachting editor of *Forest and Stream,* described those competitions.

Little by little the unfair conditions written in New York gave way to moral pressures over the years, but they have never given way altogether. No longer need the challenger submit a complete description of the challenging yacht ten months in advance with the defender not even identified until just before the start. No longer need the challenger be sturdy and seaworthy—and slow—enough to travel to the scene of the match on her own bottom.

She still must be designed and built in the country of the challenging club, however, and this condition has been stiffened since the first Australian challenge. Back in 1962 *Gretel I* was permitted to use some American-made sails and rigging—which Australia didn't have the facilities to duplicate—and her designer was given free use of the towing tanks at Stevens Institute of Technology in Hoboken.

Gretel won one race and made the other four so close that plaster fell from the ceiling of the New York Yacht Club. Never again the sporting gesture.

RUM + VODKA + IRISH = FIGHT

NOTRE DAME, INDIANA, 1977

A card on the breakfast table recommended a Fighting Irish cocktail. Perhaps "recommended" is the wrong word. The card merely announced that the confection was available at $2.50 (souvenir glass $1.75). "I'd like orange juice," a guest said, "pancakes, crisp bacon and coffee. But first, what is a Fighting Irish cocktail?" "All right," the waitress said. "One shot of rum, one shot of vodka, half a shot of Galliano, about this much orange juice and some green food coloring." There was a respectful silence. Then: "Thank God it's Sunday and you can't serve me one." "I've never tasted one," the waitress said, "but anybody I ever served one never asked for another."

This was in the Holiday Inn about three furlongs from the campus on the road to Niles, Michigan. Six days a week the Fighting Irish and

other refreshments are available here in Gipper's Lounge, a shrine
dedicated to the memory of George Gipp, the patron saint of football
and eight-ball pool at Notre Dame. Walls of the lounge are covered
with photographic blowups of football plays and players. Three dom-
inate the decor: behind the bar stands the Gipper himself, half again
larger than life, wearing the soft leather headgear and canvas pants
favored by all-America halfbacks around 1920; at his right is a huge
head shot of Frank Leahy, the late, great coach; at Gipp's left, Harry
Stuhldreher, Jim Crowley, Elmer Layden and Don Miller sit astride
four plow horses. The riders wear football regalia with cowled
woolen windbreakers, and each has a football tucked under an arm.

With the possible exception of Knute Rockne's twisted smile,
which appears on the wall of a corridor just outside, this equestrian
study must be the most readily recognized photo ever made around
here. George Strickler, who traveled with the 1924 team as undergraduate press agent, dragooned the spavined steeds from a nearby
farm and posed the picture on returning from the Army game in
New York where Grantland Rice had written the story that immortalized the backfield as the Four Horsemen of Notre Dame. On a
campus where a five-dollar bill represented wealth, Strickler sold
hundreds of 8-by-11 prints at one dollar each.

Photographic evidence notwithstanding, football played no special
part in campus affairs or discussions this weekend. Reunion '77 was
on, bringing together classes spaced five years apart from 1972 clear
back to 1927 and beyond, each group identified by baseball caps of
a certain color.

Wherever the eye turned it lighted on a cluster of gold caps covering skulls that were sent out of here stuffed with learning fifty years
ago, for something like 125 of the 400-odd members of the class of '27
made their way back. They came prepared for the discovery that
their friends had aged faster than they did in the last half-century,
and sometimes they were pleasantly surprised.

Little Eddie Broderick of Morristown, New Jersey, has retired
from the bench, yet he is the same blithe spirit who enlivened Pat
Manion's law classes. Time has not dimmed the laughter in Joe Dunn,
though the waistline has expanded a trifle since he quit Brainerd,
Minnesota, for the good life in Scottsdale, Arizona. The terra-cotta
coiffure of Red Edwards, quarterback and co-captain in 1926, has not
changed, and big John McManmon, the ag student from Lowell,
Massachusetts, who played tackle in front of Red, still discourses with
scholarship on the useful properties of manure.

It seemed improbable that the Soviet Union, Communist China, or
even Southern California could muster a more presentable clutch of
septuagenarians than the class of '27. Considering that the clammy

hand of Prohibition was on the land when these men were under-graduates, their appearance lent support to their youthful belief that barbed-wire gin, needled beer and white whisky warm from the still would make a man live long and do good deeds.

There was little talk of frivolous nature. John Harwood, now a Nashville architect, had attended a morning mass yesterday in memory of 227 deceased classmates and had doubts about returning for the reunion mass at 5:30 P.M. "If I went to church twice in one day," he said, "God might think I was pushy."

Pat Cohen of Taunton, Massachusetts, said that after a fifty-year trial he had decided to settle permanently in South Bend and had bought property for that purpose.

"Property, Pat? Where?"

"In the Jewish cemetery."

Regarding the unlined face of Joe Breig, an old crock remembered how that face had looked one evening in the spring of 1924. On the first Saturday in May—the day Black Gold won the Kentucky Derby —the Ku Klux Klan attempted to hold a state convention in South Bend. With deplorable disregard for the right of peaceable assembly, two thousand students intervened, even employing force in some instances to separate delegates from their bedsheet hoods.

A night or two later, word reached the campus that a fiery cross was burning downtown. Maybe fifty students caught a trolley car to the scene, the rest following on foot. The trolley delivered the first group into an ambush manned by thugs with blackjacks and brass knuckles along with some cops. When reinforcements arrived on foot, Joe Breig's glasses were broken, his right ear was partly detached from a bloody head, and nightsticks had raised welts across his back.

Yesterday, though, he was telling of postgraduate days on the *Vandergrift News* in his native Vandergrift, Pennsylvania. When he covered city council, members tried to delay newsworthy business until after he had left their meetings, but he was young and could wait them out if they stalled until 4:00 A.M. One day a committee waited on him at the paper to protest that day's headline, which reported that council had ignored an issue of civic importance. He explained that he had written the story because it was the truth. The councilmen argued. Joe was firm. The council president slammed Joe's desk with a fist.

"Dammit, Joe!" he said. "We didn't ignore it. We didn't bring it up!"

9.

Boxing

"I'M THE GREATEST"

Cassius Marcellus Clay fought his way out of the horde that swarmed and leaped and shouted in the ring, climbed like a squirrel onto the red velvet ropes and brandished his still-gloved hand aloft.

"Eat your words," he howled to the working press rows. "Eat your words."

Nobody ever had a better right. In a mouth still dry from the excitement of the most astounding upset in many roaring years, the words don't taste good, but they taste better than they read. The words, written here and practically everywhere else until the impossible became unbelievable truth, said Sonny Liston would squash Cassius Clay like a bug when the boy braggart challenged for the heavyweight championship of the world.

The boy braggart is the new champion, and not only because Liston quit in his corner after the sixth round. This incredible kid of twenty-two, only nineteen fights away from the amateurs and altogether untested on boxing's topmost level, was winning going away when Liston gave up with what appeared to be a dislocated shoulder.

He might have been nailed if the bout had continued, but on the evidence of eighteen frenzied minutes, Cassius was entitled to crow, as he did at the top of his voice before Liston retired: "I'm the greatest. I'm gonna upset the world."

"That's right," his camp followers howled. "That's what you're doin."

And he was.

On this score, Clay won four of the six rounds, and in one of the two he lost he was blinded. Apart from the unforeseen ending, that was perhaps the most extraordinary part of the whole wild evening.

It started between the fourth and fifth rounds. "Floating like a butterfly and stinging like a bee" as he and his stooges had predicted, Cassius had made Liston look like a bull moose plodding through a swamp.

Dancing, running, jabbing, ducking, stopping now and then to pepper the champion's head with potshots in swift combinations, he had won the first, third, and fourth rounds and opened an angry cut under Liston's left eye.

Handlers were swabbing his face in the corner when suddenly he broke into an excited jabber, pushed the sponge away and pawed at his eyes. As the bell rang he sprang up waving a glove aloft as though forgetting that a man can't call a time-out in a prize fight. In the corner, frantic seconds sniffed the sponge suspiciously.

Cassius couldn't fight at all in the fifth, but he could and did show a quality he had never before been asked for. He showed he could take the sternest hooks and heaviest rights Liston could throw—or at least this Liston, whose corner said later that the shoulder had slipped in the first round.

Just pawing feebly at the oncoming champion, Clay rocked under smacking hooks, ducked, rolled, grabbed, and caught one brutal right in the throat. He rode it out, though, and at the end of the round he had ceased to blink.

"You eyes okay, champ," they were screaming from his corner as the round drew to a close. "Everything okay."

He didn't confirm that until the bell rang for the sixth. Then, getting up from his stool, he looked across the ring, nodded with assurance, and went out to enjoy one of his best rounds, pumping both hands to the head, circling, dancing.

"Get mad, baby," his corner pleaded. "He's retreatin', champ."

It was at the end of this heat that he came back crowing about upsetting the world. Yet he couldn't have known how quickly his words would be confirmed.

Just before the bell for the seventh, Cassius sprang up and waved both hands overhead in a showoff salute to the crowd. He took a step or so forward, as the gong clanged, then leaped high in a war dance of unconfined glee. He had seen what scarcely anybody else in Convention Hall had noticed

Liston wasn't getting up. Willie Reddish, Sonny's trainer, had his hands spread palms up in a gesture of helplessness. Jack Nilon, the manager, swung his arm in a horizontal sweep, palm down. The fight was over, the championship gone.

Dr. Robert C. Bennett of Detroit, who has treated Liston in the past, hastened into the ring and taped Liston's shoulder. The former champion told him he had felt the shoulder go midway in the first round and the left hand had grown progressively number from then on.

They'll fight again to answer the prodding question of what might have been, and it will be a big one. Although return-bout clauses are frowned upon these days, Bob and Jimmy Nilon, Jack's brothers, have an independent contract with Clay entitling them to name the time, place, and opponent for his first defense.

As Bob Nilon explained this, Clay rode the ropes. "Eat your words," he bawled.

THE BIG SLEEP

Lewiston's finest stood at the doors of the hockey rink and frisked every lady's handbag for firearms before the great rematch of Cassius Clay and Sonny Liston last night. They should have searched Liston for concealed sleeping powders.

For fifteen months after Liston quit in his corner and surrendered the heavyweight championship of the world to the bluegrass bard from Louisville, the boxing public awaited a return bout.

For fifteen minutes after post time for theater-television, a sweltering little knot of customers in the Central Maine Youth Center waited for Jersey Joe Walcott, the referee, to wave the gladiators into combat.

Old Jersey Joe waved, and witnesses waited one minute more. Then they were on their feet yelling, "Fake—fake—fake," as a triumphant Clay leaned across the ropes screaming, "Where's Floyd Patterson?"

One wee righthand punch that Cassius threw from the hip had dropped his copiously sweating challenger for the quickest knockout ever recorded in a match for the heavyweight title, though Walcott didn't know it at the time. Unable to hear the timekeeper's count, the referee let Liston struggle to his feet and try to defend himself before the clocker told him Sonny had got up at the count of twelve.

Most of those who crowded down behind the press rows and bawled "fake" were young—too young, it seemed, to have been holding $25, $50 or $100 for admission. Possibly they had found a way to get in for less (pronounced nothing) when it began to appear that only about half of the 5,400 seats would be sold.

At any rate, they hollered loud enough to be in on the cuff, and a lot of them couldn't have been old enough to have seen the last fight held up here in the Moose country.

Chances are few of them even saw the punch that did the job, for it was a tiny shot that couldn't have traveled more than four inches. It didn't look like a blow to paralyze a big, brutal head-breaker who had never been knocked out in twelve years as a professional bruiser. Yet half an hour afterward, there were guys around calling it a "perfect punch."

Clay had bounced out of his corner at the opening bell to lead with a light, swinging right followed by a jab of no consequence. From then on he circled swiftly to his left as Liston chased him, hands down near his sides, his feet flashing across the canvas in showy double shuffles.

There was a look of menace in Liston's red-rimmed eyes. He was moving about as fast as he can, advancing on an angle to intercept Clay in his circling retreat. Sonny landed a jab or two of no great consequence, brought a howl from the crowd with a right swing that didn't land solidly, and banged one heavy right into the ribs.

Just once Clay paused in his flight to throw a left-right combination at the head, halting Liston for a fragment of a second. The crowd was silent then, for there had been boos for the champion as he entered the ring and cheers for Sonny when he came in with sweat dripping off his face in the punishing heat of the ring lights.

Now Sonny lunged forward to throw a left. Clay's right was level with his hip and he seemed scarcely to move it. Yet down went Liston with a massive, astonishing crash. He lay flat on his back, twitched, quivered, rolled over and hauled himself up on one knee.

The crowd drowned out Jersey Joe's count—if he had ever picked it up from the knockdown timekeeper. Sonny started to pull himself erect, pitched over and was flat again. Once more he forced himself up and this time he made it. It was a surprise when Walcott let Clay come on, for it seemed that at least ten seconds had passed.

Clay came on with a rush, punching frantically as Liston backed into his corner. For a moment Walcott left them to consult the timekeeper. Then he hustled back to declare a cease-fire.

The crowd bawled derision and anger. "The biggest fake I ever saw in my life," screamed one youngish guy with a pencil-thin mustache. Clay howled for Patterson, as if to take the former champion on then and there. Floyd joined the swirling mob in the ring, but with no intent to do bodily harm. So did George Chuvalo, another heavyweight with dreams.

Cassius paid no attention to the swelling jeers. He babbled into microphones, stayed to watch a taped rerun of his performance for a brace of strangers brought in to box after the main event. Half an hour later he was back from his dressing room haranguing what was left of the crowd through a loudspeaker.

In spite of many rumors about Black Muslim plots against Clay's life—threats which must have worried police chief Joe Farrand color-blind, for most of the handbags his minions snooped into were carried by white gals—nobody got shot. This may have been good.

ALI–FRAZIER I

1971

Early in the fifteenth round a left hook caught Muhammad Ali on the jaw and it was as though Joe Frazier had hit him with a baseball bat, Frank Howard model. Several times earlier Ali had sagged toward the floor. This time he slammed it like a plank. He went down at full length, flat on his back.

He rocked back on his shoulder blades, both feet in the air, rocked forward to a sitting position and pushed himself wearily, sadly, to his feet. He was up by the count of four, but Arthur Mercante, the referee, counted on for the mandatory eight seconds. He stepped aside and Joe came on, bloody mouth open in a grimace of savage joy.

Another hook smashed home, and Ali's hands flew up to his face as if to stifle a scream. When they came down, he had an advanced case of mumps. The comely visage he describes with such affection —"I'm the prettiest; I'm the greatest"—was a gibbous balloon, puffy and misshapen.

"Broken jaw," somebody said at ringside, but the diagnosis was not confirmed. As the fifteenth round started, Angelo Dundee, Ali's handler, had said the jaw was broken. But x-rays taken later showed there was no fracture.

On one point there was no shadow of doubt. Joe Frazier, whom they had called a pretender, was heavyweight champion of the world —the only champion of the only world we know.

Though he was on his feet at the final bell, Ali took a licking in the ring and on all three official scorecards, his first defeat in thirty-two bouts going all the way back to the days when he answered to the name of Cassius Marcellus Clay.

Losing, he fought the bravest and best and most desperate battle he has ever been called upon to make. In all his gaudy, gabby years as a professional, he had always left one big question unanswered: Could he take it? If ever he was hit and hurt, how would he respond?

He not only took it, he kept it. Each fighter got $2.5 million for his night's work, and earned it. At least they did in the estimation of 20,455 witnesses, but those beautiful people have so little respect for money that they paid $1,352,961 at the gate.

This was not only the biggest "live" gate for any indoor fight; the loot was almost twice as great as the previous record, established in the same Madison Square Garden by a double-header featuring the same Joe Frazier (with Buster Mathis). Chances are it will be weeks before the swag from television is counted up, for the match was shown on closed-circuit all over the United States, Canada and Great

Britain and on network TV in thirty-two other countries.

It was the most hysterically ballyhooed promotion of all time, and not only because of the obscene financial figures. If these men had been fighting on a barge for $500 a side it would still have commanded extraordinary attention, for never before had a single ring held two undefeated heavyweights with valid claims to the world championship—Ali unfrocked but still a champion because he had never been whipped for the title, Frazier his rightful successor because he had whipped everybody else—both at the peak of youth and strength.

So great was the interest that a bad fight would have left the Sweet Science sick unto death. A performance that left any shadow of suspicion behind might have destroyed boxing. This one destroyed nothing but Muhammad Ali.

It didn't do a thing for Frazier's health either. It did, though, prove Joe just about as close to indestructible as a fistfighter can be. He walked into hundreds of clean, hard shots, flashing combinations that drilled home with jolting force, and never for an instant did they halt his remorseless advance.

Outpointed as expected in the early rounds, he hurt his adversary in the sixth, batted him soft in the eleventh, knocked him into a grotesque backward slide along the ropes in the twelfth, and wrecked him in the fifteenth. Not many men could have survived the attack. But then not many athletes have Ali's armor of arrogance. Even in his deepest trouble, the loser pretended he wasn't losing, shaking his head to deny that a punch had hurt him, beckoning Frazier in to slug him again, trying by every trick of the theater to support the "secret" he had confided just before the start to a closed-circuit microphone:

"I predict, first of all, that all the Frazier fans and boxing experts will be shocked at how easy I will beat Joe Frazier, who will look like an amateur boxer compared to Muhammad Ali, and they will admit that I was the real champion all the time. Frazier falls in six."

Before these men ever saw Madison Square Garden, the English music critic Ernest Newman wrote of something he called the magic chemistry of genius:

> What is the artistic faculty? Is it just a knack, which some people are born with and others are not, for moving the counters of art —words, sounds, lines, colours—about in a particular way? We do not expect of a great billiards player or boxer that he shall have read Kant or Aeschylus, or understand the political problems of the Balkans. We do not even expect Mr. Joseph Louis to have studied the rudiments of that science of the impact of forces upon moving

masses, upon the correct application of which his success depends. Indeed, were he and his like to try to get their results by reason, by "culture," they would find themselves in the company of Mr. Belloc's nimble water-insect:

> *If he ever stopped to think*
> *how he did it he would sink.*

Joe Frazier has now fought twenty-seven boxing matches as a professional and won twenty-seven. The Olympic heavyweight champion of 1964 has won the championship of the professional world three times—by knocking out Buster Mathis when Cassius Muhammad Ali Clay was ostracized as a draft-dodger, by knocking out Jimmy Ellis, whom the World Boxing Association called champion, by knocking Muhammad Ali down but not out.

All his fights were cut to the same pattern, yet he could not tell you how he does it any more than Beethoven could.

Joe can talk a little about tactics, about "cutting the ring," which means advancing obliquely on a circling opponent to cut off the escape routes. As for his own bobbing, ducking attack: "I'll be smokin'," he says. "Right on." A witness within earshot of his corner Monday night could have heard his manager, Yank Durham, enlarge on this:

"Down, Joe, down ... for the body, Joe, the body ... Bring the right over ... Don't wrestle him, Joe; let the referee do the work."

What Joe says and Yank says merely brushes the surface. These two don't begin to explain what makes Joe the best fistfighter in the world at this time. Neither truly understands it. Yet one thing they do know.

If they fought a dozen times, Joe Frazier would whip Muhammad Ali a dozen times. And it would get easier as they went along.

THRILLA IN MANILA

MANILA, 1975

A gaggle of pretty girls got aboard an elevator for the press center in the Bayview Plaza Hotel, where they had been working for the last ten days. "It's over," one of them said, "and we're glad." Were they satisfied with the way it had ended? "No," they said, "no," every one of them. "How about you?" a girl asked a man on the lift. "I'm neutral," he said, "but I'll say one thing: Joe Frazier makes a better fighter and a better man of Muhammad Ali than anybody else can do." "Right," the girls said, all together, "that's right."

A small, strange scene came back to mind. It was two days before the fight and Ali lay on a couch in his dressing room, talking. If this had been a psychiatrist's couch it would not have seemed strange, but he wasn't talking to a psychiatrist and he wasn't talking to the newspaper guys around him. He just lay there letting the words pour out in a stream of consciousness.

"Who'd he ever beat for the title?" he was saying of Joe Frazier. "Buster Mathis and Jimmy Ellis. He ain't no champion. All he's got is a left hook, got no right hand, no jab, no rhythm. I was the real champion all the time. He reigned because I escaped the draft and he luckily got by me, but he was only an imitation champion. He just luckily got through because his head could take a lot of punches. . . ."

Why, listeners asked themselves, why does he have to do this? Why this compulsion to downgrade the good man he is going to fight? It had to be defensive. He was talking to himself, talking down inner doubts that he would not acknowledge. He will never feel that need again, and he never should. If there is any decency in him he will not bad-mouth Joe Frazier again, for Frazier makes him a real champion. In the ring with Joe, he is a better and braver man than he is with anybody else.

Muhammad Ali loves to play a role. He is almost always on stage, strutting, preening, babbling nonsense. But Frazier draws the truth out of him. Frazier is the best fighter Ali has ever met, and he makes Ali fight better than he knows how.

They have fought three times. In the first, Ali fought better than ever before, and lost. In the third he fought better still. This one ranks up there with the most memorable heavyweight matches of our time—Dempsey-Firpo, Dempsey's two with Tunney, both Louis-Schmeling bouts and Marciano's first with Jersey Joe Walcott.

It was really three fights. Ali won the first. Through the early rounds he outboxed and outscored Frazier, doing no great damage but nailing him with clean, sharp shots as Joe bore in.

The second fight was all Frazier's. From the fifth round through the eleventh he just beat hell out of Ali. When the champion tried to cover up against the ropes, Frazier bludgeoned him remorselessly, pounding body and arms until the hands came down, hooking fiercely to the head as the protective shell chipped away. When Ali grabbed, an excellent referee slapped his gloves away.

Then it was the twelfth round and the start of the third fight, and Ali won going away. Where he got the strength no man can say, for his weariness was, as he said, "next to death." In the thirteenth a straight right to the chin sent Frazier reeling back on a stranger's legs. He was alone and unprotected in midring, looking oddly diminished in size, and Ali was too tired to walk out there and hit him. Still, Ali won.

This evening Ali dined with President and Mrs. Ferdinand E. Marcos in the Antique House. Frazier was also invited but he begged off, sending his wife and two oldest children instead. Afterward the winner disappeared but the loser had several hundred guests at a "victory party" in the penthouse of his hotel. Like a proper host, he shaped up, trigged out in dinner clothes with dark glasses concealing bruises about the eyes.

"There was one more round to go, but I just couldn't make it through the day, I guess," he told the crowd. "Hey, fellas, I feel like doin' a number." That quickly, the prizefighter became the rock singer. "Lemme talk to this band a moment, because I sure don't want to get in another fight tonight." In a moment he had microphone in hand.

"I'm superstitious about you, baby," he sang. "Think I better knock-knock on wood." He did a chorus, he urged everybody to dance, and then a member of the Checkmates took over. The Checkmates are a trio and at the fight they had sung "The Star-Spangled Banner" in relay.

"We are all here tonight," one Checkmate said, "because we respect a certain man."

He got no argument from listeners. They all stood smiling, watching Joe Frazier dance at his own funeral.

BENNY PARET'S DEATH

1962

The pitiful case of Benny Paret moves each according to his nature. The habitually hysterical raise the scream of "legalized murder," and their number includes some who are equally quick to revile any fighter who, unlike Paret, quits under punishment. The politicians fulminate as politicians must, like that cluck in the South Carolina Legislature who wants a law requiring circular or ten-sided rings so a fighter can't be trapped in a corner.

Prodded perhaps by fear or maybe by conscience, Manny Alfaro, Paret's manager, gave a disgraceful performance trying to pin the blame on Ruby Goldstein, the referee. Nobody involved has any right to blame anybody else for a tragic accident, least of all a manager who gets his boy cruelly beaten by Gene Fullmer, then sends him back against a man who has already knocked him out.

To me boxing is a rough, dangerous and thrilling sport, the most basic and natural and uncomplicated of athletic competitions, and—at its best—one of the purest of art forms. Yet there is no quarrel here with those who sincerely regard it as a vicious business that should have no place in a civilized society.

They are wrong, of course, those who think boxing can be legislated out of existence. It has been tried a hundred times, but there were always men ready to fight for prizes on a barge or in a pasture lot or the back room of a saloon. It is hard to believe that a nation bereft of such men would be the stronger or better for it.

Still, if a man honestly feels that boxing should be abolished, he has every right to cite the Paret case in support of his position. The quarrel here is with the part-time bleeding hearts, the professional sob sisters of press and politics and radio who seize these opportunities to parade their own nobility, demonstrate their eloquence, and incidentally stir the emotions of a few readers, voters or listeners.

Some of the fakers now sobbing publicly over Paret have waxed ecstatic over a Ray Robinson or Joe Louis. It must be comforting to have it both ways.

Sometimes it seems there are more frauds outside boxing than in it. At least, the professionals are realists who recognize the game for the rough business it is, and accept the stern code which demands that a beaten man go on fighting as long as he is able to stay on his feet.

This doesn't mean that all card-carrying members of the fight mob are cut to the Hollywood-and-pulp-fiction pattern—scheming, selfish, dishonest mercenaries devoid of all decent feeling. A gentleman like Ray Arcel, the great trainer, can spend a lifetime in the dodge without dishonor, but he must subscribe to the code.

One night Ray was in the corner of a boy pacifist whose innate repugnance of violence was aggravated by the shots his adversary kept bouncing off his chin. Between rounds the boy expressed a devout wish to be elsewhere.

"Hang in there," Ray said. "He's as tired as you are."

Reluctantly the young man returned to the conflict. With a most unneighborly scowl his opponent advanced and the boy backed off warily, into his own corner.

"Ray," he said from behind a half-clenched glove, "throw in the towel, will ya?"

"Just keep punching," Ray said. "You're all right."

The tiger fled backward, buffeted and breathless. His knees were wobbly but he managed to stay up for a full circuit of the ring.

"Please, Ray," he gasped, passing his corner, "throw in the towel now."

"Box him," Ray called after him. "Stick him and move."

The pursuit race continued for another dizzying lap.

"Ray," the hero begged, "please throw in the towel. I won't be around again."

It should not be inferred that Arcel is impervious to punishment or in any degree lacking in compassion. Among the hundreds of fighters he has handled, a special favorite was the gallant Jackie Kid Berg, whom he called by a pet name, Yitzel.

Crouching in Berg's corner one night, Ray winced and shuddered in vicarious pain as a ferocious body-puncher poured lefts and rights into Jackie's middle. Sometimes the whistling gloves seemed to disappear altogether, bringing a gasp from Berg and a groan from his handler. Still up and fighting back when the round ended, Jackie did an about-face at the bell and marched back to his corner.

"Yitzel!" Ray said shakily. "How do you feel?"

"Fine, thank you," the Kid said. "And you?"

THE LITTLE CHAMP

1945

"You hafta talk to the little champ," Chick Wergeles said. "He makes a good interview on account of his Southern brawl."

The little champ, Beau Jack, was in one of the smaller salons in Stillman's Social and Reading Club getting ready for his ten-round drawl with Willie Joyce tonight. His broad, flat face was intent watching his trainer, Sid Bell, bandage his hands. He said he felt fine and had found Army life fine.

"Fine," he said. "First eight-nine months in the Army I just dig, dig all the time. Then they make me an instructor. When I went in I figure I gonna have fun. I did. A lot of fun."

"He went in on account of he wanted to," Wergeles said. "He wasn't grafted or nothin'."

"I just boxed only once in the Army," Beau said. "At Benning in Jojah. They've five hundred paratroopers going overseas wants me to box, so I boxed for 'em and afterwards after they got over there I kep' gettin' letters from 'em how they always remember what I done."

"He reads his own letters himself," Wergeles says. "He amazes me how he improved one hundred percent reading and writing in the Army. He reads his own newspaper stories by himself now."

Beau said he didn't know how much he weighed and didn't care, had no plans or preference for any weight division.

"Lightweight, welterweight, I doan know," he said. "Just so I keep on fightin' somewheres. I love to fight."

"He loves to fight," Wergeles said. "If he didn't get no pay for it, he'd still wanta fight just to relieve the monopoly. With him money is secondary. 'Money,' he says, 'is for givin' away.' How about that? Besides, he's got his family to think about."

"I got three little Beau Jacks," Beau said, grinning. "Ain't none of 'em gonna be no fighters, though. Nossir."

"He loves to fight," Wergeles said, "and he's strong and he's just coming along. He's only twenty-three."

"Twenty-five," Beau said.

"No," Wergeles said, "you got it wrong again. You was nineteen when you started fightin' and you been fightin' four years. Twenty-three."

"Look," Beau said stubbornly. He lifted an index finger and ticked it off as though counting. "April the first, 1921."

He and Wergeles and Bell were silent a moment, pondering. "Twenty-four," Bell said.

"Okay," Wergeles said, "twenty-four. Raisin' twenty-five."

Beau stood up and flexed his hands and walked upstairs to punch the small bag. He worked hard and tirelessly, flailing from all angles and laughing when he landed with extra violence.

"He's a bad bag fighter," Wergeles said. "I mean, punchin' the bag. I don't mean bag fights. I wouldn't have nothin' to do with anything wasn't on the level. I used to work for Jack Curley, the rassling promoter. Then one day I heard there was something funny about rassling. After twenty years I found out it wasn't on the level and I couldn't stand it. When Curley died I told a guy: 'He heard a couple of his guys was fakin' and the shock killed him.' "

He laughed uproariously. "What I mean, the little champ don't look good punchin' the bag," he said. "He has got to have another guy to punch. Then he loves it. Only thing, I'm afraid he might get a little tired going ten rounds with Joyce on account of he ain't boxed. But he's good and strong."

Bell said "All right" and started to detach the small bag, but Beau kept punching at it. "Quit it," Bell said, "you'll bust the bag. Quit, I tell you."

He turned Beau loose on the big bag for a while, then stepped in to swab him with a towel. Beau buffeted his trainer as he worked, slamming light punches into his middle and cutting loose now and then with a whistling hook that barely missed. Bell worked patiently, backing away. "Keep horsin' around," he warned, "and you'll bust these glasses."

"Look at him," Wergeles said. "He'll get down to a lightweight again easy, the way he loves to work. He'd work nights if I'd leave him do it. He loves to fight. He's illiterate."

DEPARTMENT OF INJUSTICE

1951

Billy Graham whipped the whey out of Kid Gavilan the other night. He earned the welterweight championship of the world. He got a favorable vote from one of the three officials, and that minority ballot went to him by a margin of one point. Not one round, but one miserable point-within-a-round. Let's get it on record right away. The score here was eleven rounds for Graham, four for Gavilan.

So Billy was robbed, and not even Frank Forbes, the judge who called the rounds even but scored a one-point edge for Graham, gave Billy anything near the credit which, in this view, he deserved.

Mark Conn is New York's second-best referee, second to Ruby Goldstein. He is cool and competent and impartial. Frank Forbes and Artie Schwartz are experienced, honest judges. To say they robbed Graham is merely to use the blunt parlance of the fight mob, for they are not robbers. To ridicule or abuse them because of an honest difference of opinion would be outrageously unfair, more unfair than what they did to Graham.

When, after announcement of the decision, Madison Square Garden boomed with an angry thunder of protest, Artie Schwartz was startled. He had left his ringside seat and walked back through the press rows, and now he returned with a shocked expression and asked a newspaperman: "How did you have it?"

"I had Graham ahead big," the reporter said.

"You did?" Artie asked, amazed, and he spread his palms in a gesture of puzzled resignation. He had scored it for Gavilan, nine rounds to six, and he could not understand how two brace of eyes could see the same fight so differently. There isn't any understanding it, but there it is. From now on, the record books, which are supposed to reflect what happened, will include a line under Graham's name reading: "August 29—Kid Gavilan, New York . . . L 15." There will be no asterisk with a note adding: "Decision smelled."

It said here in a line of pulsing prose composed before the fight that no matter who won, there wasn't going to be any great commotion about it. Like Gavilan, the Delphic oracle retains his title. Lady Godiva could have ridden through the ring without causing such commotion as the decision created.

In the tunnel beneath the seats on the 50th Street side, somebody belted somebody else. Customers funneled down to ringside, yelling and brandishing fists, and two or three burst into the ring to cuddle and comfort Graham, and in the aisle near his corner cops struggled with a large howling man who threshed and kicked out wildly in their embrace.

"We'll take care of you!" a man yelled with his face close to that of Cy Levy, an inspector for the Boxing Commission. "When we get organized, we'll take care of you!"

"Me?" Levy protested mildly. "I didn't vote."

When Johnny Addie read the last scorecard, Graham had dropped his head and half covered his features with his gloves. When he took the gloves away, his face was stricken. If he wasn't crying, he was as close to tears as a tough, game professional prizefighter ever ought to be. In the dressing room afterward he was barely able to choke out thanks to those who crowded up with words of sympathy.

"You're still the champ," some noisy guy in the dressing room kept telling him. "When you walk into a joint they'll call you 'Champ.'"

That prediction may come true, but Billy Graham fights for money and there'll be no champion's percentage in his papers next time he signs for a bout. Even if he meets Gavilan again, it'll be on a different night in different circumstances, with, maybe, a different result.

For this was Billy's night. He made Gavilan look worse than the champion ever looked before from this seat. Contrary to the majority opinion, which held that Gavilan took an early lead and then lost it, Graham always was ahead on this scorecard. As seen here, Graham's early advantage was a barely perceptible shade achieved largely by defensive skill. After a few rounds he had his man measured, his distance and timing set, and then he was in charge, making Gavilan fight his way.

Graham would jab, jab, jab and wait for Gavilan's lead. He would pick off the champion's left hook or slide inside his swinging right to the body. If Gavilan punched for the head, Graham rode with the blow, taking it above and behind the ear, where it did no harm. He circled slowly to Gavilan's right, turning his left shoulder in against Gavilan's chest, and ripping a right to the body. He had all the better of the infighting.

Billy's right to the head grew sharper as the fight progressed. Two or three times he dropped punches on the jaw which half spun the champion. They were uncommonly fine punches for Graham, who is no dynamiter.

The crowd loved the fight, though it wasn't the greatest ever seen. Today's welterweights aren't the greatest who ever lived. Still, they were fighting for the championship of the world, and if Billy had got what he deserved he'd be the champion of the world, and it's the only world there is.

PATTERN OF VIOLENCE

1951

In the third round Sugar Ray Robinson smashed a straight right stiff to the chin of Randy Turpin, knocking the Englishman halfway across the ring, but when Robinson came plunging after, to punish him on the ropes, he found a fighter there with both hands working.

That was when the pattern took shape in America's biggest fight of 1951. The former middleweight champion of the world, fighting to regain the title as Stanley Ketchel and Tony Zale did before him, would land the sharper, cleaner blows. He would go fishing for Turpin's elusive chin, angling and angling patiently, missing wildly many, many times, looking often inept and sometimes foolish against the champion's strange but efficient defense.

He would send Turpin to the floor, dropping him cleanly, while Ruby Goldstein, the referee, tolled the numbers off to nine. But whenever Robinson punched, Turpin would punch him back. When Turpin went down, he would get up. Under the severest punishment he would have his wits about him. He would be a fighting man, ready to take more and give it.

That was the pattern, but there was no guessing when it might change. Turpin is tremendously strong, and as the rounds rolled away, his youth and strength might overcome the edge the older man had in class. The longer it lasted, the more likely it seemed that Turpin might come on to win.

He was coming on. By this score he won the eighth and ninth rounds. He broke Robinson's left eye open as the tenth started—and then it happened.

It could be that Turpin's biggest mistake was to open that gash over Robinson's eye. "When that happened," Sugar Ray was asked afterward, "did you figure that was the time to go get him?"

"I figured that was the time to try," Ray said.

That's how it seemed from ringside, down in the sweltering funnel of the Polo Grounds. It seemed that when Robinson saw blood and knew it was his own, he opened the throttle all the way, reasoning that if he didn't get his man now, his neat face might come all apart soon and he wouldn't have many more chances.

He tore after Turpin, scoring well, but still unable to hurt the champion. They were in midring, closing for a rally, when Robinson's right caught Turpin's chin. It was a short punch, almost a hook, and it stopped Turpin dead. The Englishman was bent forward at the waist, feet wide, legs rigid, knees seeming locked together.

Half an instant later, Turpin was in motion again, and though Robinson went after him hungrily, it looked as though Ray might lose his victim. The victim was fighting back. But, fighting, he left another opening. Robinson filled it.

A straight right to the chin spun Turpin in the first movement of a pirouette. He pitched forward into Robinson's arms, and Ray had to step back to let him fall. Turpin dropped on his back, but at the count of two or three he rolled over, brought up his head. His eyes were clear, and you knew he was going to get up.

Robinson knew it, too, of course. And he knew what to do. He was in on his man swiftly, slugging the head with both hands, batting him around the ring. He caught him on the ropes, punching frantically at first, then suddenly changing his tactics.

It was just as you see it on the screen when the slow-motion camera comes on to show the knockout in detail. Robinson took his time, steadying Turpin's head, aiming, then letting go. Turpin was defenseless, but neither senseless nor altogether helpless. He couldn't get his hands up, but he did raise his eyes and you could see them following Robinson's gloves as he rolled and ducked and bent away from the blows. He was weaving like a cobra dancing to a flute.

At ringside they were beginning to shout for Goldstein to protect him. Then Robinson brought up a left hook and a right, and as Turpin sagged toward the floor, the referee burst in and stopped it. Ruby was right, though Turpin complained of his action in the dressing room and there will be louder protests as time goes on.

As Robinson turned toward his own corner, Turpin straightened, refusing to fall, and lurched after him as though to resume the fight. His handlers leaped into the ring and tackled him, but he wasn't trying to hit Robinson; he only meant to congratulate him, and he towed his handlers into the corner for that purpose.

It was a genuine gesture of sportsmanship from a first-class fighting man. There haven't been many better fighters than Turpin seen around here in a long time. There never has been a pluckier loser.

In the first row of ringside behind the working press, a woman was standing on a chair, gasping as her companions chafed her hands and fanned her. She seemed near to fainting. This was Ray Robinson's mother.

A few seats removed, another woman wept. Her face was wet with tears and she was crying, "The title is his!" Over and over. This was Ray Robinson's wife.

HOMECOMING IN THE SLAMMER

MARION, OHIO, 1977

For two rounds a Brooklyn heavyweight named Kevin Isaac shuffled, shrugged, feinted and circled warily while huge Stan Ward of Sacramento fixed him with a beady glare of waiting.

"Come on!" yelled a fan at ringside as the bell rang for the third round. "I've only got twenty years!"

Number 125734 was back in the slammer today, and he got a standing ovation. Up to September 29, 1971, No. 125734 was Don King, now perhaps the most widely known alumnus of the Marion Correctional Institution. Returning to alma mater where he did four years for manslaughter, the least diffident promoter in boxing presented another round in his "United States Championship Tournament" for the edification of his former classmates and the entertainment of the American Broadcasting Company's viewing audience. "King's back," read one placard held high in the bleachers. "We told you so." Another struck a note of resignation: "Some dudes ya can't chase away with a club. Welcome back, Don King."

The former resident in Room 10, Cellblock 6, stepped into the ring wearing a gold-encrusted jacket and waistcoat, brown pants with a crease that could draw blood, a frilled white evening shirt and fan-wing bow tie. His Afro haircut quivered with pride.

"I look around and see many familiar faces," he told the crowd of 1,400. "I am one of you." They cheered. "It is with mixed emotions that I am coming back to what was a trauma in my life. I am happy and proud to be able to bring back some entertainment for you because you have been part of my life." They yelled. "Wherever I have gone outside, I have never tried to hide Marion C.I. I never forgot No. 125734." That was for openers. When he went on to tell them they must "deal with the pragmatic thing realistically," they howled.

He introduced the prison chaplain, Father Fred Furey, and got mostly cheers; Pete Perini, the superintendent, who was warmly booed; his own daughter and son, Debbie and Carl, who were politely received; Joe Louis, who brought down the house. There were boos for Walter Hampton, head of the parole board, but Don reminded them: "That's the dude that sprung me."

Gesturing toward a microphone at ringside, he presented "The Mouth of Boxing—Howard Cosell." Up went placards: "Finally, Howard is where he belongs," and "Howard got in—will he get out?"

It was a homecoming to warm every cockle this side of Sing Sing.

Photographers were waiting when the returning prodigal strode through the big gate at the end of Victory Road. "I used to mow that grass," he said, pointing. Sure of his way, he walked to Cellblock 6 with the superintendent. Pete Perini was a linebacker at Ohio State, played some pro football with the Cleveland Browns and Chicago Bears and came to this post in 1967, the year Don King matriculated, fresh from command of the numbers racket in Cleveland.

"And I have to believe Don has done better," said Irving Rudd of the promoter's staff, "because he's out and Pete is still inside."

Residents recognized King as he passed. They exchanged greetings. At the door of his old quarters he spoke to the present occupant: "You're making this room famous." As he entered with the warden, the occupant, Obie Brooks, stepped out. Brooks said he was doing ten to life for murder, too. He said he had five years in, with two to go before he could apply for parole. "Did it happen in a fight?" he was asked, for it was in a street fight that King killed a man.

"During an armed robbery," Obie said.

The warden and the graduate walked together down the quarter-mile corridor to the gym. "Don didn't serve time," Perini has said. "Time served him."

Cordiality has been rampant here for days. When King arrived, the Mayor of Marion gave him the key to the city. "Mr. Mayor," Don said, "when I was here before, nobody gave me a key to anything."

Members of the press were frisked courteously on arrival and given a mimeographed sheet of do's and don'ts. "Keep track of your valuable equipment," came ahead of "do leave all weapons (knives) and medication outside the main stockade." Inside they met an old friend, Peter Rademacher, the only man who ever fought for the heavyweight championship of the world as an amateur. That was twenty years ago and Floyd Patterson dropped him seven times. Rademacher, now an Akron businessman, refereed the Isaac-Ward bout. Some of the fights were good, some funny. Mike Dokes, who lost flashily to Cuba's Teofilo Stephenson when Dokes was a flashy amateur, was in with an oval personage named Charley Jordan. Charley is known as "Big Tuna" but he is built more like an angry blowfish. Ignoring his billowing belly, Dokes aimed for his bobbing head and opened a cut near an eye. The doctor seized the opportunity to stop it, but not before Vic Ziegel of the *New York Post* had spoken: "This fight belongs here."

"Nevertheless," said Ed Schuyler of the Associated Press, one who survived the street gangs and pickpockets at last fall's Muhammad Ali–Ken Norton affair. "Nevertheless, the security is better than in Yankee Stadium, and there's a better class of people."

THE ZALE–GRAZIANO WARS

1980

In the fight mob they are saying that Saturday night's match between Pipino Cuevas and Thomas Hearns in Detroit could be another Graziano-Zale number, which is like saying Meade and Lee are hooking up again at Gettysburg. Thomas and Pipino take no prisoners. Cuevas was only nineteen when the World Boxing Association dubbed him welterweight champion of the world, and his left hook has detached ten of his eleven challengers from their intellects. Hearns has fought and won twenty-eight times, leaving two opponents still on their feet.

Rocky Graziano didn't box, he threw cobblestones. If permitted, he would cheerfully have used a knife or blackjack or grenade. Tony Zale, called the Man of Steel because he fought out of Gary, Indiana, was a body puncher. One victim said that when he fired a shot to the giblets it felt like a red-hot poker thrust clear through the abdomen. Zale was middleweight champion of the world but his title was frozen while he served in the Navy through World War II. He hadn't been seen in New York for more than four years, whereas Graziano had been a headliner in Madison Square Garden, knocking out guys like Bummy Davis, Freddie Cochrane, Harold Green, and Marty Servo.

Servo had just won the welterweight championship when Rocky caught him by the throat, held him against the ropes and, bludgeoning him mercilessly with right hands, hammered him into retirement. Naturally, New York fans made Graziano the favorite over Zale.

In Yankee Stadium Rocky gave Tony a frightful beating. He knocked him down repeatedly, battered him helpless about the ring. There was no counting the full right hands to the head that Zale took, and somehow kept. Every time the bell rang, you knew he couldn't possibly last another round, and then the bell would ring again and here came Tony out of his corner, eyes glazed, hollow-cheeked face empty.

In the sixth Zale somehow summoned the strength to nail Rocky in the solar plexus. Graziano went down, apparently paralyzed, and was counted out. Leaving the ring, he took a swing at a customer who accused him of going in the water. Zale was helped to his dressing room, limp and only half conscious but still champion of the world.

The dressing rooms presented a striking contrast. The loser sat on a rubbing table, unmarked, unhurt, cheerful. He had lost the fight but had made a good payday and assured himself of a bigger one ahead. He wasn't breathing hard.

Sam Pian and Art Winch handled Zale. The winner stood facing the press with Winch behind him, supporting him with both hands under the armpits. Tony kept trying to say something but his words were indistinguishable. Every few seconds he would sag toward the floor and Winch would straighten him up. At long last Tony got four words out. "Clean living did it," he mumbled.

That was September 27, 1946. About six months later Frank Hogan, the District Attorney, and Eddie Eagan, chairman of the New York State Athletic Commission, ran Rocky out of the boxing business. The charge against him was pure gossamer, never supported with a shred of evidence. He was set down for failure to report a bribe offer that probably had not been made to take a dive in a fight that was never held.

Banned in New York, he met Zale again in Chicago Stadium July 16, 1947. Temperatures were over 100 and the arena's makeshift cooling system did not work, yet the gate of $422,009 was the richest ever drawn indoors up to that time.

This time it was Graziano who took the merciless beating. Zale punched him stupid, clubbing the body, cutting up the face. When an eye swelled shut, Rocky's trainer broke the swelling with a 25-cent piece. Time and again Rocky started to fall and each time he dragged himself erect as if he had seen the face of Frank Hogan or Eddie Eagan on the floor.

He kept fighting back. The heat drained both men but it seemed to take more out of Zale, who was thirty-four years old to Rocky's twenty-five. In the sixth round Tony was helpless, and with fifty seconds to go, Johnny Behr, the referee, stopped it.

Rocky was middleweight champion of the world. "I like Chicago," he said. "They trut me good." They still trut him as an outcast in New York, though. He and Zale went to Ruppert Stadium in Newark for their third meeting.

Somehow, from some source, Rocky got the notion that he was a boxer with the polished skills of a Ray Robinson or Willie Pep. With the airy grace of a water buffalo, he tried to use the ring, sticking and moving. Zale regarded him with curiosity for a moment, then moved in and slugged at will. He needed less than three rounds to render Rocky a former champion.

Four years passed before Graziano had any more truck with the championship. Meanwhile, the title passed from Zale to Marcel Cerdan to Jake LaMotta to Ray Robinson. By that time Sugar Ray stood elected by acclamation as the finest fighter alive, pound for pound. "I wanta see what makes him tick," Rocky said, getting a match with Robinson in Chicago.

Leading citizens introduced from the ring before the main event included Zale, retired. He shook hands perfunctorily with Robinson, then strolled over to Rocky's corner with a smile that lit up his face. When two men have had the sort of fights Tony and Rocky had, there is a bond between them that nobody else in the world can share. The pain and the triumph were theirs and theirs alone.

Beaming, Zale took both of Graziano's hands in his, leaned over him and spoke. It wasn't necessary to hear the words. You knew he was saying, "Give him what you gave me, Rock."

Rocky tried to comply, but in the third round Robinson caught him coming in. One shot to the chin and the fight was over. One more bout and Graziano's career was over.

If, as they are saying, Cuevas and Hearns are clones of Graziano and Zale, there are interesting times ahead in the welterweight division.

DURAN NO QUITTER

1980

This is the first opportunity for comment on the ending of the Roberto Durán–Sugar Ray Leonard bout since Durán, then the World Boxing Council welterweight champion, told the referee: "No más, no más. No more box." It would require a deal of convincing to shake the conviction here that Durán had to be sick or injured, because Roberto Durán was not, is not, and never could be a quitter.

The Sweet Science is a harsh mistress, and under her cruel rules the deadliest sin is to give up under punishment. The most damning criticism that can be made of a fighter is to say, in the parlance of the fight mob, that he is a bit of a kiyi or that he has a touch of the geezer in him, meaning a streak of cowardice. The fact that no coward walks up the steps and into the ring isn't good enough for the fight mob. It is further required that when his number comes up, the fighter must endure pain and punishment without complaint as long as he is conscious.

"Do you want me to stop it?" Harry Kessler, the referee, asked when Archie Moore was being slugged senseless by Rocky Marciano.

"No," Archie said. "I want to be counted out." He was.

"I'm going to stop this," Joe Gould, Jim Braddock's manager, told his fighter when Joe Louis was pounding Jim loose from the heavyweight championship of the world.

"If you do I'll never speak to you again," Braddock said.

This is the code. Exceptions are made only if a fighter surrenders for dishonest reasons, as Sonny Liston almost surely did in his two engagements with Cassius Clay-Muhammad Ali. (The name changed between bouts.) In other words, quitting is a disgrace, deeply to be deplored unless it is done to discharge a business obligation.

Liston's motives have never been made public, but suspicions raised by the first match were confirmed beyond reasonable doubt by the second. Liston was heavyweight champion of the world up to and including his first six peculiar rounds with Clay in Miami Beach. The bell for the seventh found him sitting sullen on his stool while the title changed hands. He said an injury had rendered his left arm useless.

They met again in Lewiston, Maine. In the first round, which was also the last, Liston went in the water with a splash that washed away whatever doubt the first performance had left.

Memory retains only one other case of a champion surrendering his title, and that was strictly on the level. In 1949 Marcel Cerdan was defending the middleweight championship against Jake LaMotta in Detroit when the supraspinatus muscle at the back of his right shoulder came loose. Right arm hanging at his side, he fought on left-handed and LaMotta was having all he could do to beat one side of Cerdan until the tenth round, when the Frenchman's seconds persuaded him to leave the rest of his fight for a better time.

The better time never arrived. Booked for a rematch, Cerdan died in the crash when the plane bringing him back to the United States flew into a mountain in the Azores.

LaMotta, the Bronx Bull, was as tough as any man of his time, yet he quit in the ring at least twice. One was for business reasons. He had agreed to a barney to ornament the gaudy record of one Blackjack Billy Fox, but Jake had never been off his feet and was too proud to hit the deck. He floundered along the ropes impersonating a carp out of water until a faint-hearted referee stopped the performance. Even when Ray Robinson pounded him loose from the middleweight title in thirteen rounds in Chicago, LaMotta was still on his feet when the referee stepped in. But in his next match he gave up. Irish Bob Murphy, who wasn't great but could hit, punished Jake until he quit after seven rounds.

That scene was reminiscent of a night in Jersey City when Max Baer, a former champion, hurled invective and righthand shots at Tony Galento until Tony, sick from swallowing his own blood, gave up. Baer didn't know it, but he had an accomplice. On the eve of the fight, a barfly in Galento's spa in Orange, New Jersey, had asked Tony for tickets, had received a predictable answer and had shoved a beer glass into Tony's profile. Several stitches were required to close the wounds before Baer reopened them.

Willie Pep and Sandy Saddler fought for the world featherweight championship four times. All four bouts were memorable and one can't be forgotten because Willie quit when he was winning. Saddler had knocked him out and taken the title in their first match; in a gallant performance with one brow gaping like a third eye, Willie outfought Saddler to regain the title; Pep lost it back in the third meeting when he did or did not tear a muscle; in their fourth match Willie took an early lead and was winning on all cards when the ninth round ended. "No more," Willie said.

At least one onlooker who had never before and has not since seen a boxer quit while winning was reminded of Willie's story of his beginnings in Hartford. As soon as school was out, he said, he would take off on the run. He didn't have to look back; he knew bigger kids would be chasing him. On his good days he was able to run home and slam the door before his pursuers could lay hands on him. Tiring of this one-sided game, Willie went to a gym to learn boxing. There he came under the tutelage of Bill Gore, and in Gore's hands he developed into the supreme artist of the ring.

Now in his fourth fight with Saddler, the artist blotted his sketchbook. "Again this night," an onlooker thought, "he ran home and slammed the door."

NIGHT FOR JOE LOUIS

1951

Joe Louis lay on his stomach on a rubbing table with his right ear pillowed on a folded towel, his left hand in a bucket of ice on the floor. A handler massaged his left ear with ice. Joe still wore his old dressing gown of blue and red—for the first time, one was aware of how the colors had faded—and a raincoat had been spread on top of that.

This was an hour before midnight of October 26, 1951. It was the evening of a day that dawned July 4, 1934, when Joe Louis became a professional fistfighter and knocked out Jack Kracken in Chicago for a fifty-dollar purse. The night was a long time on the way, but it had to come.

Ordinarily, small space is reserved here for sentimentality about professional fighters. For seventeen years, three months, and twenty-two days Louis fought for money. He collected millions. Now the punch that was launched seventeen years ago had landed. A young man, Rocky Marciano, had knocked the old man out. The story was ended. That was all except—

Well, except that this time he was lying down in his dressing room in the catacombs of Madison Square Garden. Memory retains scores of pictures of Joe in his dressing room, always sitting up, relaxed, answering questions in his slow, thoughtful way. This time only, he was down.

His face was squashed against the padding of the rubbing table, muffling his words. Newspapermen had to kneel on the floor like supplicants in a tight little semicircle and bring their heads close to his lips to hear him. They heard him say that Marciano was a good puncher, that the best man had won, that he wouldn't know until Monday whether this had been his last fight.

He said he never lost consciousness when Marciano knocked him through the ropes and Ruby Goldstein, the referee, stopped the fight. He said that if he'd fallen in midring he might have got up inside ten seconds, but he doubted that he could have got back through the ropes in time.

They asked whether Marciano punched harder than Max Schmeling did fifteen years ago, on the only other night when Louis was stopped.

"This kid," Joe said, "knocked me out with what? Two punches. Schmeling knocked me out with—musta been a hundred punches. But," Joe said, "I was twenty-two years old. You can take more then than later on."

"Did age count tonight, Joe?"

Joe's eyes got sleepy. "Ugh," he said, and bobbed his head.

The fight mob was filling the room. "How did you feel tonight?" Ezzard Charles was asked. Joe Louis was the hero of Charles' boyhood. Ezzard never wanted to fight Joe, but finally he did and won. Then and thereafter Louis became just another opponent who sometimes disparaged Charles as a champion.

"Uh," Charles said, hesitating. "Good fight."

"You didn't feel sorry, Ezzard?"

"No," he said, with a kind of apologetic smile that explained this was just a prize fight in which one man knocked out an opponent.

"How did you feel?" Ray Arcel was asked. For years and years Arcel trained opponents for Joe and tried to help them whip him, and in a decade and a half he dug tons of inert meat out of the resin.

"I felt very bad," Ray said.

It wasn't necessary to ask how Marciano felt. He is young and strong and undefeated. He is rather clumsy and probably always will be, because he has had the finest of teachers, Charley Goldman, and Charley hasn't been able to teach him skill. But he can punch. He can take a punch. It is difficult to see how he can be stopped this side of the heavyweight championship.

It is easy to say, and it will be said, that it wouldn't have been like this with the Louis of ten years ago. It isn't a surpassingly bright thing to say, though, because this isn't ten years ago. The Joe Louis of October 26, 1951, couldn't whip Rocky Marciano, and that's the only Joe Louis there was in the Garden. That one was going to lose on points in a dreary fight that would have left everything at loose ends. It would have been a clear victory for Marciano, but not conclusive. Joe might not have been convinced.

Then Rocky hit Joe a left hook and knocked him down. Then Rocky hit him another hook and knocked him out. A right to the neck knocked him out of the ring. And out of the fight business. The last wasn't necessary, but it was neat. It wrapped the package, neat and tidy.

An old man's dream ended. A young man's vision of the future opened wide. Young men have visions, old men have dreams. But the place for old men to dream is beside the fire.

10.

Pals, Colleagues, and Himself

FIRST ANNIVERSARY

1940

It is just about a year now since great, living, fearless, human literature started appearing in this space as a regular daily feature. To be
sure, it could be eleven months or maybe thirteen, but there's no
point in getting technical about it now, because August 15 has been
designated officially as the anniversary of this column's birth. This
was established at 6:30 A.M. daylight time—and we mean daylight—
on Thursday. At that hour it suddenly became desirable to have a
good story, quick. A question had been asked, rather frostily, we
thought.

"And what was it this time, pray tell?" the questioner inquired.
"Sitting up with a sick fight manager, perhaps? Or interviewing an
insomniac batboy? Or possibly you were celebrating something?"

"That's it," we said. "Celebrating. We were celebrating our anniversary."

"Our anniversary? Our anniversary is in February, and for your
information this is—"

"Not your anniversary," we said haughtily. "Our anniversary. The
first anniversary of the day when the product of this observer's
trenchant pen became an indispensable adjunct to the breakfast
tables of the land. It was exactly one year ago that American journalism was enriched—"

"If you want breakfast," this acquaintance of ours said,
"you'd better get it now before you go to bed. I'm not going to have
anybody messing up my kitchen when it's time for the children's
lunch."

That is the true story of how Journalism Enrichment Day came to
be instituted as a national holiday.

Now, looking back over the year that led up to this occasion, we
are compelled to report that it has been disturbingly undisturbed.
Threats of libel action have been few and far between and very few
women and children have been killed in the crush around the news-
stands when this department reached the street in the Bulldog Edition.

Oh, there have been some letters beginning genially, "Dear Rat:
All you knockers make me sick—" and one that we particularly
treasure read: "I and many others know you wisht you had some of
Joe Louis cash. Dont be jelus. He is only a Negro but he never pick
cotton.—(Signed) A friend."

But reports that Judge Landis always consults us before making
World Series plans and that Mike Jacobs wouldn't dream of schedul-

ing a title fight without our written approval are not more than half true.

And our fearless and forthright predictions that Galento would flatten Baer and the Yankees and Cardinals would win the pennants and that Seabiscuit would lose the Santa Anita Handicap and Bimelech win the Kentucky Derby exerted only a minor influence on the actual contesting of these events.

In short, the public seems able to take us or leave us alone. Sometime during the holiday celebration, we expressed our dissatisfaction with this state of affairs to a gentleman we encountered in a noted spa adjoining a parking lot.

"I'll give you a tip," he said. "No columnist ever amounted to anything unless he believed in something, with his whole heart and soul. What do you believe in?"

"The immortality of Connie Mack," we said. "Let's you and me drink to good old Connie."

"That won't do," said the man, who is a True Believer himself. For years he has believed, with a faith unsupported by evidence, that two dollars planted with a bookie will bear fruit in riches, happiness and a life free of pain.

"That won't do. Everybody believes in Connie. You've got to believe in something controversial. Something you can write about and make people think about. Now take Heywood Broun—"

"Let's have a drink to good old Heywood."

"All right. He believed passionately in the brotherhood of man."

"Let's have a drink to the brotherhood of man, on you."

"All right," the man said, "now you take Eleanor Roosevelt. She—"

"Good old Eleanor! Let's have a drink to Eleanor on the house."

"—believes in Young People. All right, to the Young People then. But you don't believe in anything."

At the time we had to confess this was so. But that was a long while ago. We have lived since then, and no longer are we the carefree, superficial wastrel of last Wednesday night.

Now we believe, with passionate sincerity, in abstemiousness, clean living, regular hours, and a healthy, normal home life. With our whole heart and soul, we believe in national prohibition.

HAPPY BIRTHDAY, GRANTLAND RICE

1954

Since it was only Sunday evening when it began, chances are Grantland Rice's birthday party will be settling into stride about the time these pages become a shroud for some obsolete haddock. There have been some memorable wingdings in Mr. Toots Shor's fish and chips hutch, but none topped this and none ever could.

It wasn't the people present who made it the best. It was the man who was not there, though he wasn't really absent, either. What happened more than once since Grant died last July kept happening again and again Sunday night; you found yourself gazing around the merry room in absent-minded questing, expecting to see Granny at the merriest table.

It was amusing to see men who live all their lives in a swarm of autograph-seekers going around this time collecting signatures from others, signatures that would fill the register of a Hall of Fame in any sport or almost any other field from show business to politics.

Yet what else would you expect? Jack Dempsey, Gene Tunney, Earl Sande, Gene Sarazen, Vinnie Richards, the Four Horsemen, Johnny Weismuller, Herman Hickman, Lou Little, Tommy Henrich, Yogi Berra, Eddie Arcaro, Ted Atkinson, Hank Greenberg—where else would they be on a night the clan was lifting a tall one to Granny?

Wherever they were, in Miami or Nashville, Cleveland, Chicago or California, they dropped what they were doing and came on. There wasn't one among them, however famous, however successful, who doesn't owe much to Grantland Rice.

It was the biggest haul of debtors this side of Old Bailey, and they were there to pay up in the only coin Granny would ever accept—affection and laughter.

This was the party Granny's friends had been planning for several years. It didn't come off earlier because they'd never got together on a date and, anyway, there was grave doubt that Granny would have attended an affair in his honor at gunpoint. This date sort of picked itself; it was the eve of the seventy-fourth anniversary of Grant Rice's birth and the night before publication of his memoirs, *The Tumult and the Shouting.*

There was nobody to sing "Happy Birthday" to, but they could have sung it loudly, for it was a happy occasion. Granny is missed but he is not mourned. There was no tear-jerking; that would have embarrassed Granny.

Rube Goldberg thought of this while watching Douglas Fairbanks, Jr., on Ed Sullivan's television show. (Some of the guests went to the studio before dinner and the others watched from the party.) Fair-banks was giving a graceful reading of Granny's moving verse "Ghosts of the Argonne":

> You can hear them at night when the moon is hidden;
> They sound like the rustle of winter leaves . . .

The party was quiet. "If Granny were here now," Rube said to Colonel Red Reeder of West Point, "he'd be talking."

"Right," another said, "he'd be asking Red here, 'Hey, how about that Virginia team pretty near beating Army?' Or he'd want to know what you thought about the election, Rube. Or he'd be talking about some book he'd just read, not his."

General Rosie O'Donnell was across the room. He and his West Point sidekick, General Blondie Saunders, were two of Granny's all-time favorites. Mrs. Kit Rice tells of the morning her squire got home showing traces of wear, but full of reassurances.

"Everything's all right, honey," he said. "I've been out with Rosie and Blondie."

Everything's still all right with Granny. Nothing can be said of him now that he didn't say better of somebody else. For example, there is a verse he addressed to Charon, the boatman of the Styx, after many of his friends had died:

> The Flame of the Inn is dim tonight—
> Too many vacant chairs—
> The sun has lost too much of its light—
> Too many songs have taken flight—
> Too many ghosts on the stairs—
> Charon—here's to you—as man to man—
> I wish I could pick 'em the way you can.

JOE PALMER DAY

1957

In the dining room at Belmont, Joe Palmer's friends were swapping stories about him. It seemed only a little while ago that Joe was there, holding up his end of the conversation to say the very least, but the feature race this day was a handicap named in his memory and it was not the first or the second or the third so titled. If figures matter, it will be five years, come Halloween, since the *Herald Tribune*'s wonderful racing writer left an unfinished column in his typewriter.

"It keeps happening all the time," one fellow was saying, "that something comes around the track and I think, What a shame Joe isn't up here to write about that. For instance, I guess the two forms of animal life that he loathed most were state racing stewards and people who watered down whiskey.

"Well, since he died there's been a man around who lost his license for cutting the whiskey he served, and he was also a state steward. If Joe had been around to work him over—"

"That reminds me," another began, and while he told a story the others waited, with no especial patience, to get in one of their own. As the day wore on, truth did not necessarily prevail, which would have been all right with Joe Palmer.

"This department," Joe wrote, "had a reputation for unswerving truthfulness until approximately the age of seven, and would no doubt have it still except for leaving Kentucky temporarily at that age. But since then various things have happened, and now a certain admiration is felt for a well-told falsehood. This is wrong, of course, but there you are."

Belmont is a pleasant place and this was a pleasant, uncrowded day. Some millions were spent on physical improvements since last season, but the changes hardly show. To the casual eye this old cavalry post looks just about as it did when Joe temporarily shared Greentree Cottage there with John Gaver and would occasionally watch the morning works before bedtime.

Actually, the most noticeable change isn't on the course at all, but in Creedmoor, the big mental hospital beyond the far turn. There've been additions there, a skyscraper construction that gives the patients an unimpeded view of all the racing, even that on the Widener Chute. Almost certainly Joe would have approved.

Conn McCreary dropped by to chat. He was one of Joe's favorite guys, though they were relentless adversaries at poker. The broken leg which Conn suffered this summer when a horse banged him against the starting gate has just about repaired itself.

Joe DiMaggio, an infrequent visitor, was in a box with friends, taking a somewhat more modest profit than he used to get from an afternoon at Yankee Stadium. "I only wish," he said, "that I'd do as well as I know the Yankees are doing."

At the moment the Yankees were playing the White Sox. There had been no report as to the score. They won, of course.

Sammy Renick, the little man who does television at the races, said he and DiMaggio had just paid a call in the jockey's quarters.

"I took Joe in there a couple of years ago," Sammy said, "and one of the jocks looked up and said, 'Here comes God.' Today when he walked in, one of 'em said, 'Here comes God—with Renick.' Do you think that moves Joe up, or back?"

"A man who spends his life poking around racetracks," Joe Palmer wrote, "gets, in addition to a view of human nature which is at once more tolerant and less rosy than any endorsed by the clergy, a rather unreasonable fondness for certain places. I say unreasonable, because it does not seem to be dependent upon architectural or horticultural attractiveness, on setting, on comfort, or even on the quality or cleanliness of the racing at these places."

There were five fillies and mares in the Joe Palmer Handicap, all connected with somebody who had been Joe's friend. Jimmy Jones had two from Calumet Farm, just down the Versailles Pike from Joe's home in Lexington, Kentucky. These were Amoret and Beyond.

Attica was running in the silks of Kentucky's Hal Price Headley, and George B. Widener, president of Belmont in Joe's time, had Rare Treat. Jack Skirvin saddled the other, named Gay Life.

"On Joe's account," a man said, frowning at past performances, "I've got to bet Gay Life. I can't find any excuse for it here, though, and there are some awful nasty comments about his races."

The comments were justified. Gay Life ran out of speed early. Attica and Rare Treat ran Amoret down in the stretch and raced to a rousing finish, with Rare Treat the winner in a photo.

Joe's friends tore up their tickets and went downstairs for a bourbon—even those who preferred Scotch. They lifted their glasses silently.

THE COACH

1962

It was a little country baseball field near the highway somewhere in rural Massachusetts, much closer kin to a pasture lot than to Yankee Stadium. "See that field?" Stanley Woodward said, pointing from the car. "I started the sweetest riot there you ever saw in your life."

At that moment he spotted a Cooper's hawk or a loggerhead shrike or something, and his interest in birds distracted him from his sinful past. For anybody who knew him, though, it wasn't hard to guess what had set off the riot.

He would have been pitching for the visiting team, and the chances are he chose a strategic moment to stick the ball in somebody's ear. For as a young pitcher Stanley was—to borrow a line from Uncle Wilbert Robinson of the old Dodgers—fast and "pleasingly wild," and any good hitter coming up with big runs on base had better stay loose.

The fierce combativeness that has characterized Rufus Stanley Woodward for sixty-six years is one of many reasons why he has been one of the finest all-around newspaper men and far and away the greatest editor and department head I have ever known. In a sandlot ball game or as a rough tackle at Amherst or in a friendly "wrestling" match with Jock Sutherland (the only honest rassling match I ever saw) or in the highly competitive newspaper field, he came to play and he played to win.

Now, after two hitches on the *New York Herald Tribune,* the Coach is benching himself. He'll be back in the game from time to time, and if the rest of us try hard enough to approach the standards he established, it ought to remain a good game. But pretending it will be the same game is self-deception.

Mere truculence, of course, doesn't make a man great. The qualities of greatness in Stanley are a rich and brilliant mind, a supple wit, uncompromising integrity, broad knowledge and understanding, and a ferocious dedication to the job. Sometimes the best of these— integrity and dedication—were a cross on his shoulders, for they got him into rows with publishers and executives who did not understand that when he fought them he was fighting to give them a better newspaper.

"Woodward did not come to us by accident," the editor of the paper in Worcester, Massachusetts, wrote in effect when Stanley left his home town for Boston. "He came because newspaper work is the only field that interests him."

"He is often contemptuous of his superior officers," Joe Palmer said, "barely tolerant of his equals and unfailingly kind and considerate to his subordinates."

Joe Palmer, greatest of turf writers, had seen at first hand how Stanley battled for his men. Rebuilding after World War II, the Coach hired Joe in 1946 and this rounded out what may have been the finest sports staff ever assembled. "Holy mackerel!" Tom O'Reilly said when he heard that Palmer was coming. "Next week they'll hire Thomas A. Edison to turn out the lights."

It was not the intention of Stanley's father to raise up a newspaperman. He wanted a big-league catcher, and as soon as the boy could walk, his sire and Jess Burkett, the mighty hitter who lived in Worcester, began training him. Reluctantly they converted him to pitching when, about high school age, his eyesight began to fail.

For a year he was blind. Unable to pitch or catch, he played the fiddle. If he attacked the violin as he attacks a typewriter, he must have been hell on G strings.

Operations restored his vision but he had to wear glasses playing football at Amherst. He was self-conscious about the cheaters; he would tuck them into the knee of his football pants, jog blindly on to the field with an end at one elbow and a guard at the other, then surreptitiously slip the glasses on.

He tried this before the big game at Williams, or maybe Wesleyan. He did not see the low rope stretched along the sideline. The busted shoulder finished him for the season. It is unlikely that Amherst's rivals were displeased, for Stanley was not then and is not now a cuddly adversary. Once when he and his friend Dan Parker were peppering each other in their columns for the fun of it, Stanley was warned that he had picked a formidable sparring partner.

"Oh," he said mildly, "I know Dan's smarter than I am, but I fight dirtier."

Sometimes it has seemed that Stanley had a quality of second-sight which enabled him to be on the scene when unexpected news broke. He wasn't born with a caul, though; he just knows his business.

Thus he would pass up an Army-Navy football game to be in Boston when Holy Cross brought off an unforgettable upset of unbeaten Boston College. Though no racing fan, he managed to be at Suffolk Downs when rioting horse players tore the joint apart. When Philadelphia's mounted cops rode valorously across Franklin Field clubbing young Penn and Princeton skulls, Stanley was perched on Thrumbull Terrace watching with a connoisseur's keen apprecia tion.

Thus also as a war correspondent, in both the European and Pacific theaters. When the 101st Airborne landed behind German lines, Stanley dropped out of the sky with them. When the carrier *Enterprise* got racked up, Stanley was on the next wave.

Though no baseball scout ever had a more discerning eye for talent in his field than Stanley in his, the Coach has a blind spot where his own writing is concerned. When Army coaches decided that a slaughter by Michigan was due to the West Point center's failure to give the football a quarter-turn on presenting it to the quarterback and he observed that this is like blaming the Johnstown flood on a leaky toilet in Altoona, he doesn't consider it wonderful.

He has written that to let Jack Kramer, that gold-plated debaucher of amateur youth, coach the Davis Cup tennis team, is like electing Jean Lafitte commodore of the New Orleans Yacht Club. And when the Cornells railed at him for misquoting their anthem, he replied that he had visited their campus often and in his considered judgment it was higher above Cayuga's water than far above.

WILLARD MULLIN

1971

The National Cartoonists Society is running a hog-killing in the New York Hilton tonight saluting Willard Mullin, a member, as "sports cartoonist of the century." With him on the dais will be the greatest of heavyweight champions, Jack Dempsey, and Mrs. Charles Shipman Payson, the gracious lady who owns half of Greentree Stable and most of the New York Mets.

Nobody will quibble with the society's designation of Dempsey as "athlete of the century" or Joan Payson as "No. 1 Lady in Sports," but "sports cartoonist of the century" is poppycock. Willard Mullin, as any fool should know, is the sports cartoonist of all human history.

From the hairy ancestor who scratched his picture stories on the cave walls right down to this moment, there never has been another like the square-rigged squire of Plandome, Long Island. Call the roll from Bud Fisher, Bob Edgren and Tad Dorgan, to Murray Olderman and Bill Gallo, and nowhere do you find all the qualities that distinguish Willard Mullin.

With his perception, wit and marvelously comic pen, he was much more than an illustrator or a caricaturist. He was a warm but penetrating critic of the human scene, and each of his drawings was an editorial. I would hate to admit how many times over the years I swiped a whole column from one of his cartoons.

The past tense is employed here, not because Willard has lost the hop on his fastball but because he is quitting these parts to go sand-painting or something on Fort Myers Beach, Florida. Newspapers today won't provide the big block of space that Willard's commentaries occupied in the *World-Telegram,* six days a week for thirty-three years.

That's too bad for the newspapers, too bad for their readers and too bad for the New York scene which Willard has brightened since escaping from California in 1934. He'll be missed in many places, perhaps most of all by surviving members of the Village Green Reading Society.

This was an informal group that met two or three times a year in New Haven when the late Herman Hickman was Yale's football coach. Along with Herman and Charley Loftus, then in charge of public relations in the athletic department, there were Grantland Rice, Frank Graham, Tim Cohane, Willard and Joe Stevens, of the sports catering clan.

At meetings the order of business included drinking, eating, literary and poetic composition and recitation, laughter, argument, and song. Nobody ever had more fun.

It was a privilege and an education to sit with Willard in a press box and watch his imagination work. For seven or eight innings he would watch, say, a baseball game in Ebbets Field, alert to all the nuances of the occasion. Then he might say, "I think I'll have the Bum coming into a saloon and saying . . ." Laughing, he would describe some comic bit of business that would capture the essence of the event he was watching.

Everybody remembers with pleasure the characters he had created to represent various teams—the Brooklyn Bum with toes peeping from cracked shoes; the big, dumb oaf who was a New York Giant; St. Louis Swifty, a steamboat slicker who portrayed the Cardinals; and the St. Louis Brown, po' white trash with a jug of corn squeezin's.

When the Bum moved from Brooklyn to Los Angeles, he went Hollywood on the drawing board, putting on sunglasses, a beret and Bermuda shorts. When the Boston Brave took his breechclout to Milwaukee, his speech took on a trace of German accent and a beer belly grew steadily rounder.

Willard was fun to work with and a joy to read. He is the best of companions, though it isn't always easy to stay the course. We don't have many guys around who can live it up with Willard and keep going at his pace into the tiny hours.

Stanley Woodward could. That old Amherst tackle was a great bear and Willard, designed on a less massive scale, is broad-shouldered and muscular. One night at Bear Mountain Inn they were hand-wrestling for the drinks. Stanley exerted sudden pressure, and dislocated Willard's thumb.

It was the right thumb, the one on Willard's drawing hand. Stanley oozed remorse from every pore. "Hit me, Willard," he begged, "please hit me!" He offered his face unprotected, removing his glasses first.

Not that there were any hard feelings. Another night when the three of us were together at the same cheerful watering hole, we convinced Willard that his genius wasn't appreciated on the *World-Telegram* and Stanley hired him for the *Herald Tribune*. Next day Stanley and I dragged ourselves out of bed in the Forest Lodge, where Jack Martin had planted us, cocked a bleary eye at deer grazing outside, and summoned the new employee: "Come, Willard, we've all got to get down to the office."

"I'll start next week," Willard said, burrowing deeper.

CRUMBUMS

1969

Fourteen hundred people with a price on their heads slithered through the winter's first snowstorm the other night to graze together in recognition of Toots Shor's forty years in New York.

The price was $100 a head, which seems slightly ridiculous when you consider that celebrating forty years of Toots Shor is like celebrating a broken hip. Actually, the crumbums came to salute themselves for survival.

The roster of crumbums present—i.e., friends of the saloonkeeper —ranged from District Attorney Frank Hogan to former Chief Justice Earl Warren, from Bob Hope and Pat O'Brien to Joe E. Lewis and Gordon MacRae, from Horace Stoneham to Horace McMahon, from Johnny Rotz to Johnny Lujack.

Indeed, there's a former haberdasher out in Independence, Missouri, who probably would have been there a few years ago when he was in his early eighties. As a Senator and Vice President, Harry Truman was a licensed crumbum, and he pouted a good deal when the Secret Service told him the old joint on 51st Street was off-limits for the President.

The improbable scope of Toots Shor's friendships flabbergasts people from narrower worlds. They don't understand that in forty years in the saloon business it is impossible not to meet everybody, and Toots never forgets anyone. Years ago this fact was remarked on by Bill Veeck, the free spirit who used to operate baseball franchises the way Shor runs a bar—noisily.

"What I love about him," Veeck said, "he's no front runner. When I was a busher in Milwaukee, he was just as obnoxious to me as when I had the world champions. He's a foul-weather friend, which is the worst kind."

A few hours after the Yankees mopped up the Phillies in the 1950 World Series, Toots sat chatting with a customer in the dining room when a waiter whispered that Joe Page had just come into the bar. Hastily, the proprietor excused himself and went out front. For three seasons and two World Series Page had been undisputed king of the Yankee bullpen, but 1950 had been a bad year for him and he was ignored during the Series. In no mood to attend the team's victory party, he had left the Stadium by himself.

Pretty soon the waiter came back smiling. "The boss gave him a hero's welcome," he said.

Bernard Shor is not necessarily better for people than whiskey. Not as good, he would say, and he would say it out of respect, not false modesty.

On Grantland Rice's seventieth birthday, he was inexpressibly pleased to receive seventy red roses from Toots Shor. "Gee, that was thoughtful, Toots," a friend said. "Wish I'd thought of it."

The saloonkeeper made a brushoff gesture, backhanded. "Whiskey," he said. "That's all it takes—whiskey, and heart."

A few nights later there was a birthday party for Granny in the Coffee House, a quiet gathering of a dozen or so. After cocktails— Toots always remembered there was just one apiece—there was dinner at one long table. Then Eddie Rickenbacker got up and made a spread-eagle speech knocking labor. Roy Howard got up and damned the administration. Somebody else was clearing his throat when Toots bounced up.

"You creepy bums," he said with the Old World grace that has always distinguished him, "I thought this party was for Granny Rice." He walked around the table, bent and planted a kiss on the pate that Granny used to say looked like a half-picked cotton patch. "I love ya," Toots said, and resumed his seat. It was the closing address of the evening.

Toots Shor has had many fights but only two feuds—with Sherman Billingsley and a man in Philadelphia named Paul Harron.

" 'Hate,' " he said one night in philosophy class, "is a word I don't use. I say 'dislike.' One time my little girl Kerry was sick, in a coma. I prayed to God.

"I told God, 'If this little girl gets better, I'll never dislike anybody again as long as I live—except two guys.' "

He had to level.

AL LANEY'S PROSE

1978

Twenty-five years late but still not too late, the Metropolitan Golf Association has chosen Al Laney to receive the organization's Distinguished Service Award. The choice speaks well for the literary taste and for the memory of the selection committee, for more than a decade has passed since Al's sensitive reporting and beautifully crafted prose last appeared in the daily press. He covered sports in America and abroad for the *New York Herald Tribune,* retiring in 1966 when the paper died. Now eighty-two, he lives quietly in Spring Valley, New York. When Al was a schoolboy in Pensacola, Florida, the Cleveland baseball team, called the Naps after their manager,

Napoleon Lajoie, pitched its spring training camp there. "It was a thrilling enough experience," Al has written, "to speak with Joe Jackson and Napoleon Lajoie, but of course they were not the Giants. In those days Christy Mathewson was a shining knight, and if the Giants won, then were the gods just and life a lyric."

Equal in stature with the princely Mathewson in Al's young eyes was the dramatic figure of Maurice McLoughlin, the "flame-thatched" California Comet of tennis. In 1914 Al was on vacation in New York and sat in the stands at the West Side Tennis Club in Forest Hills watching McLoughlin defeat Norman Brookes of Australia, 17–15, 6–3, 6–3, in the historic match in the Davis Cup challenge round that did for tennis in America what Francis Ouimet had done for golf a year earlier by beating Harry Vardon and Ted Ray in the United States Open.

Al already had a regular after-school job on the *Pensacola Journal* and that afternoon at Forest Hills he conceived an ambition to become a tennis writer. In time he covered all sports but it was tennis and golf that brought out his most graceful writing.

The Metropolitan Golf Association citation notes that "despite his international reputation—or because of it—Mr. Laney worked just as hard at covering Met area events as he did at the Masters. No one knew more local golfers and no one made more visits to local clubs than he. He made his readers aware of golf in their area and thus set a standard that forced other newspapers to re-evaluate their local coverage. Mr. Laney covered golf on the *Tribune* for more than forty years. His collective efforts during that span form a body of work that stands as a major contribution to the game of golf."

Before World War I Al worked on the *Dallas Dispatch* and the *Minneapolis News*. He fancied himself as a tennis player in those days, but a wound incurred with the 308th Infantry of the 77th Division put an end to his playing. Back in the United States he landed on the *Evening Mail,* and in 1925 he returned to France, where a job on the *Paris Herald* opened hours before his last francs slipped away. He was night editor but got away to cover golf and tennis championships for the parent paper, the *Herald Tribune.* He and O. B. Keeler of Atlanta were the only American reporters who covered the British Open and Amateur in 1930, the year of Bobby Jones' grand slam. In the middle thirties he returned to New York but for some years went abroad each spring to do Wimbledon, the British Open and similar events.

By that time, the place in his esteem once occupied by Maurice McLoughlin had been taken over by Bernard Darwin, the great British golf writer. They became friends, and Al's writing may have been influenced by his admiration for Darwin. Maybe not, too. Perhaps his graceful style was a natural expression of his own courtliness. What did he write like? Well, in 1954 he covered Babe Didrikson Zaharias's twelve-stroke victory in the Women's National Open just a year after a cancer operation.

"She acted the part of a champion to perfection," he wrote, "and her progress twice around the course was a queenly procession with her nearest pursuers, already dimly seen in the far distance at the start, fading more and more out of the picture as the day wore on."

Al is a gentle man, fanatically neat. On the golf course you would usually see him walking alone, always wearing a snap-brim hat of Confederate gray and, in the most stifling weather, a jacket and tie. He spoke in a voice so gentle it was often barely audible. "Dammit!" his sports editor, Stanley Woodward, shouted during one effort at conversation. "I'm going to have you wired for sound!"

In several winters when he wasn't covering hockey, Al wrote a series of where-are-they-now features about sports stars of the past. He spent weeks scouring through Harlem in search of Sam Langford, the old Boston Tar Baby, whom some considered the greatest fighter the ring ever knew. Again and again Al was assured that Sam was dead but he found him at last, penniless and blind and lonely, in a dingy room on 139th Street.

The story Al wrote had no trace of mawkishness, but it so moved readers that voluntary contributions poured in, creating a $10,000 trust fund to take care of Sam.

On the day before Christmas Al visited Sam again. The room was gay with decorations and Sam sat surrounded by gifts—a guitar, three boxes of cigars, a bottle of gin, that sort of thing.

"You tell all my friends," Sam said, "I'm the happiest man in New York City, I got a geetar and a bottle of gin and money in my pocket to buy Christmas dinner. No millionaire in the world got more than that, or anyhow they can't use any more. Tell my friends all about it and tell 'em I said God bless 'em."

WRITING LESS—AND BETTER?

1982

Up to now, the pieces under my byline have run on Sunday, Monday, Wednesday, and Friday. Starting this week, it will be Sunday, Monday, and Thursday—three columns instead of four. We shall have to wait and see whether the quality improves.

Visiting our freshman daughter (freshwoman or freshperson would be preferred by feminists, though heaven knows she was fresh), we sat chatting with perhaps a dozen of her classmates. Somehow my job got into the discussion. A lovely blond was appalled.

"A theme a day!" she murmured.

The figure was not altogether accurate. At the time it was six themes a week. It had been seven and when it dropped to six that looked like roller coaster's end. However, it finally went to five, to three and back to four, where it has remained for years.

First time I ever encountered John S. Knight, the publisher, we were bellying up to Marje Everett's bar at Arlington Park. He did not acknowledge the introduction. Instead, he said: "Nobody can write six good columns a week. Why don't you write three? Want me to fix it up?"

"Look, Mr. Knight," I said. "Suppose I wrote three stinkers. I wouldn't have the rest of the week to recover." One of the beauties of this job is that there's always tomorrow. Tomorrow things will be better.

Now that the quota is back to three, will things be better day after tomorrow?

The comely college freshman wasn't told of the years when a daily column meant seven a week. Between those jousts with the mother tongue, there was always a fight or football match or ball game or horse race that had to be covered after the column was done. I loved it.

The seven-a-week routine was in Philadelphia, which reminds me of the late heavyweight champion, Sonny Liston. Before his second bout with Muhammad Ali was run out of Boston, Liston trained in a hotel in Dedham.

I was chatting about old Philadelphia days with the trainer, Willie Reddish, remembered from his time as a heavyweight boxer in Philadelphia.

"Oh," Willie said apropos of some event in the past, "were you there then?"

"Willie," I said, "I did ten years hard in Philadelphia."

There had been no sign that Liston was listening, but at this he swung around. "Hard?" he said. "No good time?"

From that moment on, Sonny and I were buddies, though it wasn't easy accepting him as a sterling citizen of lofty moral standards.

On this job two questions are inevitably asked: "Of all those you have met, who was the best athlete?" and "Which one did you like best?"

Both questions are unanswerable, but on either count Bill Shoemaker, the jockey, would have to stand high.

This little guy weighed 96 pounds as an apprentice rider thirty-two years ago. He still weighs 96 pounds and he will beat your pants off at golf, tennis, and any other game where you're foolish enough to challenge him.

There were, of course, many others, not necessarily great. Indeed, there was a longish period when my rapport with some who were less than great made me nervous. Maybe I was stuck on bad ballplayers. I told myself not to worry.

Some day there would be another Joe DiMaggio.